Sir David Russell's St Andrews links

CIT 10/3/95

One of the greatest occult stories of modern times, involving people from St Andrews is told for the first time in the newly published biography of Sir David Russell (Canongate, £14.99) by Lorn Macintyre, who lives in St Andrews.

Sir David, who died in 1956, was a model employer who built up the family paper mills of Tullis Russell at Markinch into among the most modern and progressive in Europe.

Sir David installed a sun clinic (the equivalent of today's sun beds) for debilitated workers, and in the 1920s equipped the mills' houses with the most up-to-date appliances, including electric irons. Much more than paper mills, the Fife works were a small town, with a brass band, an Institute with books and newspapers, proud gardens and a well cared-for and contented workforce.

The biography discloses that Clarence Hatry, sentenced to 14 years penal servitude in 1920 when his six companies collapsed with liabilities of over £29 million, and who had reorganised the Dundee jute mills, had tried to buy Tullis Russell.

A man of wide learning, Sir David was a major benefactor to St Andrews University, through his own personal generosity and through family trusts which continue to support the university, including the Walker Trust. The interior of St Leonard's Chapel was refurbished by Sir David and Lady Russell as a memorial to their son Pat, a former student of St Andrews University, killed with the London Scottish in Italy in 1944.

Lorn Macintyre had exclusive access to the 200 box archive of Russell papers in St Andrews University Library in the writing of the biography, which reveals how Sir David helped his close friend Professor James Irvine to become Principal of St Andrews University. The book evokes leisured life of St Andrews between the wars, with golf matches, and piano recitals in the Principal's fine residence on The Scores.

The most fascinating chapters in the biography tell the story of how Sir David Russell and his closest friend, the famous psychic Wellesley Tudor Pole, persuaded Professor James Baxter of St Andrews University to head the excavation of the Great Palace of the Byzantine Emperors in Istanbul. Though this was ostensibly an archaeological dig, involving huge outlays by Sir David, and the uncovering of exquisite mosaics, the excavation was undertaken because information received psychically indicated that priceless items were buried under part of the Great Palace.

Sir David Russell

Sir David Russell
A Biography

LORN MACINTYRE

Canongate

First published in Great Britain in 1994 by Canongate
Frederick Street Books plc,
14 Frederick Street,
Edinburgh EH2 2HB

© Lorn Macintyre 1994
All rights reserved.

This book is published with help from
The Russell Trust and from Tullis Russell & Co. Ltd,
who donated the 115gsm Mellotex superwhite paper
on which it is printed.

British Library Cataloguing-in-Publication Data
A catalogue record for this book is available on request from
The British Library

ISBN 0 86241 463 6

Photoset by Servis Filmsetting Ltd, Manchester
Printed and bound in Great Britain by Bookcraft Ltd, Midsomer Norton.

Foreword

The privilege of introducing such a remarkable and uncommon biography is one which greatly honours me.

My earliest memory of David Russell is of a visit, bearing presents, to my father's house in Thames Ditton in the early 1930s. I must have been 11 or 12 years old, and already had learnt to call him "Uncle David", as was the custom in those days among family friends.

On later occasions in Scotland and in London, where in my time he invariably stayed at Brown's Hotel, I came all too gradually to realise that Uncle David was a quite exceptional person. In the immediate post-war years when I was a young man recently demobilised, Sir David (as he had by then become) gave me encouragement in face of the grim realities of civilian life, and showed me creative kindness of inestimable value. In my mind's eye I can see him still, pacing beside the burn which traversed the garden of his house in Fife, a tall figure, ever somewhat shy, speaking very quietly.

It is in the light of such memories as these that I am particularly moved by the publication, some 40 years after his death, of Dr Lorn Macintyre's exposition of so many recondite themes.

The range and scope of Sir David's interests are here admirably recalled. He was a man far ahead of his time in his interest in what today is termed holistic medicine, while remaining a brilliant businessman, always concerned with the development of the Tullis Russell paper mills and ancillary companies, and with the well-being of all who worked in them. He was an outstanding benefactor of St Andrews University (an older foundation than England's Oxford or Cambridge), where today generations of students have manifold cause to remember him. In the revival of the isle of Iona as a spiritual centre of importance to Scotland, and far beyond, he was a prime mover, a full account now for the first time being given. Likewise in what the author describes as "one of the great untold stories of the twentieth century"—the mysterious Quest which took Sir David to Constantinople, and which my father, Wellesley Tudor Pole, was so closely involved.

Running through all that is unfolded in this biography, like a golden thread, is Sir David's understanding of what truly is meant by the phrase *service to others*, be those others high or low, of service understood by him in the light of his deepest convictions and insights.

This is a highly unusual book, of course, packed with fascinating incident (some of it very amusing), and touching upon a multitude of people who lived out their lives more than half a century ago. One wants to learn more of almost all of them!

Yet, when the last page is turned, there lingers with the reader—or certainly with this one—an impression of something quite elusive and indefinable about David Russell, as also of Wellesley Tudor Pole. What, exactly? I can only say that to me it seems to partake of a quality, of an inner orientation (if those are the right words), to convey some glimpse of which demands the pen of a poet. As it happens, G.R.H. Wright, with whose lines I venture to close, himself is an archaeologist working in the Middle East, and he is just that poet:

> The sun returns from sea to land again
> And turns the shadowed mountain on the plain;
> Lighting its moment for a little while,
> Nor counts the loaves and fishes which remain.

DAVID TUDOR POLE
June 1994

Author's Acknowledgments

Many people have helped me with this book. I owe special thanks to the late Dr David Russell, who commissioned this biography of his father, and who gave me so much help and hospitality, along with his wife Catherine, at Rossie House. My thanks also to: Mrs Sheila Erdal and Mrs Anne Macaulay, for recollections and suggestions; Mr David Tudor Pole for recollections, suggestions and hospitality at Flete, Devon; Mr Robert Smart, Keeper of Manuscripts and University Muniments, St Andrews University, for leading me into the massive Russell archive and guiding me through to the proof stage; Mrs Christine Gascoigne, Keeper of Rare Books, St Andrews University Library, and Mrs Priscilla Jackson for lugging so many boxes from the Russell archive, and general help; Mr Kenneth Fraser, Senior Assistant Librarian, St Andrews University, for much help with research; Dr Mary Whitby, School of Greek, Latin and Ancient History, St Andrews University, for allowing me to draw on material she wrote for the Byzantine Conference at St Andrews University, helping me to prepare the plan of the Great Palace, and also for reading the Great Palace chapters; Professor Reginald Christian, honorary professor of Russian, St Andrews University, for making available his published work on Alexis Aladin and reading the relevant chapter; Mr Dugald MacArthur, Iona expert and former Librarian, St Andrews University, for reading the Iona chapters; Dr Ronald Cant, historian of St Andrews University, for reading the relevant sections of the manuscript; Mr Leonard Sleath and Mrs Willa Sleath, Chalice Well, Glastonbury, for help and hospitality; Mr James B. Rae, former managing director of Tullis Russell Limited, for his recollections and for hospitality; Mrs Eugenia Recchi Franceshini, for permission to draw on her published writings on the Great Palace; Messrs Weidenfeld & Nicolson, for permission to quote from Lord Sieff's Memoirs (1970); Roger Billcliffe for the use of the photograph of Clarence Hatry; the late Mrs Tamara Talbot Rice, for help with the Great Palace chapters, and for the use of the photograph of her husband in Istanbul in the 1920s; Lady Jean Carroll, for permission to use photographs of her father, Wellesley Tudor Pole; and Mrs Katharine Eden, my editor, for much help and guidance.

Contents

	Introduction	xi
1	Schooldays at St Andrews	1
2	Convalescence in Sweden	10
3	A Papermaking Family	20
4	Wellesley Tudor Pole	31
5	Post-War Problems	40
6	The Paper Millionaire	49
7	A Russell Buy-out	58
8	The General Strike	68
9	The Romance of Esparto	77
10	St Andrews Benefactor	87
11	Alexis Aladin	96
12	Iona	105
13	The Quest Begins	118
14	Italian Affairs	129
15	Sunlight and Enlightenment	138
16	The Quest Continues	151
17	Excavating the Great Palace	159
18	The Romeland Investment	172
19	The Expropriation Question	182
20	The Iona Dream	193
21	Another War	204
22	A Grievous Loss	213
23	The Dig Resumed	225
24	In the House of Justinian	233
25	A Life Concluded	241
	Index	254

Introduction

The library of St Andrews University contains a collection of over 200 boxes of papers and photographs, the business and personal archive of an extraordinary man, the Fife papermaker Sir David Russell, who died in 1956. For years there have been rumours of a mysterious Quest which took Sir David to Constantinople, and there were requests for access to his papers. These were refused because Sir David's family, and particularly his elder son Dr D. F. O. Russell, felt that only a full-scale biography would do him credit. I was asked to undertake this task three years ago.

It was both a privilege and a revelation. Sir David's combination of business acumen and care for his workers allowed him to develop his inheritance into one of the largest and most progressive privately-owned paper mills in Europe.

But he was also immersed in philosophy, literature, art and religion, a man whose mind ranged far beyond the mundane in his search for a meaning to life. Central to these interests was Wellesley Tudor Pole, a man whose undoubted psychic gifts had won him admirers in many countries. For almost 50 years they wrote to each other on a near daily basis — both sets of correspondence have been preserved, as Sir David kept copies of all the letters he wrote. Their belief in the Quest took them to Constantinople, and led (albeit inadvertently) to the restoration of an art treasure to the world.

The archive also contains information never before made public, about Sir David's instrumental role in the renovation of the monastic buildings on Iona, based on unpublished correspondence with the late Lord MacLeod of Fuinary.

Sir David Russell liked fitting ends. Though his son Dr D. F. O. Russell died before he saw this book in print, he approved the manuscript.

1
Schooldays at St Andrews

In the early mornings the boy wandered among the dunes of St Andrews Bay in Fife. He might have a hand-lens for studying the flowers, or a golf club to improve his game. If it was summer David Russell had to join 50 shivering boys in the North Sea, for Clifton Bank was a typical Victorian boarding school, determined to turn out hardy sons for the Empire. Douglas Haig was to be one of its success stories.

Dr Paterson had left his teaching post at Madras College to build a prep school on the Scores, the row of houses and hotels overlooking the sea. But he was canny: the school was two houses linked internally, so that if the enterprise failed, the properties could be sold off separately without loss.

Clifton Bank flourished, with many of its boys coming from Fife. The three Russell brothers, George (born 1869), Robert (born 1871) and David (born 1872) were from Leven. They were boarders because 15 miles was a considerable drive in Fife weather, in the days before motor cars and well-made roads. There were four Russell sisters, Mary (born 1874), Christian (born 1876), Jenny (born 1880) and Agnes (born 1883).

In 1854, at the age of 23, their enterprising father David Russell had bought and rebuilt the property of Silverburn at Leven, setting up "certain red roofed works and other erections" for flax retting. Later, he realised that the ancient flax industry had had its day, and he moved ahead of the times by taking the lease of the old spinning mill at Largo. He started the manufacture of cotton cake at the Largo Oil Mills, a new venture for Scotland. He also acquired the old sugar mill at Burntisland, where his business of seed crushing and the manufacture of linseed oil and cotton cake prospered.

In 1874 he had branched out into papermaking, with a partnership in the mills at Rothes and Auchmuty with his Tullis relations. Tea in Assam, sugar in Australia and timber in the USA completed a substantial business portfolio. In 1868 he had married Janet Hutchison, daughter of Robert Hutchison, founder of a large firm

David Russell Senior (1831–92), who adapted his business from flax retting to papermaking.

of corn and grain merchants in Kirkcaldy. By the time a family started to arrive, Silverburn was the spacious and comfortable home of a successful businessman.

David Russell was a young boy when his trunk was carried into Clifton Bank by the Silverburn coachman. But he was not homesick. There was plenty to do and see in the medieval town of St Andrews, where horses clattered along broad North Street, and ladies with bustles chose golf clubs as carefully as they chose their hats.

The boy who was to take part in one of the greatest esoteric-cum-archaeological quests of the twentieth century wandered among the ruins of the cathedral, looking for the site of the shrine of Scotland's patron saint, the apostle and martyr Andrew. In October 1884 he wrote home excitedly: "They have been digging up at the cathedral and have found a subterranean passage from the castle to the cathedral."

There was more digging in St Andrews in 1886, as the railway line was being completed. The Russell brothers saw a man killed during its construction, and sent an account to Silverburn. In March of the same year George reported another tragedy: "There was a little girl going to school, last Tuesday, between Brownhills and St Andrews, when she was caught in a snowdrift, and was found dead next day."

Silverburn had acclimatised the Russell brothers to the east wind. "I have got my semmet but I have not got on my drawers yet as I do not feel cold," George assured his parents, and David boasted: "I am never cold in bed." As the days lengthened, it was light enough to read in their rooms in the early morning. The boys were allowed to put up pictures in the schoolroom. David sat gazing at the minarets on a six foot long photograph of Constantinople, a city he was to become closely associated with in his Quest.

Astronomy was on Clifton Bank's testing curriculum, and George told his parents what to look out for at Silverburn. "Saturn is seen right overhead at about seven, Mars rises between seven and eight." David had more down-to-earth concerns. "The eels will be all dead in the pond for want of water and fluid," he wrote anxiously, and attached a sprig (too faded now to identify) to a letter to his mother as proof of his love as well as his botanising.

The boys were encouraged to take an interest in the family business. "There must be a great change at the mills now with all your alterations and improvements," George complimented their father. They witnessed more change, when Principal Tulloch's funeral procession passed through the streets of St Andrews. The young David Russell, who was to become one of the great supporters and benefactors of the "college of the scarlet gown," stood watching the cortège, his school cap in his hand.

From an early age he was fascinated by the latent powers of the mind and sat wide-eyed at a thought-reading performance in St Andrews town hall. Blindfolded, Mr Alfred Capper found a ring taken off a lady's finger. Two professors bound him, but intellect had to give way to illusion, for the performer was able to take off his coat though his hands remained tied.

David was concerned with his brother's hands, because he told their sister Christian to "look sharp" in knitting gloves for George, perhaps to keep his hands warm while he golfed and skated. But lessons were just as important as games at Clifton Bank. As well as Greek, Latin and algebra, the boys had to know the Bible.

David Russell's essay on "The Easter Holidays" explained his lifelong love of nature. "I never used a gun in the holidays for the birds were all building just beside us. There were five woodpigeons' nests in the fir trees, and I knew three robins' nests, and a great many more other nests." He got 8 out of 10 for his care. The boy who would become a bibliophile also wrote his "Thoughts in a Library," enthusing:

Books are a never-failing companion to many people. They give you good advice and never get angry. Let us look along one shelf and see what there is. We see the Bible which is the best book in the library but which too many despise. Then we see volumes on botany. It is very nice to study botany and to go on botanising excursions. Then there are a great many books on natural history which is very interesting. Then you see books on astronomy, geology, chemistry and other things.

But the English master was not impressed. "Very careless," he wrote, and gave young David Russell half marks. In another essay, "When there's a will there's a way," David Russell wrote confidently: "When there's a will there's a way also applies to lessons and although a boy is far back he can learn his lessons quite well."

On one excursion by train to Edinburgh the three Russell brothers had only money to buy one newspaper. George and Robert took their pick of the pages, leaving David very contented with the book section.

At Silverburn all the Russells were anxious weather-watchers, filling their diaries with records of the persistent sea-mists and precious hours of sunshine. They were frequently in bed with colds. But Christian's ailment in January 1885 was much more serious, probably typhoid. David Russell senior wrote to reassure Robert: "There is really no risk of infection in a letter from your mother or me from Silverburn. Mrs Campbell is never in any room but Christian's and never enters the kitchen. Every plate and article that comes out of their room is disinfected with carbolic acid."

The Russell family were seasoned travellers in Britain and abroad. In 1886 they were at Lausanne, and in August there was another great adventure as David set off for London with Robert to see the Museum of Natural History and the Crystal Palace. Their father applied the thoroughness of his business management to family matters. On their way home from London his sons were to hire a hansom to take the big portmanteau. "I suppose it will cost you about 3/6 or 4/-." There was an overnight stop at the Station Hotel, Doncaster.

Tell the Boots to call you at 3 in the morning. Get a cup of coffee and as much as you can eat of breakfast. The train starts at 3.45 and reaches Edinburgh at 9.55. Go straight to the Royal Hotel if no one is to be meeting you at the train. Leave your luggage in the Left Luggage Room. You will have to pay 2d for each bundle.

But it was time to discuss further education. David Russell senior wrote:

My Dear Boys, I was making enquiries about the Science classes in Edinburgh and saw the Principal and will hear from him tonight again as to the classes in Edinburgh. There are other very good classes in Glasgow which open on September 1st but I would like you in Edinburgh. Those in Edinburgh open in October, I think.

All three brothers attended George Heriot's School, Edinburgh, for a short time. A certificate of merit for class V for session 1888 survives in the name of David Russell. He showed "diligence and proficiency" in mathematics, chemistry and freehand drawing. In those days it was possible to take summer classes at university. At Heriot-Watt College and Edinburgh University David Russell acquired an impressive portfolio of first class certificates in a wide range of subjects. Of the 6126 candidates who sat the elementary stage of animal physiology in the nationwide examinations in 1890, 544, including David Russell, obtained a first class.

He gained certificates in organic chemistry, practical plane and solid geometry, applied mechanics, magnetism and electricity. His certificate from the City and Guilds of London Institute for the Advancement of Technical Education, first class in the ordinary grade, electrical lighting and transmission of power, was no doubt taken with his future place in the mills in mind.

But David Russell was also interested in more subtle forms of energy. On 3rd December 1890 the 18 year old student had his horoscope drawn up. It was to prove uncannily accurate with regard to his future character.

Those born under Leo are generous to a fault, and they are sincere, faithful and earnest. Although idealistic they do not struggle after the unattainable nor do they talk of their ideals; but they quietly and silently try to make their ideals into realities. They have strong feelings and are very sincere in their affections, but express them by acts rather than by words. They have great faith and are said to be more thorough than those born under the other signs.

In the summer session of 1891 he studied elementary practical botany at Edinburgh University and gained first class certificates in the faculty of medicine. Later in life he was to say that if he had not been a papermaker, he would have been a doctor, but as a student examining specimens at the university he knew that the family business had to be his destiny.

He stayed on in the capital, living at the substantial villa at 7 Strathearn Road owned by his father, getting experience of the paper trade by working in Tullis Hunter, paper merchants, and enjoying the cultural life, the concerts and exhibitions. His little sister Agnes was at St Katharine's School, St Andrews. She wrote to her brother, asking him to get her "a little red demon on a bicycle" from a shop in Princes Street for a "very nice girl's birthday . . . Please try and send it in time, sweet, little, darling brother (I am using sweet words so as you will get the thing for me)."

Mary also stayed in Edinburgh. David was at home in Fife when she wrote from Strathearn Road about "a very sad event that has happened and I hope you won't be very angry." Apparently he had given her a pot of seeds he had obtained at a lecture, with instructions on steeping the pot in a tub. The seeds were washed out. David Russell was also developing a consuming interest in photography, and Christian was sent precise instructions on where to point the camera in the Silverburn garden.

As his sons matured David Russell senior was able to share business problems with them. The Silverburn flax work account at 29th June 1889 survives, showing the now forgotten processes of scutching, stricking and rolling, shaking tow and carding tow. Flax straw was resold to Dundee, leaving a debit balance of £5480 5s7d. In March 1891 David Russell wrote to his son David:

> George Wallace who was assistant agent in the bank has disappeared. He had been behaving himself very badly in many ways and many will suffer at his hands. Mrs Campbell has lost £120 by him and I have lost a good deal more as well as your aunts Innes and Tullis. You will hear more when we meet.

Arthur Dace of Queen Street, Edinburgh, gave the Russell family music lessons. Christian wrote to her brother David from Brighton, where she was pursuing her piano studies: "I haven't any more to say; at least, I can't be bothered saying any more." Mary, also in Brighton, was more forthcoming: "We have a very lively lady staying here just now. The three things she hates are: plain boiled rice, cold mutton and matrimony! She regards a bride as 'a hero for an hour and a victim for a life-time' (NB: take this to heart)." David was teased by Christian about a young lady in Edinburgh: "Have you seen dear Nellie lately? Have you ever happened (!!) to pass the house again on your bicycle?"

Christian had a leg deformity and had to walk with two sticks, but she nonetheless managed to have an extraordinarily active life in Brighton. On one occasion she laid aside her sticks to play a rousing duet on the piano with her sister Mary. However, "I haven't fallen in love yet, and am not likely to," she assured David.

George was out in Canada in 1894, riding across the wide open spaces, having made it clear that he was going to be a farmer, not a papermaker. But Robert was proving a brilliant engineer at the mills, and assured David: "Everything is going well and the Soda Recovery Plant working very satisfactory."

David and Robert Russell were close. They shot partridges together at Cadham Farm near the mills. The company was the tenant of Cadham, and George would manage the farm. In July 1894 David and Robert Russell holidayed at Loch Maree. Their mother wrote: "The combination of colours, such as Walter Paton paints, must be very beautiful." It was during a holiday at Loch Maree that David discovered an unknown sub-species of plant, and his contribution to botany was published.

But Janet Russell suffered heartbreak at home as 14 year old Jenny got weaker with consumption at Silverburn. On 4th March 1895 Mrs Russell wrote to David:

Thursday she came down as usual and took a faint turn after dinner. She said 'Our Father' after me on Saturday morning, and then the faint, so gently taken, no suffering. And her radiant look on Sunday night, how wonderful, as if she had seen a vision, and her "Oh Mother, Oh Mother" her last words.

The following day she added: "You understood Jenny better than anybody. She was always very sensitive and had a very highly strung temperament."

David was also highly sensitive. He attributed his stammer to the fact that although he was left handed, he had been made to write with his right hand. The difficulty he had with spelling would now be diagnosed as dyslexia. The stammer, combined with his naturally quiet speaking voice, sometimes made him inaudible in company. The new telephone installed at the mills made him apprehensive. How could he conduct business, face to face or at a distance, with his impediment? He was already showing the thoroughness of his approach to the ordering of his life when he arranged to have speech therapy. He chose the Brampton Park clinic at Huntingdon, an expensive institution which took members of the landed class, the sons of army officers and professional people.

His father assured him in September 1896:

I am very glad to hear you are getting on so well with all your exercises and are getting able to control your articulation now. I am sure you are working on the right lines now . . . and will go steadily on to feel quite easy about speaking and do it without almost any effort . . . I don't grudge the £70 a bit and will be quite glad to write out another cheque at any time you think and as often as you like.

He offered to send on botanical papers and books.

Beasley, the proprietor of Brampton Park, had a drink problem, which did nothing for the confidence of his patients. But at least David Russell made friends. Reginald Graham, another pupil, wrote from Brampton Park: "We have all of us been here in sackcloth and ashes since you departed, and Alice refuses to be comforted, (although Carr is doing his best). We are now supposed to have speeches 3 nights a week. A new pupil has arrived, by name Piper (horrid word to say)." Another letter informed David Russell: "The old man was drunk 3 times last week. *Hope you are speaking well.* You must speak slow."

James Carr was a kindred spirit who travelled for the family firm of millers and corn merchants and who was self-conscious about going into shops to take orders. He wrote to David Russell in December 1896: "I always thought you had gone away from B.P. leaving a little bit of your heart behind, and seeing a letter directed to Miss Sutherland the other day, confirmed my thought, but I must say I was a bit surprised. She is a very nice little girl, but a pity she is so young." There seems to have been some confusion, for Carr wrote again at the close of the year: "I am afraid you have a wrong idea of what I have been saying to Miss Sutherland about you."

By Christmas 1896 David Russell was losing confidence in the Beasley system, but another of his correspondents, Stuart Duncan, urged him to remember: "Beasleys is the best because it is the simplest." He advised him to keep up his exercises. Pupils go wrong, he argued, because they let things slip. Confidence is the key word. "A stammerer can never afford to talk off rule. EXAGGERATE. SLOW INSPIRATION, MODIFIED SIGH."

David Russell seems to have given Brampton another chance, for Beryl Beasley wrote on behalf of her father in January 1897, sending a prospectus with terms. David Russell wanted to keep up his lessons when he returned to Edinburgh, and asked for details of Miss Herbert's tuition for stammering at 25 Gilmore Place.

But Brampton must have helped, for David Russell had managed to communicate his feelings to not one, but two young women. In 1903 Mary Anderson wrote to him from the Queen's Bay Hotel, Joppa, outside Edinburgh. She appreciated "how lonely in spirit" he had been all his life. She was going to return the circlet he had given her, but she would keep the little safety pin "as it embodied a secret." Apparently David Russell had found someone else.

As for the name of course I don't want to know, not yet at any rate. And aren't you nearly 31, David? Well you do know that song. It's an Irish one and Pat says to Mary that her father and mother won't agree to it, and Mary says: 'If me father and mother's so cruel—You'd better, you'd better ask—me!'"

2
Convalescence in Sweden

Like his brother David, Robert Russell had had his horoscope drawn up. "Considerable enthusiasm and some practical ability for public work. An agitator. Carves his own fortunes." But as the century turned, Robert was showing more signs of the deepening depression that was to keep him away from his duties at the mills for weeks, even at periods of major modernisation, when his presence as engineer was required. Since David Russell senior had suffered a stroke and could not attend to his business, the burden of running the mills fell on his son David, though he did have the Tullis partners.

The inevitable result was a serious nervous breakdown. But whereas Robert lay in bed at Silverburn, David Russell went in search of help, on his sister Christian's recommendation. "I've felt very worried about you very often; you are never as well as you ought to be," she wrote to him. She had been to the Kellgren Institute in London to have her leg treated by Dr Harry Kellgren. "He's a wonderful man. I feel utterly different inside!" she told her brother.

The Kellgren cure had started in Sweden. Frustrated by his lack of success as a poet, Per Henrik Ling (1776–1839), the fencing master at the University of Lund, devised a system of gymnastic exercises for therapeutic purposes. In 1831 he founded the Royal Gymnastic Central Institute at Stockholm and became its principal.ß

A former student at Lund, Jonas Henrik Kellgren finished off his army officer training at Ling's Institute in Stockholm. Kellgren believed that practically all disease could be cured, partly or completely, by physiotherapy. He maintained that since the functions of the body were largely under the influence of the nerves, they could be controlled by treatment in which the physiotherapist worked with a light touch, stimulating the neural pathways. In "suction-vibration," for example, the manipulator spread out his fingers on the patient's skin as if playing the piano. Kellgren was not daunted by infectious diseases, or cancer and glaucoma. Gymnastic treatment was even administered during childbirth to combat loss of blood.

Jonas Kellgren moved to London in 1874, opening an institute which proved so successful that he decided to set up a series abroad; at Norderney, Germany, in 1877, Baden-Baden in 1883, Paris in 1884. In 1886 he established a summer sanatorium at Sanna near Jonkoping in Sweden.

The London institute was run by Jonas's elder son Harry Jonas Henrik Kellgren, a licentiate in medicine and surgery of the Society of Apothecaries, London. There was opposition among university medical graduates to such licentiates using the title of doctor, but Harry Kellgren was known as Dr Harry by his many patients, and his healing skills were never in doubt.

Christian seems to have been the first of the Russell family to have turned to alternative medicine. She had treatment for her leg from Dr Harry in London before going out to the summer sanatorium in Sweden in the summer of 1903, where she made such improvement that she was able to tell her astonished family that she was riding a piebald horse. She wrote to her brother David: "Well, sir, I have a proposal to make—when you take your holiday to come here for a fortnight. You would find it A1. You could boat, ride, botanise, geologise, etc."

Harry Kellgren warned his new patient that it would take him three years to get back to normal after his breakdown and suggested that he spend the summer of 1904 at the Swedish sanatorium. Jonkoping, the capital of the old province of Smaland, lay at the southern end of the 79 mile long Lake Vattern and on the shores of the little lakes Munksjon and Rocksjon. The ancient town owed its modern prosperity to the opening of the Gota Canal, the 347 mile waterway which crosses Sweden from Gothenburg. As well as being the principal centre of the Swedish match industry, Jonkoping was famous for its paper mills, a good reason for combining business with treatment.

Sanna was between Husqvarna and Jonkoping. The Kellgren sanatorium was a complex of wooden villas, with national names—a German villa, an Austrian villa, and even a billiard villa. In the villa occupied by David Russell, Christian and their aunt Joanna Hutchison, the bedrooms had a balcony outside, reached by a glass door from David's room, which Christian had occupied on her previous stay. They also had a table to themselves in the dining-room.

One of the sanatorium buildings at Sanna, Sweden, where David Russell went to take the Kellgren cure as a young man.

Klass the coachman helped David Russell to acquire a hammock, which he slung alongside the others hung from the lombardy poplars round their villa. The lilac scent was heady. Reading and relaxing were part of the therapy of Sanna, but he roused himself to ride Dr Harry's horse, or to row on the lake. After his Russian dancing lesson he wandered the hilly countryside, noting how poor the sandy boulder-clay soil was for crop growing, and that the fields were separated by ditches. A lover of trees, he wrote wistfully to Silverburn: "I have not seen any woods like the woods of home." But he was glad that he had brought his botany books so that he could study the water plants on the marshy sides of the river. "The flora is practically the same as in Britain. I have only found one plant not included in our own flora."

Conscious of the cost of his stay at Sanna, David Russell wrote to Robert: could he arrange for him to see over the paper mill at Jonkoping, which his brother had already visited? The Swedish mill, which took its generating power from the falls at Husqvarna, was fascinating to this student of electricity, since the electrification programme for the Fife mills had started before the end of the century under Robert Russell's supervision. David Russell added a

PS to his letter to his brother. "I am very glad to hear that your new motor car is going so well. How do you like the solid tyres?"

In July David Russell visited the Monksjon mill with George Tullis from the Rothes and Auchmuty mills, and Tom Hunter, another business associate. But David Russell was worried about his lack of progress after five weeks at Sanna, and disappointed that Dr Harry had been so long in getting away from London. "All three of us prefer his treatment to the others. He is expected on the 1st and I hope nothing will prevent his coming." As he anxiously awaited Dr Harry, David Russell noted a drawback in the use of electric power in industry: with the Husqvarna falls low in the drought, the works were affected.

David Russell senior received regular letters from his son and daughter at Sanna. Christian wrote in the first week of July to tell him how busy the sanatorium was.

We now sit down about 50 to meals, which is more than is usual so early in July. They have had more people wanting to come than they have room for this year. Eight arrived from London on Sunday evening. There are two very nice ladies here, including a Mrs Broklejem and her daughter. Mrs B is really Scotch, her parents lived in Dundee before emigrating to Sweden.

In return for his letters to his father, David was sent the *Fife News* and copies of the *Scotsman* containing the long-running saga of the Free Church dispute. In 1900 the Free Church and the United Presbyterian Church had amalgamated. But all the property had been appropriated by the new United Free Church, and the minority of members of the Free Church who had declined to go into the union had raised a legal action in the Court of Session, Edinburgh, over its former property. The decision went against the Free Church, and an appeal was made to the House of Lords.

Though it was days late, David Russell avidly read the *Scotsman* for 2nd August 1904 as he lay in his hammock at Sanna. "Never for a quarter of a century have the doors of the final Court of Appeal in the country been besieged by so many members of the general public, eager to learn at first hand the pronouncement of a decision fraught with such consequences to Scotland." The Lords had decided in favour of the Free Church minority.

It was so hot at Sanna that the farmers cutting rye grass by the scythe, could only work for half the day. Dr Harry was expected daily, David Russell wrote to his father. "It is said that the run of patients in London was from the Stock Exchange people. A Stock

Exchange man who had been lame for 2 or 3 years and was told by his doctor that he would be lame for life went to Dr Harry who discovered what was wrong and after 15 minutes treatment he was all right."

Aunt Joanna left in late July and, at last, the harassed Dr Harry arrived at Sanna on 8th August, probably as much in need of a rest as some of his patients. But David Russell planned to consult him on behalf of his father, as he told Robert. "I have been thinking of asking him if he would advise us to have an assistant north in autumn to give father treatment for a month or so."

In another letter David Russell cited the example of an officer, deprived of speech for 11 years after a shock, and considered a hopeless case by his doctors, who was on his fifth visit to Sanna. "He speaks perfectly and although his arm and leg flap a little he takes long walks."

On 11th August 1904 ("Mother's birthday") he wrote to his father, giving a detailed Swedish weather report: showery, with chilly mornings. He recorded the changing colours of the poplars and birches with the approach of autumn. There seemed to be a biblical message in his news. "Four or five miles from this the birch trees were almost leafless in July, due to some fly. They have been the same for three years and it is said the fly always destroys them for 3 years running and disappears on the fourth."

The oats and barley were being cut, but it was a thin harvest. "I changed from my room into Aunt Joanna's (next to Christian's) at the end of last week." A consumptive clergyman from Cambridge, a brother-in-law of the Duke of Hamilton, now occupied his room. They found a common interest, fishing Loch Maree.

There were now 90 patients in the sanatorium, of whom about 70 were resident. "Dr Harry gives me twice or three times as long as the average patient and his treatment is most thorough. The ordinary treatment has hardened all the nerves that were so sensitive at first in my back and body and altogether I am really very much better." His pulse had settled at a normal 70, though it could reach as high as 100 for brief periods. He was 9 stone 11 lb and felt sure that he would make rapid progress, with the cool weather and Dr Harry's treatment.

Jonas Kellgren the patriarch had not studied medicine, but was determined that his family should be well qualified in applying his homoeopathic treatment. His daughter Annjuta, who was married to Dr Edgar Cyriax, was taking her examinations to become a licentiate of both the Royal Colleges of Physicians and Surgeons,

Edinburgh, as well as of the Faculty of Physicians and Surgeons, Glasgow. Christian Russell told her sister Mary proudly that their brother David had become a "walking advertisement" for Sanna.

The Kellgrens believed that pleasure was an important part of treatment. Dr Karin's engagement party was held by brilliant moonlight, with plenty of champagne, and Chinese lanterns hanging from the balconies of the villas. An enchanted Christian wrote to Silverburn in mid August:

last night after supper Dr and Mrs Harry, Mrs Olson and Hedvig Kellgren danced a Russian dance for us in the gym, in costume. It was very pretty. The gentlemen were in red uniform with gold braiding and trimmed with fur—white riding breeches, top boots and spurs. The ladies were in white and pale blue, very pretty old style with Queen Elizabeth's collar behind.

The patients and the Kellgren clan went camping, consuming a hundred crayfish for breakfast. "I'm sure Dr Harry's liveliness will have a good effect on David as well as the treatment. It certainly has on me! He is very good to David," Christian reported. The dashing Count Hamilton went horse-riding, and took a hand at bridge in the evening.

It was the custom for patients to give the assistants a supper, but David Russell wanted to leave them a more tangible memento of his appreciation, so he asked Robert to collect and dispatch four gold safety pins from Hamilton & Inches, the Edinburgh jewellers. The same letter contained a recommendation from Dr Harry. "He would much prefer to have father under his own care in London but if that cannot be he would come to Silverburn and go over everything with the assistant for two days, and he has no doubt that would do father a lot of good."

David Russell used the knowledge he had gained in his classes in Edinburgh to give Robert advice on sizing paper, with precise chemical instructions about the use of acid and alum. In late August he wrote to his father: ordinary labourers in Sweden got up to 2s 9d a day. However, the rate for labourers in the Husqvarna foundry was double that. "Work is so severe that few can stand it for long." According to Dr Cyriax, there was something else bad for the health: strong coffee. In the same letter David Russell asked nostalgically "What is doing in Fife?"

David and Christian Russell planned to leave Sanna on 8th or 15th September, since Dr Harry was due to start work in the London institute on 1st October. David told his father that he hoped to start work at the mills at the beginning of October, after his six months' absence. "The busy season will soon be round again." His mind was already on business: he referred to two scientific papers about the production electrically of nitrate of soda, and of electricity from water power. But his father's muscular power was of much more importance. "I hope you are making good progress and improving every week."

On 27th August David Russell inspected the bicycle and sewing machine factory at Husqvarna. On 30th August, the night of the sanatorium's fancy dress ball, Christian wrote excitedly: "I have got my fish-wife costume finished, all but the creel! David has got a Russian costume of Dr Harry's to wear!" That day a band had appeared outside the gymnasium, and Dr Harry had requested a waltz, followed by a polka for his patients to do their exercises to.

By 1st September most of the patients had left. David Russell weighed 10 stone 5 lb and was looking forward to going home, travelling first to Stockholm by rail, or by steamer through the Gota Canal. He and Christian were urged in the sanatorium to go by water, since the boats were comfortable, the scenery interesting. They would then proceed to Copenhagen and Hamburg.

Dr Harry left for London on 14th September. Apart from memories of the bonhomie of Sanna, David Russell was taking something else home. He had been studying the treatment given at the sanatorium, and had had practical lessons on its application. He would be able to help his family when they had headaches, toothache, or neuralgia, he told them confidently.

But the aftermath of Sanna was a disappointment. Dr Harry wrote to David Russell in November 1904:

I am sorry to hear that you have not progressed much since you came back to Scotland. As to the question of Graves' disease or exophthalmic goitre as you say your condition is supposed to be, I think it quite possible that your thyroid may be somewhat affected. This is not however the seat of your trouble; it is in the medulla of your brain and the gland is only secondarily affected. The best thing you could do would be to come down for a short aftercure.

The early months of 1905 were spent in London, getting more treatment from Dr Harry, who warned him that certain nerve centres had "given way" and that fatigue was preventing their restoration. David Russell stayed at Morley's Hotel in Trafalgar Square, then moved to the Star and Garter Hotel, Richmond Hill, to a room more than 100 feet above the river. It had a piano and a good fire. He did some business for the mills, but most of the

CONVALESCENCE IN SWEDEN

time was spent in walking in the parks, or being driven through Slough and Cranford, at that time leafy suburbs with large green spaces.

On 20th February he wrote to his father:

Motorising suits me very well. I get a lot of fresh air and I enjoy it. Dr Harry says he has no doubt some weeks of treatment would do you a lot of good. He thinks the vibrator should be used, not to continue it for too long at one time; that is, never to go beyond the point of stimulation.

He had become close to the Kellgrens, and they dined together.

Dr Harry's wife is very nice. She got into disfavour with the Russian police before she was married for trying to educate the peasants. She has not been back to Russia, since she was married, till last year, when she was surprised to find how much more freedom was allowed than formerly. She is not at all sorry to see Russia in difficulties now.

Dr Harry predicted that the Tsar would be "got rid of."

In the city David Russell saw one of the hazards of the modern science that fascinated him so much, when a pavement burst open through a short circuit, causing an "electrical explosion."

The Russell brothers took to the automobile. In this photograph from 1905, Robert Russell is at the wheel of his brother's Albion. Dr Harry Kellgren is sitting beside him, and David Russell is in the back.

Meanwhile, Christian was finding romance through her affliction. Gunnar Chronander, one of Kellgren's Swedish assistants, was falling in love with her. He told her stories about the eccentric Duke of Hamilton, who was one of his patients. When His Grace was in the navy he would dive from one side of a ship and come up the other. He had rescued a lost torpedo by diving with a rope and securing it to the weapon. After getting sunstroke in Burmah, the Duke lost consciousness and was paralysed and speechless for six weeks. Captain Sinclair the Liberal whip was also attending the Kellgren Institute for nerve treatment, perhaps because the parliamentary majority had been brought down to 24.

But David Russell was gaining in confidence. He was having more therapy for his stammering and played the piano with Mr Stahl, a fellow guest who had known Wagner and who had a Stradivarius. A sultan with a Mercedes was a figure of fascination in the hotel.

David Russell reported Dr Harry's charges to his father: 1st month, 25 guineas; 2nd month, 20 guineas; 3rd and after, 15 guineas. On 8th March he wrote again: "I asked Dr Harry what he thought of me going home next week, that is after 4 weeks treatment. He said he thought it would be much better if I could arrange to stay a fortnight longer. What would you like me to do?"

He stayed on in London because the glands on the right side of his head and neck were swollen. Dr Harry assured him that it was the result of the treatment, and not a relapse. The nightingales sang as he went to bed in Richmond. Some days he missed treatment to do business calls, answering customers' complaints about paper not taking ink well. He saw an exhibition of paintings by the Pre-Raphaelite brotherhood of Rossetti, Millais and Holman Hunt, and sent his mother violets from Haywards Heath, with the hope that Robert was better. "I always feel that I should be at home and that he should have a good holiday but I hope it will not be long now before I am able to do a good day's work."

He went north in late April, and resumed work at the mills. Early in 1906 Dr Harry came up to give David Russell senior treatment at Silverburn, and Gunnar Chronander stayed there in May to continue the physiotherapy. Chronander wanted to open his own practice in Edinburgh. "Do you think the doctors would make it too difficult to start there?" Christian asked her brother anxiously.

But not even the skilled fingers of Gunnar Chronander could bring back David Russell's life-force as he lay on his bed in Silverburn. He was 77 when he died, "gathered like a shock of corn fully ripe," as one of his obituary notices eloquently put it. His funeral was one of the largest in Fife, with a hundred of his workers walking with him to the end. At the head of the procession his son David knew how hard it was going to be to take his father's place.

3
A Papermaking Family

Fife flows with history. From her prison on Loch Leven Mary Queen of Scots had tried to escape, disguised as a washerwoman, but her beautiful white hands betrayed her. The River Leven rises from this loch, running 12 miles to the Firth of Forth at the town of Leven. In the early eighteenth century Daniel Defoe (whose Robinson Crusoe was based on Alexander Selkirk, of Lower Largo) noted that "the Salmon of this River are esteemed the best in this Part of Scotland."

But the Industrial Revolution gave the salmon competition. The local poet William Ranken made the Leven speak:

> I bleach the linen fair and clean,
>   To pure angelic hue,
> And from Earth's centre, far unseen,
>   I raise the coal-pit too.
>
> I spin the flax, whose canvas proud
>   Britannia's thunder spreads,
> Confirms her empire o'er the flood,
>   Or wafts where glory leads.
> (*Poems on Different Subjects*, Leith, 1812)

At the beginning of the nineteenth century the Leven supported 7 bleachfields, 2 large cotton mills, 3 mills for spinning flax, 12 corn mills, 3 fulling mills, 7 lint mills, 2 flour mills, 4 barley mills, one mill for manufacturing linseed oil and 3 coal engines. Auchmuty meal mill on the south bank was leased from the Countess of Rothes by James Stronach, but the wheel was stopped abruptly in 1809 when he went bankrupt. That April, in a sale by public roup, Robert Tullis of Cupar purchased the remainder of the 99 year lease.

Books, not millstones were Robert Tullis's business. A well-known bookseller and publisher, at one time printer to St Andrews University, he brought out editions of the classics: Caesar, Horace and Sallust. Tullis probably took the lease of Auchmuty Mill to supply paper for his publishing business, since Auchmuty was converted into a four-vat paper mill which began to produce handmade paper in 1810.

Six hundred yards lower down the river at Rothes there was another paper mill, started in 1804 by William Keith, whose father Archibald was a papermaker at Newbattle, Midlothian. But it was a risky business; between 1804 and 1836 three papermakers went bankrupt at Rothes Mill. But upstream at Auchmuty Robert Tullis's mill continued to turn out paper. In 1822 Tullis expanded his interests by establishing the *Cupar Herald*, one of the first weekly newspapers in Scotland, which a year later became the *Fife Herald*. He also acquired partners, the firm becoming Robert Tullis & Company (altered to R. Tullis & Company in 1845). In 1836 it purchased the bankrupt Rothes Mill.

In the 1820s one of the first paper machines in the country had been installed at Rothes, followed by another, 10 years later, at Auchmuty Mill. Both machines were driven by water-wheels. The web was carried into a loft, cut by hand and hung up to dry. The opening of the Thornton and Cupar Railway in 1847 and the laying of the branch line from the Leslie railway to the mills about a decade later brought the installation of plant to meet the demand for machine-made paper.

Midway between the two paper mills, Rothes Bleachfield was being operated by William and Robert Russell, manufacturers in Kirkcaldy, who might have been distantly related to the David Russell of this biography. In 1846 R. Tullis & Company acquired the business, becoming not only papermakers but yarn merchants and bleachers. But even after the installation of the second paper machine at Auchmuty in 1856, there was little increase in the production of paper. Apparently the firm was afraid of flooding the market, and for some years the machines ran only from breakfast to dinner time.

Up until the 1870s, rag and flax waste were the raw materials used in the mills. But in the Great Exhibition of 1851, samples of esparto grass, a sub-desert plant from North Africa and Spain, had been shown, and in 1857 Thomas Routledge brought to his mill at Eynsham the first consignment of this grass to be tried on a commercial scale. Thirty years later esparto was used at Auchmuty Mill.

George Smith Tullis, the eldest son of Robert Tullis of Cupar, died in 1848; in 1872 his son Robert was admitted a partner. Two years

SIR DAVID RUSSELL

later David Russell senior of Silverburn, Leven, and Arthur Russell, banker, Cupar, also became partners. As a schoolboy wandering the cathedral ruins at St Andrews David Russell had seen the weathered tombstones of Russells and Tullises lying together and realised that his father's new partnership went far back, into friendships between the two families. There was an even closer tie: William Tullis, a senior partner in the papermaking firm, was the second son of Robert Tullis the founder, and brother of George Smith Tullis and Robert, both deceased. William had married Agnes Russell in 1846. They were young David Russell's uncle and aunt.

As heritors and tenants of Fife lands, the Russells had been "inwrought with much of the Kingdom's best estate," and David Russell's branch had farmed around Cupar for generations. But he was a papermaker now, and the mills had not kept up with industrial development. On Monday morning the one engine at Auchmuty had to be lubricated by hand with Russian tallow "with two eccentric tramps coming up through the floor." The esparto grass was hand-picked, the paper cut with a knife or hand guillotine. A ton of paper was reckoned a good production per shift. There was a gas supply, but when it failed parts of the mills had to be lit by candles, and at the bleachfield men continued to use long poles to turn over the yarn laid on the grass.

In 1887 the firm bought the lands on which the paper mills and bleachfield stood from the Countess of Rothes. Three years later a symbol of the mills' growing prosperity was erected. The new chimney stack at Auchmuty to serve the expanding steam boiler plant was heightened to 225 feet in a friendly competition with Fettykil Mill. For sixpence, men and women could ascend the new chimney by hand windlass for a spectacular view of Fife. Children went up for half price and were twice as impressed.

In 1891 Arthur Russell died, leaving Robert Tullis and David Russell as sole partners. There was another change: the old waterwheels at Auchmuty and Rothes were replaced by water turbines. David Russell senior viewed these improvements proudly as he was driven from Silverburn to the mills by his coachman, or rode his own horse. He believed that many "rogue" horses had become that way, not because of their nature, but because they had been handled badly by previous riders. He had a succession of "rogue" horses which he turned into docile obedient mounts.

The mills had become a small community. In 1892 Rothes and Auchmuty were employing 270 people, about 80 of them women and girls, their wages gradually getting better, though not as good

The Russells' partner, Robert Tullis, painted in 1919.

as the men's. But money had to be ploughed back: in 1894 a new beater house was built, and the following year £5000 was laid out on a soda recovery plant.

David Russell could take it easier because he had two sons in the business. David and Robert Russell brought to the mills the energy and knowledge required, not only to modernise them, but to put them ahead of the competition. They were present at the Spithead naval review of 1897 to celebrate the Diamond Jubilee of Queen Victoria. Charles Parsons had designed the first steam turbine ship in the world, and the Russells watched the *Turbinia* causing a sensation by racing down the line of warships at a speed greater than that of any other naval vessel afloat.

But the Russell brothers needed the authority to implement their ideas. In 1898 Robert was made a partner, followed by David the next year. At the Paris Exhibition of 1900 David Russell saw the Parsons steam turbine which the firm was one of the earliest to introduce into a paper mill. It was delivered out of stock, price £2608. Inspecting German scientific inventions at Berlin in 1903, he had a letter from Robert, telling him that the three year old turbine was already out of date. The mills needed more power.

Robert wrote: "We wired Christy yesterday, confirming the order for the 300kW. Parsons Turbo generator . . ."

There was another innovation. A system of bribery was well established throughout the paper trade, and to get an order, the salesman had to give a backhander to the purchaser. David Russell's refusal to do this put the prosperity of the Tullis Russell mills at risk, but gradually buyers came round because they needed the paper. He had brought about the end of bribery in the trade.

In May 1906 the firm ceased to be a private concern and became a limited company, Tullis Russell & Company Limited, with David Russell senior as chairman, though he only had a month to live. Robert and David Russell were appointed to the board. George, the elder brother, was now supervising Cadham Farm for the company, and would become a farmer in his own right by succeeding his Uncle George at Hatton.

There was black crepe at Silverburn for Christmas 1906, after David Russell's death in the summer. Gunnar Chronander was trying to bring down Christian's temperature from 100, but by Hogmanay he himself was ill. However, both recovered and in the new year Christian went out to Sanna, Sweden, to work treating patients for knee swellings in the gymnasium. But relationships had changed from the summer of 1904. "I am afraid there is something wanting in the Kellgrens' business capacity," she wrote to her brother, complaining about how little Gunnar was getting paid for long hours and heavy work. In May David Russell took a well-earned holiday in Switzerland, inspecting alpine plants on the mountain paths.

In 1907–8 Rothes Mill turned in the first profit for many years, but a heavy loss on the bleachfield because of the unexpected plunge in the price of yarn wiped out both the Rothes and Auchmuty gains, and there was no ordinary dividend. Nonetheless, David Russell and his partners continued the process of expansion and modernisation, with an electric power house, new engines and boilers.

At last trade began to pick up, and in the centenary year of 1909–10 production at Auchmuty Mill reached the record figure of 100 tons a week, when in 1900 the combined output of Auchmuty and Rothes had been 800 tons a year. David Russell had not forgotten his chemical studies in Edinburgh. The mills were probably the first in the country to appoint a chemist, and in 1910 David Russell set up a laboratory for quality control and research.

Modern accounting practices were introduced into the mill

Rothes Mill in 1906

Auchmuty Mill in 1913. Note the line of railway wagons.

offices. David Russell had his stutter under control, for telephone conversations and business trips to London in search of new orders and processes. But he was conscious that he was approaching 40 and still single. Who was to succeed him at the mills, with Robert mentally unstable, and George more interested in farming?

Since his father's death David Russell had become the head of the family, the person his sisters and brothers turned to increasingly for help with their financial and domestic problems. He would supervise his sisters' marriage contracts and make sure that they had their share in the inheritance of the mills. He always treated them as equals, not dependents, at a time when women were still to win their due place in society.

In July 1907 Christian wrote with news she had not even told her mother.

Mr Chronander and I are engaged, and I am so happy in spite of the fact that he has gone home to Sweden for several weeks, perhaps three or four months. The doctor he consulted said he *must* give up work and go for a rest. You don't know how good Mr C is. I know we shall be tremendously happy together, and you will see now what stuff he is made of.

Mrs Cyriax of the Kellgren Institute gave Christian treatment before and after the birth of her son Robert in 1910, though £58 was "rather a lot to charge an old assistant," Christian noted indignantly. She turned to David: "It doesn't matter does it, if I spend a little more than my income now? Now that Gunnar has begun work I'm quite sure he'll soon have quite a good practice and then it will be all right." But Gunnar himself needed treatment because of his poor health. Christian rebuked her brother in a letter from Burley, Hants, where the Chronanders were living in September 1910: "I do think you might take *some* interest in Gunnar and send some of your patients to us. I don't think it is quite kind of you. You think nobody can give treatment like Harry but I know lots of patients prefer Gunnar to Harry." She added: "We were awfully surprised to hear of Mary's engagement to Capt. Chill. I must say I had never thought of it. But I'm awfully glad for her, she seems so happy."

Stationed in St Andrews, Captain Walter Chill of the West India Regiment had become a regular visitor to Silverburn. He joined the smoking concerts of the local Territorial unit in which the three Russell brothers were officers. Like his father, David Russell rode daily from Silverburn to the mills, but was not as adept as his father had been in handling "rogue" horses. The one which young David Russell rode refused to turn right, and whenever he was on mounted parade, he had to get his horse away from the right hand end of the line.

On one occasion, riding home from the mills, he found that his horse would not turn right at the top of the hill leading down to Milton, so he let it go left, as it habitually wanted to do. They ended up on a side track, and though he galloped it to a standstill at the entrance to Montrave, the horse did not learn a lesson.

But "horsepower" had its advantages. Almost every morning as he rode to the mills he met a steam-driven motor bicycle. It would overtake him as he left Leven, but he would pass it at Milton, where it invariably broke down.

Robert Russell was repeatedly absent from the annual Territorial camps. Bessie, George's wife, wrote in despair to David Russell from Cadham in May 1908: "You seem to be the only one who can persuade Robert to do anything." Robert had spent part of 1909 in St Petersburg, but the fur-wrapped countesses speeding in their troikas only made him pine for one of his cousins. He had proposed to her in 1907. In December 1909 he confided to David: "[She] has been within my heart more than anyone else and until I am well again I cannot talk about it."

But Robert did make attempts to return to business, and when he was at the mills, showed his sensitivity to the emotional problems of others. When Summers the mill engineer lost his son, Robert wanted to send the heartbroken parents to Pitlochry for a week's holiday. But he was also unpredictable, obsessed with the state of the country as well as with his cousin. David Russell received a letter from Morley's Hotel, Trafalgar Square, London in December 1910.

You will have heard about me running off to London. I came because of the very serious political situation, there is real danger of Home Rule in Ireland without another election and I called at Mr Balfour's house and saw his secretary and had a talk with him. I sent a short letter on Thursday night urging him to accept office for a short time only (one year) and save the union. I am staying till tomorrow as things are not satisfactory. Asquith declared in Fife that it was his intention to give Ireland Home Rule and I feel quite convinced that the unionists must meet that declaration by offering to accept office to save the union only, and let all other contentious things wait till after another election.

In a following letter he complained: "my effort produced nothing." Then, ominously: "You will have heard I have not been doing much work, hardly any. I am sorry and I may be able to begin."

David Russell had presents to buy in October 1910. On the 11th Agnes married Benjamin Blyth, who was connected with the engineering firm of Blyth & Blyth. On the 29th it was Mary's day, with Captain Chill. David Russell was shy, but Agnes's wedding provided an easy introduction to the Blyths at their substantial house in Erith Road, Belvedere, Kent, and he began to show an interest in Alison Blyth, the third daughter of Francis Creswick Blyth, a City businessman. The family, which had "genteel" connections, were somewhat disconcerted to see the suitor from Fife wearing boots, though he did have a Daimler with chauffeur at the gate.

When he was in the south David Russell accompanied Alison to garden fetes and watched her play tennis. Her mother, Mrs Debbie Blyth, wrote to him at his Hindhead hotel, telling him that she had to take a day in bed after her "unwonted dissipation" of an excursion with him on one of these flighty things called motor cars. She added:

You are always very good for the girls, and it is a pleasure to see you here: I only wish I could feel *quite* happy about it and that I could be sure you only come as a *friend*. I know Alison has told you how I feel about it, so you will not misunderstand, or resent my saying this I hope.

His sister Mary wrote encouragingly from Aviemore in May 1911: "I wonder if you go on to Belvedere. I hope you will get on well if you do and you have my best wishes for your happiness." From Penang, where she was holidaying in October 1911, his cousin Mary teased him. "How are your plans progressing? I must say I think a certain Miss is very dilatory. I hope she has nothing else 'in the bush.' It was very sweet of you to take me to Romeo and I enjoyed it awfully."

David Russell was persistent and patient. He continued to call on Alison, and the Blyth family came to accept his quiet charm as well as his footwear. But his sister Christian was desperately in need of his support. Gunnar Chronander had never kept well, and had not managed to establish his own physiotherapy business. He died in June 1912, leaving a two year old son and a heartbroken widow, who, in the course of a long life, would come to depend on her brother.

But David Russell realised that if he was to give his family support, he needed support himself. He and Alison Blyth were married at Tunbridge Wells on 6th November 1912, and went to the Hotel Continental, Paris, for their honeymoon, then on to Italy. As they were motoring to Ravello boys crowded round the car, clamouring to show them the church. Hearing David Russell's Scottish voice, one boy shouted to him: "I'll show you round, Sir, and I don't want nothing for it!" He was a little Cockney, the son of an Italian in London. The boy had been sent out to Ravello for his education.

The newly married couple could not stay at Silverburn, since Mrs Russell and Robert were there. They chose instead to live at Rothes House near the mills. David Russell had the kind of open mind that welcomed coincidences, and family continuity meant much to him. After their marriage William Tullis and Agnes Russell had set up house at Rothes in 1846. They had no children, and belonged to the Free Church. But Rothes was never a gloomy house in their time. They had filled it with flowers, and with artists, writers and painters from Edinburgh, and scholars from St Andrews who came to discuss the ideas of the day over lavish hospitality.

Rothes House was done up with David Russell's characteristic attention to detail. Whytock & Reid, Edinburgh, supplied the parquet flooring. Liberty sent lights, and furniture from Heals arrived on the London train. A harmonium was installed in the

An evocative study of David Russell, home lover and book lover.

dining-room for family entertainment. The staff in the kitchen were not forgotten: an electric kettle, "the 20th century method of boiling water," was invested in.

As David Russell walked to work each morning, it looked as if the two mills would soon meet because of the expansion, but there was still ample space for the birds and flowers he stopped to admire before the day's business. The huge investment programme continued: the new power plant cost £38,000, and a new power house was completed in 1912. Old hands at the mills who had tended the water-wheels had laughed at the Russell brothers' obsession with electricity. Now the smooth running machinery and the continuous paper proved the Russells right.

The numbers employed at both mills continued to grow, and the bookshelves at Rothes began to fill up as David Russell followed his many other interests while his wife tended the garden. He was fascinated by esoteric matters, and was about to meet a man with astonishing powers who would become his closest friend and who would lead him on a quest that would have been incredible in any book.

4
Wellesley Tudor Pole

In 1904 a young man made a pilgrimage to the sleepy Somerset town of Glastonbury. Having seen the Abbey ruins, where King Arthur is reputed to have been buried, he went up Chilkwell Street and knocked on a door, asking permission to visit Chalice Well below the hill called the Tor. A member of the French Roman Catholic order which owned the property admitted the visitor. As he drank from the pure well the young man recalled the legend: Joseph of Arimathea had brought to Glastonbury the Cup used at the Last Supper, burying it for safe keeping beneath Chalice Hill, close to the well.*

Wellesley Tudor Pole returned to his desk in the family business of Chamberlain, Pole & Company, flour, grain and cereal merchants, Bristol. On the wall in his office there was a large-scale map of the Chalice Well property and the surrounding country. One day in 1906 Tudor Pole saw light emanating from the site of Bride's Well on the map, not far from Chalice Well. He sent his sister Katharine and two friends to Glastonbury. They dug with their hands in the mud of the well and uncovered a sapphire blue bowl which was taken to a small oratory in an upper room of the Tudor Pole house in Clifton, Bristol.

Meantime at Rothes House in Fife the new bookshelves were filling up with esoteric works. David Russell had become president of the Leven Lodge of the Theosophical Society, formed in New York in November 1875 and incorporated at Madras in April 1905 as "an absolutely unsectarian body of seekers after Truth, striving to serve humanity on spiritual lines, and therefore endeavouring to check materialism and revive religious tendency."

The first annual convention of the Scottish branch of the Society was held in Edinburgh in June 1911, with Mrs Annie Besant presiding. Earlier that week David Russell had heard her public lecture in Scoonie Kirk Hall on "Man the Master of his Destiny". He had great faith in her message. The following year he was asked to join the national council of the Theosophical Society in Scotland.

---

*Accounts of these events differ. See Patrick Benham's excellent *The Avalonians* (Gothic Image Publications) for an account of the Glastonbury attraction.

David Russell read about the discovery of the bowl at Glastonbury and decided to go down to Bristol to get more information. He was lucky to meet Tudor Pole, who had been booked to take a business trip on the *Titanic* that April. He had cancelled, not through psychic forewarning of the disaster, but because there was a carters' strike at the family firm, and his father was frightened that the horses would be injured in any disturbance.

David Russell handled the bowl and talked with Tudor Pole in the Clifton oratory. It was the beginning of the closest friendship of David Russell's life. Almost every day until his death he and Tudor Pole corresponded in letters that mixed business, esoteric subjects, philosophy and family news. David Russell was to give Tudor Pole encouragement and financial backing for his esoteric and spiritual interests, including the great Quest that was to come to obsess Tudor Pole.

Tudor Pole saw the closest psychic connection between the bowl and Chalice Well, Glastonbury, though that was not the well where the bowl had been found. In March 1913 Philip Oyler the architect wrote to David Russell, informing him, no doubt with financial support in mind, that "the property containing the Holy Spring and owned by the Catholics has been offered to me for £2500, which will have to come in a few weeks in answer to combined prayer." Oyler had a scheme for "a school for religion, art, oratory, healing, painting, folk song and dance." David Russell was requested to come to Chalice Well for the month of August, for "a gathering to represent those who can present high ideals in simple constructive fashion through any form of religion or art." Tudor Pole's sapphire blue bowl would have a central role in the proceedings. That year the Chalice Well property was purchased by Miss Alice Buckton, poet, dramatist, mystic.

The First World War was to change the lives of David Russell and Tudor Pole, as well as those of millions of other people. David Russell was at his desk in the mills when war was declared on 4th August 1914. But the room of his brother Robert, the joint managing director, was empty. The brilliant engineer had patented some of the improvements he had made to the mills, and other mills had implemented his inventions and processes. But because of his mental instability Robert had begun to live a nomadic life accompanied by a series of attendants appointed by Dr George Robertson, superintendent of the Royal Asylum, Edinburgh. The alternative was confinement to an institution, which David Russell did not want. He arranged the payments of the attendants, who included two Edinburgh University medical students.

The three Russell brothers were all over 40 in 1914. As a Territorial, George Russell wanted to go on active service, but was debarred by a serious operation, and instead went south to train men for overseas. Robert was a captain in the Volunteer Fife Light Horse, but instead of reporting to his unit in early August, he was being rowed on Ullswater by Charles Lewis, a medical student. Robert's papers were passed to Dr Roberston, and he satisfied the authorities that his patient was not fit for service.

In 1914 Rothes and Auchmuty were among the best equipped paper mills in the country because of the massive investment programme. But as employees left for France and Belgium, production began to drop, though sales were not badly affected because the mills were carrying substantial stocks. Investment continued, with over £19,000 spent in 1914–15. With zeppelins in mind, consulting engineers suggested bricking up a window between the mechanics' shop and the switchboard in order to save the power supply from fire.

Because his milling company was engaged in Government work, Tudor Pole was exempt from military service. Nevertheless he meditated: "Is it worthwhile enlisting as a Tommy, and one wonders what alternative there is? . . . one longs to help at any point where 'vision' as well as commonsense would be valuable!"

The Russell's first child, Catherine Alison (Ca), had been born in October 1913. She had hydrocephalus, water on the brain. When she was a few months old the leading brain surgeon of the time operated on her, but the operation was only partially successful, and she was not expected to survive infancy. Alison Russell did not find life at Rothes House easy in wartime. The restrictions on petrol consumption meant that she could not visit her friends, and it was dark before her husband arrived home from the mills, by which time his daughter was already in bed.

Resident at the Marine Hotel, North Berwick, Robert Russell was also trying to do his bit for the war effort by applying his engineering expertise. He had noted that some Edinburgh buses had been converted to gas, and had decided to have the same done for the Daimler. He kept his indulgent brother informed about the expensive modifications, which resulted in a 30 feet long, 6 feet wide trailer that had to be towed to power the car.

Because of Catherine's condition, "caring" friends had advised her parents not to have any more children. But David and Alison

Russell had faith, and their son David Francis Oliphant (Dadie), a healthy child, was born in September 1915. However, the strain of wartime was beginning to tell, and in January 1916 both parents had to go to London for treatment from Dr Harry Kellgren, who was himself under considerable stress. Writing from 49 Eaton Square in April, he asked for his patient's help in getting settlement of an account for £58 8s which David Russell's mother at Silverburn owed, but which was not overdue. "The income tax people are over me and threaten to distrain my furniture if I don't pay before the 14th so I must scrape together all the money I can."

Robert had now moved south to be near another former Edinburgh medical student, Captain A. S. Glynn, RAMC, who had been posted to Brocton German prisoner-of-war camp near Stafford in 1916. Complaints reached David Russell about the way the Daimler was being driven around Brocton. "I would have thought the police here would consider me a very careful driver", Robert wrote from the Station Hotel, Stafford. Though admitting that he had been stopped for having "dim numbers", he added plaintively: "I have not run into anything or run over anything here."

Robert's other medical attendant, Dr Charles Lewis, was now a surgeon stationed with the fleet at Rosyth on the Forth. When he came ashore they went for drives in the Daimler. Robert was waiting with the car on the evening of 31st May 1916, but Dr Lewis did not show up. The previous evening at 6 o'clock the ships had received orders to raise steam for full speed ahead with all dispatch. The Grand Fleet under Jellicoe and Beatty was gathering for the great naval battle of Jutland. A shell blew up the magazine of the battle cruiser *Queen Mary* on which Dr Lewis was serving. On shore Robert waited for news, hoping that somehow the young man had survived. The following year Robert wanted to spend £20 on a Jutland gold medal, in memory of his friend, but his attendant George Maxwell dissuaded him.

Tudor Pole enlisted in the Royal Marines in November 1916. In the course of the war it would become clear that he did not want to return to the family business, even as managing director. In his absence David Russell took on the responsibility of corresponding with the Chamberlain, Pole lawyers to arrange an allowance for Florence, Tudor Pole's young wife, since there were problems about his army pay coming through. Tudor Pole repaid his staunch friend by sharing with him his paranormal experiences. In 1917 Tudor Pole was commissioned into the Cheshire Yeomanry and immediately posted to the Middle East. During Allenby's advance

Wellesley Tudor Pole in 1918, as Staff Captain (Intelligence) at General Allenby's HQ.

on Jerusalem that year he was seriously wounded in action, spending long weeks in military hospital.

Home on sick leave, Tudor Pole was walking at Bournemouth on 12th March 1917 when he felt the presence of someone.

I looked round; no one was in sight. All that day I felt as if someone were following me, trying to reach my thoughts. Suddenly I said to myself, "It is a soldier. He has been killed in battle and wants to communicate!" That evening I happened to call upon a lady who possesses some degree of clairvoyant power. I had forgotten about the soldier, until she described a man dressed in khaki, sitting in a chair near me. He was gazing intently in my direction. She said he was mature, wore a small moustache, and seemed somewhat sad. Not a very intelligent character apparently, but an honest one. I came home and sat down at my writing-table. Immediately my pen moved. Did I move it? Yes, in an involuntary sort of way. The thoughts were not my own, the language was a little unusual. Ideas were mainly conveyed in short simple phrases. It would really seem as if some intelligence outside myself were speaking through my mind and my pen.

Some of the ideas are not in conformity with preconceived notions of my own.

The messages I received in this manner from "Thomas Dowding," recluse, schoolmaster, soldier, are set down exactly as they reached me.

Private Dowding, the personal story of a soldier killed in battle, was first published in August 1917, and by the following year had gone into four editions. Those bereaved by the war found much comfort in Dowding's testimony that there was life after death. David Russell was moved deeply by the story, and arranged publication of editions at home and abroad, as he was to do with other Tudor Pole writings. Years later he lent a copy of *Private Dowding* to his teenage daughter Sheila, as an introduction to the truth of life after death. It influenced her for the rest of her life.

In January 1918 Tudor Pole was posted to the General Headquarters of General Allenby in Second Echelon of the Occupied Enemy Territory Administration as Intelligence Officer. In March he was promoted director of OETA. By April he was a staff captain; by November a major. In his Memoirs (London, 1970), Israel Sieff (Lord Sieff) of Marks & Spencer recalled an invitation to the house-boat that Tudor Pole lived in on the Nile at Cairo.

"Delighted you have come," he said, with his usual courtesy. "I hope you won't mind if I have to break off for a spell around eight-thirty. I shall be in France. If I seem distrait, do not worry; just sit there quietly, I shall soon be back." I hardly knew whether to take him seriously, but sat down, took a drink, and behaved as if I were accustomed to being welcomed with such information. We had a pleasant and interesting conversation for an hour or so, but at eight-fifteen he turned down the lamp, an oil lamp, I remember, and lay back slowly against his cushions. His face became pale and his breathing deeper. He was obviously in, or pretending to be in, a trance. I sat there quietly and rather frightened. Fifteen minutes later he sat up, quite composed, and turned up the lamp. "I've been to France," he said, in a grave but otherwise normal voice. "It's the Somme. The Germans have broken through; we're having a terrible time of it, there are frightful casualties." His clairvoyance was beyond dispute. The Germans had blown a huge hole in the British lines and in a matter of days had pushed through many miles. We resumed our conversation and shortly after I left.

I saw Tudor Pole once or twice again before we left Cairo. After the war we kept up our acquaintance and we met from time to time in the post-war period. One day he said to me suddenly: "Israel, I'm sorry to have to tell you, but shortly there is to be a tragedy in your life. Somebody you know and love is going to die. I wish I could tell you who it is; I can't." Two weeks later there was a telephone call from Algeria. It was Tudor Pole. "Israel," he said, "I must tell you that your sorrow is about to fall on you." That was all, he said, he could say. The next morning, one of my sons died in an accident. I cannot explain either Tudor Pole or his extraordinary communications. I report them exactly as my memory records them.

David Russell was privy to an example of intuition, if not clairvoyance, during Tudor Pole's time in Egypt. In 1908 in Constantinople Tudor Pole first heard of a group of Persians, known as Bahais, who were associated with a movement for the promotion of peace and brotherhood among members of all religious faiths. On further enquiry he discovered that their leader, known as Abdu'l Baha (Servant of God), had been a prisoner for nearly 40 years and was still confined with his family in the fortress city of Acre in Palestine. Abdu'l Baha regained his freedom following the Young Turkish Revolution, and Tudor Pole became a close friend, struck by his spiritual strength and clairvoyant powers. In November 1917 Tudor Pole wrote to his wife from Palestine: "A goldfinch sits on my knee as I write this and lizards run round my feet . . . it is a glorious life. We shall be in Abdu'l Baha's land probably when you get this and I look forward to that beyond words."

But in the spring of 1918 Tudor Pole began to feel acute anxiety for the safety of Abdu'l Baha and his family and followers in Haifa. The espionage service warned Tudor Pole that the Turkish commander-in-chief, whose headquarters were between Haifa and Beirut, had sworn to kill Abdu'l Baha and his entourage if the Turkish army was compelled to evacuate Haifa and retreat north.

David Russell was kept informed of the rescue mission, and was ready to provide funds if necessary. Using friends at home as channels, Tudor Pole got a warning through to Lloyd George, Lord Balfour, Lord Curzon and other members of the Cabinet. A dispatch was sent to General Allenby, instructing him to ensure the safety of Abdu'l Baha, his family and entourage, as soon as the British army captured Haifa. But no one in headquarters at Cairo had heard of the Bahai leader, and the matter came to Tudor Pole for his attention. He had General Allenby briefed, and immediately Haifa was captured, a guard was posted round Abdu'l Baha's house. Their leader's safety made Bahais venerate Tudor Pole.

In 1919 Abdu'l Baha was made an honarary KBE, accepting the insignia at a ceremony outside the Dome of the Rock in Jerusalem. Today the Bahá'í faith (as it is called) is the eighth-largest religion in the world.

David Russell was making his own contribution to the war, as a platoon commander in "D" Company, Markinch detachment, of the 1st Battalion Fifeshire Volunteer Regiment. The part-time soldiers of Fife had their own marching song:

> We are hefty sonsy laddies, though
>   we're forty-twa;
> Some are ten year mair, I trow—o' that
>   we dinna blaw.
> Oot we tramp ilk ither nicht, when
>   ither chiels sit doon;
> Left right, left right, on we march,
>   and aye we troll this tune:
> Roamin' in the gloamin' roond the
>   bonny Ridin' Schule;
> Roamin' in the gloamin' till we're
>   stoury as a mill.
> When the sun has gane to rest,
>   That's the time we a' lo'e best—
> O! it's lovely, dreelin' in the
>   gloamin.'

At the instigation of Lieutenant David Russell, Lieutenant Kincaid-Smith lectured to the Markinch detachment on bomb-making. "At one time men made their own bombs, using any kind of old tin etc known as Ticklers Artillery from the name of the makers of the jam which some of the cans originally contained. Nowadays there are any amount of efficient bombs."

On 14th April 1918, Lieutenant Russell received his orders for the capture of Leslie. Nearly half the platoon were to be on cycles, until someone noticed section 54, para. 3 of Training and Manoeuvre Regulations, 1913. "No personnel, motor cars, or other vehicles, cycles or horses in excess of those allowed in the official establishment, are permitted to take part in manoeuvres, nor are private servants (in excess of those authorized), private motor cars, or other private vehicles, allowed to accompany the troops."

However, imaginary aircraft were allowed in the race to reach the South Lodge of Leslie policies before the "enemy" who were holding the "Cow Bridge position." But how to supply the noise of a machine gun in action? "This might be done by a hand 'corncrake,'" the instructions suggested. Birds' nests had to be protected, and there was no hiding in the winter wheat fields. The code word in the event of an invasion was "Vampire."

The Russells' second son, John Patrick Oliphant (Pat) was born in April 1918. Robert was still a problem, continuing to wander the country in his Daimler with his attendants, though he had a base in Falcon Avenue, Edinburgh. His medical supervisor Dr George Robertson warned David Russell in May 1918: "The different companions who have been in charge of your brother have apparently at different times, so far as rumour goes, induced your brother to spend considerable sums of money entirely in their own interest."

There were other family problems. David Russell's sister Christian had to go into a sanatorium with lung trouble and his sister Mary Chill, who was living at Thornhill, Dumfriesshire, needed his help with her business affairs since her husband was away in the south, in charge of a prisoner-of-war camp.

David Russell had tried to buy shares in Tudor Pole's family business to look after his interests in case he decided to return to business after the war. He also kept in touch with Florence and the two children at Penlee, near Dartmouth, where, as she reported, the influenza epidemic was "killing people." But Tudor Pole had been detained in Egypt. By January 1919 he had become Deputy Assistant Adjutant General of the Occupied Enemy Territory Administration. David Russell had news for him about a new recruit: on New Year's Day 1919 three year old Dadie had presented the prizes after a shoot at Leven Town Hall, saluting each prize-winner.

David Russell had made changes at the mills: from May they started up at 6 a.m. on Monday instead of midnight, Sunday, with no loss of pay. But pay was about to become a major problem in the post-war mills.

5
Post-War Problems

One hundred and sixty-eight men had gone from Rothes and Auchmuty mills to the war. Twenty-four had been killed and 26 wounded. The firm kept its promise that those who came back would have jobs. But as he went round shaking hands, welcoming the workers home, David Russell knew that the machinery would not run smoothly in the post-war world.

There is an enduring misconception about the world before 1914. It is recalled nostalgically as a peaceful scene of young men harvesting green fields, of young women working efficiently in factories before the waste and slaughter to come. But the three years preceding the outbreak of war had been disrupted by an unprecedented wave of strikes as industrial relations became more and more troubled.

Between 1914 and 1918 the cost of living had more than doubled, and it would treble by 1920. Those employed in essential industries during the war had become used to decent wage rates, and those returned from the battlefields were looking for the implementation of Lloyd George's pledge of "a land fit for heroes."

In 1913 trade union membership had totalled 4 million; by 1918 it had reached 6.5 million, including women. They had played their part in the war effort, taking over from the men who had gone to fight. At Tullis Russell women packed, baled and wrapped, looking self-conscious in their trousered garb when the camera caught them. But female labour was not new in paper mills.

Women and children were employed in the rag houses of the late Victorian mills. Girls worked 66 hours a week—a 10 to 12 hour day. Winter hours were shorter because of the dangers of using candles among the heaps of rags. Holidays were practically non-existent, varying from one day a year—Christmas or New Year's Day—at most mills, to eight days at the most enlightened mills.

When workers approached the management of mills for better conditions, they were met with more than refusals: one mill declared a lock-out, demanding that its workers should undertake not to join a trade union. The men responded by forming a new union in Edinburgh in February 1890. The National Union of Paper Mill Workers had an initial membership of 3106 and catered for all unskilled and semi-skilled workers in both hand-made and machine mills. The Amalgamated Society of Paper Makers (ASPM), founded in 1894, was for skilled workers, and was more a trade benefit society than an industrial union.

In 1913 paper mills in Lancashire and the north were disrupted by the unions, principally the ASPM, until employers conceded a 2 p.m. close on Saturdays. In November 1913 there was a short and successful strike over wages at the Guard Bridge Mill, near St Andrews. To counteract union pressure employers formed a national Federation of Paper Makers.

As soon as the war was over disputes broke out again. In the wider union movement pressure was put on the Government for protection from a sudden cut in wages, which resulted in the Wages Temporary Regulation Act. But its duration was limited, and the rank and file wanted tangible improvements in conditions of employment. In January 1919 the shipyards and engineering shops of the Clyde and Belfast were brought to a standstill by an unofficial strike, and that same month the miners threatened a national strike that could bring the paper mills to a stop through shortage of coal.

In March 1919 the Sankey Commission published an interim report which conceded the miners' claims for higher wages and a seven hour day. The unions in the paper mills were also looking for more money, though they had had substantial increases through bonuses and voluntary increases in the course of the war. In early April the Government appointed a Committee to enquire into the paper industry. Its terms of reference were "To consider and report on the conditions prevailing in the paper industry, with particular reference to the restriction of manufacture in British mills owing to competition of imported paper and the resulting unemployment of labour; and to make recommendations."

In May 1919 David Russell was laid up at St Fillans for a fortnight with a quinsy throat. The cause was not only the strain of running the mills at a time of threatened disruption; because of its closeness to the River Leven Rothes House was proving an unhealthy place to bring up a family, and the Russells never seemed to be clear of colds. But David Russell could no longer consult his medical mentor, Dr Harry Kellgren.

It had seemed that the Kellgrens had magic hands, as healers and moneymakers. When the wealthy Jonas Henrik Kellgren decided to retire to his native Sweden, his grateful pupils had a gold medal struck in his honour, carrying the patriarch's likeness. Replica medals in silver and bronze, struck at the Royal Mint in Sweden, went on sale to patients, and David Russell had paid £1 5s for a silver one, including case, in 1907.

Two years later, a movement was started by some of those who had experienced the benefits of the Kellgren treatment to found a hospital, "to provide the poor and those of small means with the advantages of the Kellgren Treatment at nominal fees, and to train students and nurses in its methods," according to the promotional literature. The sponsors were so confident of the project that a lease of a suitable house in Queensberry Place, South Kensington had been taken.

The Duke and Duchess of Hamilton were among the patrons. Funds were raised, and the hospital was opened. But the war in Europe destroyed the Kellgrens' international chain of clinics by depriving them of patients. Jonas Kellgren was left stranded at the deserted summer sanatorium at Sanna, Sweden, and in 1917 the London institute at Eaton Square was abandoned. Dr Harry took consulting rooms at Sloane Street. Early in 1918 the Kellgren Hospital closed its in-patients department. The circular which an anxious David Russell received at Rothes informed him as a subscriber: "The reason for this decision was due partly to the decreased number of applications for admission, caused by the air raids, partly to monetary difficulties and partly to the difficulty of obtaining people suitable for the domestic and nursing staff of the Hospital, caused by the War." The lease had been terminated, and in November 1918 the work in connection with the out-patients department was "suspended," and the furniture sold off.

Dr Harry was striving to keep his own patients. A chain-smoker who had always driven himself hard, he became a victim of the influenza epidemic and died in April 1919, "after a most terrible illness," as his wife Vera told David Russell. "I cannot even explain to you in words what the last 8 weeks were. His mind gave way. It was the end of that beautiful career. All the books we were going to write and all the things we were going to tell and teach the world."

When his estate was wound up it became evident that Dr Harry had lived beyond his income, keeping too many assistants. His only asset was a sixth share in the summer sanatorium at Sanna. He left

POST-WAR PROBLEMS

Mrs Dryburgh and Mrs Brown, two workers at Auchmuty Mill in 1917

four children. David Russell was the godfather of seven year old Jonky, and in effect became his guardian, paying his school fees at Bedales. Vera was a woman of strong opinions and maintained a vigorous correspondence with David Russell on female labour, asking about the prospects for promotion for women in the Markinch mills.

Prospects for peace at the mills were not good. At the end of June 1919 David Russell wrote wearily to Tudor Pole:

I spent the whole day on Monday and the whole of Tuesday till after 5 o'clock on the wages question. On Wednesday forenoon the union workers in our mills and, I believe, in every other mill in the country, handed in notice to the effect that, unless the demands made at a meeting held in Manchester last week were granted within a week, they would cease work.

As regards the position in our works, there appears to be no strong feeling. It may be that a few of the younger men feel strongly, but so far as I have been able to gather the main feeling is rather of anxiety in the prospect of the possibility of the works being shut down. Three of the four machinemen at Auchmuty Mill will have nothing to do with the Union.

Note the dress of the young women sorting paper in the mills in the 1920s.

The fourth man, who is a member, appears to take an entirely reasonable view and considers that the Union is forcing matters unduly. Some sections are practically unaffected, but, as the move is a national one from the Papermakers' point of view, the issue does not lie in our hands and, unless the representatives of the Employers' Federation can come to an agreement with the representatives of the Union, all paper mills throughout the country will be shut down.

Some mills were disrupted by industrial action, but the Ministry of Labour intervened, and in July 1919 the first national agreement in the history of the papermaking industry was signed. The new agreement put the industry on a three 8-hour shift system with an average week of 44 hours for shift workers and 48 hours for day workers. The wages per normal week for a day worker and shift worker in the same class of occupation were identical. Minimum rates of wages were also set, with a skilled machineman getting 1s 8d per hour, and an unskilled labourer 1s 2d per hour. Provision was made for a week's holiday.

The agreement was hailed by the unions as the "Paperworkers' Charter." Collective bargaining had arrived as a force. Though

Tullis Russell would not join the Employers' Federation until 1947, the firm honoured the new national wage agreements as they were made.

During the war the firm had encouraged its employees to save by opening a Savings Fund. At the worker's request, a deduction was made from his or her wages, and, in addition to interest, the firm added 1 shilling for every 19 shillings saved by the individual.

The first post-war year, 1919–20, brought an economic boom in papermaking and other trades, fuelled by pent-up consumer demand and high incomes. "Anything could have been sold that year" was the recollection. That included the 4000 acre Leslie estate. David Russell revered Scottish history, and was saddened that the 17 year old Earl of Rothes, the twentieth of his line, had decided to sell the last family estate and quit Scotland. Cadham House and farm had been held on lease since 1888, and Tullis Russell bought the property for £5200 at the public roup, and contributed to a farewell dinner to the departing earl at which David Russell proposed a loyal toast.

But Tullis Russell did not enjoy the full benefits of the economic boom. The mills were running with a much reduced output in the autumn of 1919. A national railway strike was declared on 26th September, resulting in a shortage of coal and other materials at the mills. After the relief of the wages settlement, David Russell was disconsolate. "All the indications here are that the men do not understand what they are striking for, or have a quite distorted idea as to the position."

For some time he had been contemplating quitting papermaking. In March 1920 Tudor Pole wrote from Cairo: "Will you *really* be able to get out of business? I think the time is coming for you . . ." But first David Russell was looking for a new home to get his family away from damp Rothes House. They had been troubled by tonsillitis, and little David had had to have his tonsils removed in 1919. David Russell had considered the mansion house of the Leslie estate during the sale, but it was too large and impractical. The Russells had no wish to acquire an estate in order to advance their social status. They would remain plain-speaking Fife mill owners.

The country house of Aithernie at Lundin Links was for sale. Apart from its view of the Firth of Forth, it had the added attraction of being only a mile from Silverburn, where old Mrs Russell was living, with infrequent and difficult visits from her son Robert. Though he liked Aithernie, David Russell thought the asking price of £8000 exorbitant.

In April 1920 the bank rate was suddenly raised by 1 per cent to 7 per cent, coupled with systematic cuts in public expenditure, and Britain entered one of the worst recessions of its recent history. In 1920–21 there was a severe loss on the Auchmuty Mill and Rothes Bleachfield accounts, and Cadham Farm also lost money. Only Rothes Mill realised a small profit that depressed year. David Russell had to go round the firm's suppliers with his cheque book, to clear off outstanding liabilities on cancelled wood pulp contracts.

He wrote despairingly to Tudor Pole in March 1921:

When is the depression going to come to an end? A great stumbling-block appears to be the retailer, who is doing his best to realise his high-priced goods at a profit. I came across one case this morning where higher prices are being quoted for paper to the consumer than at any time during the war, and yet our prices have in some cases fallen to about half of what they stood at eight months ago, and probably every paper mill in the country is running at a very serious loss. It was estimated at the meeting of paper makers in Edinburgh last week that some mills must be running at a loss of £30 per ton of paper made, and that is not taking short time into account.

But in March 1921 a 1000 ream order from Japan was received, and through Tudor Pole there were prospects for business diversification, with a proposal to make centrifugal hollow concrete building blocks out of an accumulation of the estimated 500,000 tons of waste lime and waste ashes at the mills. David Russell was to be given the Scottish rights to manufacture the blocks from the Hume Pipe Company in which he had shares. Glasgow Corporation was showing an interest in the blocks for its post-war housing programme.

There were also attempts to find export markets for the firm's paper. Having decided not to return to the family milling business in Bristol, Wellesley Tudor Pole had set up his own firm, W. Tudor Pole & Co. in St James's Street, London. In the years following the war he became involved in a series of international deals, including negotiating direct trade to Russia and Europe, particularly in tea, a commodity David Russell was interested in, since his family were shareholders in the Dooria Tea Company in Assam, owned jointly by Russells and Drysdales.

Tudor Pole, who was dealing in clothing with a Dutch group associated with the Soviet Government, had urged David Russell: "I feel that you and I with the ideas we hold about Russia and her future, should lose no opportunity, commercial or otherwise, in linking up with Eastern Europe." David Russell wanted to do business with the new Russian Government in both paper and tea, and he pointed out that his wife's brother, Ben Blyth, whose firm was depressed by the lack of contracts, could be of use in a Russian engineering reconstruction programme.

The gregarious Tudor Pole had also become an art dealer. He was convinced that he had come across a portrait by Gainsborough of his wife. It was in a bank in Berne, and was offered to Sir Charles Allom in the USA for £12,000 plus a percentage. There was another picture which Tudor Pole was certain was a genuine Turner. David Russell advanced him £250 to help buy it.

But David Russell had laid out money elsewhere, having taken Aithernie on a six-month lease, with an option to purchase at the end of March 1921. He bought it jointly with his brother Robert, having beaten the price down to £7000. The house, which had an extension by the fashionable Scottish architect Sir Robert Lorimer, was in very poor condition externally, and needed a considerable sum spent on it. But it was a spacious family home of seven bedrooms plus servants' quarters, lit by an oil engine. It had a tennis lawn for the children and a south-facing verandah where they could take the air.

But David Russell did not have the time to settle into his new home. Men were leaving the mills for the pits, and through the "Triple Alliance" of the unions a general strike was threatened. On the eve of the strike the railwaymen and transport workers called off their action, leaving the miners to go it alone.

They were out for two bitter months. There was an anxious night for David Russell that spring when miners caused a disturbance at Thornton Junction, three miles from Rothes, and in the surrounding countryside, strikers set fire to haystacks. The mills had sufficient stocks of coal to last six to eight weeks, but practically no orders for paper. They closed down at the end of a week with, for the first time, no certainty of reopening the following week.

David Russell wrote to Tudor Pole:

in this part at least the railwaymen seem up against the miners, and it is difficult to see how a really effective strike can be realised at the present time. We occasionally hear, principally from sisters of miners, of the dissatisfaction high wages have brought, and of their want of consideration for their parents, and the more moderate men appear to be bitterly up against the younger hotheads.

Owing to the coal shortage, some paper mills were being shut down indefinitely. This brought Tullis Russell more orders for paper, though they only had two weeks' supply of fuel themselves. If no further supplies became available, David Russell estimated that the mills would have to reduce to half-time working in a month.

During the war George Russell had arranged the collection of straw from farms. After the armistice he left the dampness of Fife for his farm, Eldoret, in Kenya. He seemed to be following in the family tradition as a flax grower. He had 500 acres of the crop, but the price had slumped. He had advice for his brother David back in Scotland.

My opinion is that for a long shot land well chosen now is well worth buying to hold. This is *not* the country for the small man with only a few hundreds to put into land. Canada is the place for him where he can take off his coat and work hard, and where he gets 160 acres of land free.

He hoped to have cattle for export when the country had cold storage facilities. Kenya was a perfect climate of sunshine, he reported. "Everyone must wear a sun helmet and I always wear a *red* undervest."

With the mills depressed, David Russell was making his own economies. He had on order a new Rolls-Royce, but wrote to the company, asking them if they could resell it. Its value was £2400, but trade in luxury cars was also depressed. He rented out Aithernie to cover the cost of painting and the removal while he holidayed with his family at Braemar in June and July 1921. He had the loan of the Glastonbury sapphire blue bowl, to test its psychic effect, but had left it in the safe at the mills. The Russells were expecting another child, and Tudor Pole used his powers of clairvoyance, or an inspired guess, to tell the father-to-be: "I think your new star will be clothed in a girl's form but better not raise Alison's hopes too strongly!"

As he made a bed of bracken on Royal Deeside so that his little son Dadie could have a sleep, David Russell was considering an intriguing business proposition—one that would give him much more time with his family while saving himself and Tullis Russell from the strains of competition when markets were difficult.

6
The Paper Millionaire

Clarence Hatry was the most handsome, flamboyant man in the City, a tycoon who had made his fortune by promoting and refinancing industrial undertakings, either on his own account or through the Commercial Bank of London Limited which he controlled. He was also a large and successful speculator in oil shares, including Shell and Mexican Eagle.

Hatry took an office in Dundee. In October 1920 he was the mastermind behind the formation of Jute Industries Limited in which some of Dundee's most prominent textile families (including the Grimonds) merged their fortunes. Hatry had a new scheme: to bring the manufacturers of esparto papers in Scotland together in a combine, and Tullis Russell was the first company he had in mind.

Clarence Hatry.

Tudor Pole made discreet enquiries in the City about Hatry and reported back to David Russell: "Not one single commercial combination brought into being during the past eighteen months by Hatry and his people is paying its way at present, or has done so since the various schemes were put into operation, and in some instances considerable watering of stocks is believed to have taken place."

But in May David Russell had written to Hatry: "We are confident that by bringing together all the large esparto mills in one group considerable economies in production would be effected and additional profits realized." There was a series of meetings with Hatry in Dundee. "He has made a very favourable impression," David Russell told Tudor Pole.

He seems straight and is undoubtedly able. We have not come to any definite agreement, but we do not appear to be very far apart, and his ideas as to the advantages of an amalgamation are on the whole sound. From talks we had with him about others in the trade, he appears to have a wonderfully good insight into character. He undoubtedly has ability to pick the right men and, if no hitch occurs, I think he should be able to organise successfully an amalgamation on sufficiently sound lines to make it a success.

In June 1921 Hatry sent a contract to Braemar for David Russell's signature. David Russell evidently had the agreement of the Tullises, for he and all the other shareholders in Tullis Russell were to sell out to the new combine, to be called Esparto Paper Mills Limited. The price was to be £592,000, and David Russell was to lend Tullis Russell £192,000—with interest.

But David Russell would not be leaving papermaking immediately. Accepting the appointment of managing director of Tullis Russell for several years at an annual tax-free salary of £3000, he wrote to Hatry: "I had hoped to be able to give more time to other interests but I am willing to continue as managing director for three years, provided that it is understood that during the first year, means will be taken to relieve me of many of the details connected with the routine of business."

The general depression in papermaking was described by Sir Charles Chalmers of Loch Mill, Linlithgow, in a letter to David Russell.

If one could foresee the future of the paper trade it would be a great guide. If it is likely soon to return to being a pleasant and fairly remunerative occupation, I would be pleased to hold on for a few years yet, but if one has to face a year or two of present conditions I would be glad to clear out.

David Russell suggested to Chalmers that if the Hatry negotiations fell through, several mills should consider working together, initially with the object of comparing costs. But the future looked brighter in September 1921. He reported to Tudor Pole:

We are running Auchmuty Mill for the fourth week, and we see some prospects of being able to run next week and, as for many months we have only run every other week, this is a great improvement, although our out-turn is still far below normal. But we find a considerable improvement in trade generally, and I am hoping that it may be possible now to get back to continuous full-time working.

Alison Russell gave birth to another daughter, Sheila Felicity Oliphant at Aithernie on 24th October 1921, and her father spent as much time as possible visiting the new nursery. But he was needed at the mills. Engineers from London were working on the expensive new grass boiling plant, trying to get it into smooth operation. He told Tudor Pole:

Business is as depressed as ever. We are getting more orders by severe cutting of prices, but the class of business we are doing would be ruinous if continued over a long period and, as the competition is largely among "ourselves" so to speak, I have urged upon Hatry the advisability of completing the agreements and eliminating competition.

Abdu'l Baha "passed peacefully to the Wider Life" (Tudor Pole's expression) at Haifa on 29th November 1921. But David Russell had little time for spiritual reflection. At a meeting in Edinburgh at the beginning of December some papermakers indicated that they were turning against the idea of a combine. David Russell had not signed the agreement Hatry had sent to Braemar, but on 21st December, against the advice of his legal advisers, he signed an amended agreement because he wanted the negotiations finalised.

The Russell and Tullis interests were disposing of Tullis Russell to the new company for £600,000, £240,000 in cash and £360,000 fully paid up shares of £1 each in the new company. Similar arrangements were being made with other mills which were joining the combine. The Inveresk Paper Company Limited, Musselburgh, was to be sold for £250,000, £100,000 in cash and £150,000 in shares. Henry Bruce, Kinleith & Sons Limited, Currie, Midlothian, would change hands for £200,000, £80,000 in cash and £120,000 in ordinary shares. Watsons of Bullionfield Limited was to be sold for £125,000, £50,000 in cash and £75,000 in ordinary shares. The Carrongrove Paper Company, Denny, declined to deal with the combine except on a cash basis, and was offered £500,000 for the whole shareholding.

Two days before Christmas Tudor Pole cautioned David Russell:

One can see how Hatry and his friends have used your mills all through as a weapon in the negotiations and have taken rather an unfair advantage of you when the crisis arose. I strongly advise you from the first to make Hatry and Co realise how awkwardly you are placed vis a vis your co-directors in your successful effort to prevent the whole scheme collapsing.

Sir Frederick Becker and David Russell were to be among the directors of the new Esparto Paper Mills company. James Rae, the Tullis Russell office junior who was to become the firm's managing director, recalled seeing Becker at the mills in the 1920s, looking more like a stage actor than a businessman in his black hat and beard. A barrister's clerk, Becker had turned his attention from legal briefs to wood pulp and was one of the first to recognise the potentialities of the Canadian wood pulp industry, the products of which he shipped to Britain by chartered steamers.

Becker & Company Limited became the largest pulp selling concern in the United Kingdom, if not the world. During the First World War he had placed at the disposal of the Government the resources over which he had command, for experimental purposes required by the Paper Controller. Becker's Scottish address was Ellon Castle, Aberdeenshire, where he was chairman of Donside Mill. An issue of *The Times* was produced on paper made chiefly from sawdust at Donside. He was also managing director of Watsons, Bullionfield, a member of the Esparto consortium.

Becker's business acumen and patriotism were rewarded in January 1922, when he was knighted. But at the end of that month there was a crisis, with Hatry phoning David Russell to say that he was "out of all the negotiations." David Russell was suspicious of Becker's manoeuvres, but he was under pressure, since the new Esparto Paper Mills company had to be registered within the week. He told his brother George, who, while enjoying the sunshine of Kenya, was wondering about his own shareholding in the mills: "I would not proceed without Hatry's approval, and blocked proceedings, causing great unpleasantness and much friction."

There were stormy meetings, with all agreements cancelled on 8th February 1922. "The key to the whole situation then was the position of the Carrongrove Paper Company, which had to be paid for in cash on 21st February," David Russell explained to George.

Becker said he could have provided the money for the whole Combine, and believed Hatry to be absolutely out, owing to his other difficulties in the City. We had seen Hatry before the meeting, believing that Becker's whole object was to secure Carrongrove Mill for himself and to use it as a weapon to destroy other mills, or to secure them at lower prices.

William Tod Jun'r & Company Limited, Polton, Midlothian, and Hendon Paper Works Limited were also included in the new company. The combined assets of the participating mills were listed at nearly £5 million. At a meeting in London of Esparto Paper Mills Limited, in February 1922, Sir Frederick Becker was appointed chairman, and Sir Walrond Sinclair, a nominee of Hatry's, intimated that he was considering accepting a seat on the board. An agreement was to be entered into with Becker for the acquisition of the shares in Watsons of Bullionfield for £115,000. But the price of Tullis Russell had dropped to £550,000.

David Russell gave a guarantee to the Commercial Bank of Scotland for £116,250 of a special account of £465,000 for Esparto Paper Mills Limited. But there was Robert's position to consider. In a pencilled note dated March 1922, David Russell debated with himself: "For my brother's best interests, what should my attitude be towards him? Is it right that I should proceed with the arrangements I am contemplating for running of the business? Should I continue to do everything I can to complete the transfer of the business to Hatry and his interests?"

But there were diversions in the midst of the protracted negotiations. Tudor Pole proposed a motor tour of Germany to collect 100,000 marks' worth of objets d'art and antiques. David Russell had surplus marks, having bought them to cover the cost of plant ordered from Germany, and replied eagerly:

The proposed trip to Germany attracts me. I wonder if I could get away. I have to be at St Andrews on the 7th August, to receive an LLD degree; at least, if I go off before then I suppose I will have to leave the LLD behind, but that would not matter much in the long run. It would give us an unusual opportunity of observing the conditions in Germany. I shall be glad to have further particulars.

But the negotiations with Hatry were becoming acrimonious. He accused David Russell of supplying inflated figures for the mills, and by April 1922 the price for Tullis Russell had dropped to £400,000, half in shares and half in debentures. David Russell could not agree to this. "The figure of £550,000 was already a modified figure, and for us to discuss a further modification would give the impression, which I did not at all like, that we had all along been pressing for a most inflated price, and had been found out!"

Should he stay in the negotiations, or pull Tullis Russell out of the combine? Hatry's warning in May sounded like a threat: "It is only fair to let you know that if something is not done almost immediately, there must inevitably be unpleasant complications between you, the Becker group and the Commercial Bank of Scotland. Do let us have this thing settled once and for all."

Since he had signed legal papers, David Russell turned to lawyer James Watt, the senior partner of Davidson & Syme, Edinburgh, for guidance. They had first met when Tullis Russell had lost an esparto case which Watt was handling for another client. David Russell was so impressed by James Watt's understanding of the papermaking trade that he made him the firm's lawyer. Watt did not keep well, probably because he drove himself so hard, but when he had to go into a nursing home from time to time, he surrounded himself with telephones, boasting that he could conduct a board meeting from his bed.

James Watt was a match for Hatry's manoeuvres. "The more you run after them the more will the position be that the price will become thinner and thinner, and less and less will be paid in cash and more and more on paper," was his blunt warning to David Russell in June 1922. That same month the Hatry side capitulated, cancelling the agreement. They delivered the guarantee given to the Commercial Bank of Scotland and repaid the £6000 advanced on account of the initial expenses. Tullis Russell was well out of the combine. The loss had been of time and David Russell's energy.

But there were other amalgamation schemes afloat, with a plan to combine several English mills by a group negotiating with Inveresk, which was sold in the summer of 1922. At the same time George MacElwee of Associated Paper Mills Limited approached David Russell with a scheme for a combine of Scottish esparto mills which would cost 1 million pounds to arrange.

As always, David Russell gave the matter his most careful scrutiny, but he had been neglecting the mills while he negotiated with Hatry and his associates. Besides, the workforce was unsettled through rumours of sell-out and amalgamation, and his brother was an anxiety. Though drawing a full salary as joint managing director, Robert Russell had not been near the mills for years, and when he did return, caused disruption. James Watt had cautioned David Russell: "there is no reason why there should be a forced sale of the business because of your brother's interference."

The senior partner in the firm, Robert Tullis, the son of George Smith Tullis, had stood aside from the management of the mills for many years, but his sons George and Robin Tullis were in the business. Robert Russell did not get on with them, and had made difficulties over the sale of the mill to the Hatry interests, including laying down rules about how Tullis Russell was to be managed by the combine. When the Hatry deal collapsed Robert Tullis wanted his son George as joint managing director in place of Robert Russell, but with George subordinate to David Russell, whose experience and restraining influence he acknowledged readily. In the autumn of 1922 it was proposed that Robert Russell and George Tullis should each take six months' holiday. But by September it was evident that Robert would have to go into a nursing home.

However, David Russell was later able to report to Tudor Pole: "Everything is going well . . . The new conditions have made everyone cheerful, and it is a pleasure to go through the mills." There was an intriguing proposal on his desk about making paper containers to hold petrol. A record 230 tons of orders had been dispatched from Auchmuty Mill, and Robert was much better.

David Russell could at last turn his attention to other schemes. Tudor Pole had suggested the formation of a St James's Literary Agency, to help authors place their manuscripts, particularly those with spiritual interests, and David Russell was pleased to back the scheme financially.

There was further financial involvement with Tudor Pole. The motor tour of Germany he had earlier proposed had not come off, but an associate of his had gone to Berlin to try to invest David Russell's 2.6 million inflation-hit German marks in valuable objets d'art. His German currency had been used to purchase armour, swords, pistols and china. The cargoes arrived at London Docks in mid October. The following June Christie, Manson & Woods would sell several items, including "A three-quarter suit of fluted armour, in the style of Maximillian, of bright steel" and "an early 17th century wheel-lock sporting arquebus."

Old Mrs Russell was growing frail at Silverburn. She had a fall, breaking her arm, and told her son David, her confidant and adviser, that she wished she could "pass on," because she felt she had lived long enough. Robert was still a constant worry. Furthermore, because of the disputes David Russell knew that he had to do something to secure the stability and future expansion of the business. He decided to buy out the Tullis interests, but like the Hatry negotiations, the Tullis ones were to be protracted and acrimonious.

Meantime, he had neglected his wife and children, and wanted to make it up to them. They went on holiday to Perthshire in May 1923, and Alison wrote to her husband from Old Faskally House:

> It is snowing hard, and the ground is white. The children are playing out in the snow, fearfully pleased! We are none the worse of our walk yesterday, which seemed quite a short way really. We all enjoyed it ever so much, but after saying goodbye to you I had a lump in my throat and felt very choky. It seemed *awful* to say goodbye under just those conditions. The larch wood smelt just how larch woods do smell on a wild spring day after rain: the flowers were so lovely; enormous anemones, violets and primroses. It was all so achingly lovely, I just longed to have you there to enjoy it all and get peace and healing and strength from it all.

David Russell was never one to draw strength from the misfortunes of others, no matter if they had treated him badly. At the annual meeting of Becker & Company Limited in 1913 Sir Frederick Becker had tempted fate by making the astonishing declaration that "up to 1924 the position of the company was already assured, and there were few companies in any trade, and especially in the pulp trade, who could say that profits of upwards of £120,000 were already earned." In October 1923 a receiver was appointed for his company. A victim of the depression, it had over-extended its interests through advancing cash and acquiring paper mills.

It would take six years before the Hatry success story ended. On Saturday, 21st September 1929 David Russell opened the *Scotsman* to read: "Stock Exchange Sensation. Dealings suspended in 'Hatry Group' shares. Slump in Prices." The gross liabilities of Hatry's six companies were stated at a staggering £29.5 million. In January 1930 Hatry received 14 years' penal servitude, with a concurrent sentence of two years' hard labour. The judge told him: "You stand convicted of the most appalling frauds that have ever disfigured the commercial reputation of this country."

It emerged that at the time of his negotiations with the Dundee jute mills and the Scottish paper mills, Hatry had been trying desperately to make a new fortune as quickly as possible, since he had taken over debts of the insolvent Commercial Bank to the extent of £1.5 million.

In his memoirs, written for the *Sunday Express* in January 1930, Clarence Hatry confessed: "My efforts in Scotland were only partly successful. I was able to make a certain amount of money, probably between £30,000 and £40,000, which enabled me to keep my creditors at bay, and exist. This money I made in connection with an amalgamation of paper manufacturers in Scotland . . ."

However, the headlines of a document called "Eight Current Misconceptions" compiled in his defence argued: "There is no justification for the belief that Mr. Hatry's business career was of short duration and that he was identified only with failures. Altogether over 150 companies acquired or capital issues placed, total sum exceeding £100,000,000. Vast majority of these transactions unqualified success."

David Russell did not condemn Clarence Hatry. For Christmas 1933 he sent him a cake of shortbread to Maidstone prison, but the authorities would not allow the fallen tycoon to have the gift. Mrs Hatry wrote to thank David Russell for his thoughtfulness, and he replied: "I only knew Mr Hatry over a short period. The negotiations were sometimes difficult, but all my contacts with him were pleasant. I always felt in some strange way an affection for him, and his fate seemed desperately hard for both of you."

7
A Russell Buy-out

The negotiations with Hatry's esparto mills combine had brought to the fore the tensions between Robert Russell and George and Robin Tullis. After the collapse of the negotiations it was clear that the two families could no longer work together. David Russell offered to leave the business, but Robert Tullis would not hear of it because he had no wish to increase his responsibilities at the mills. The best course for the preservation of the business seemed to be a Russell buy-out.

But David Russell knew that it would be an expensive and risky undertaking, given the fluctuations in the papermaking business. The Russell and Tullis families each held 30,000 ordinary shares; but the Russells held 63,000 preference shares compared to the Tullises' 39,000.

In February 1923 the Tullis family set out their terms. They wanted £4 10s per ordinary share, a total of £135,000. Their preference shares, estimated at £39,000, were to be purchased at par plus any accrued dividends within five years. The other condition of sale was that the Rothes Bleachfield was to be leased to Robin Tullis.

David and Robert Russell, who were buying out the Tullis interest jointly, had to arrange a personal loan of £60,000 and a company loan of £50,000. But there were difficulties over the negotiations and, as always, Tudor Pole was ready with advice. He wrote to David Russell in July 1923: "I wonder whether the Tullis interests are taking a more reasonable line and am sure the time has come for the launching of a firm ultimatum by you. This impasse cannot be allowed to continue." Several weeks later Tudor Pole had a proposition. "I am awfully sorry there is no Tullis Russell settlement yet. Would it expedite matters were I to get you a firm offer in cash for the whole business? I could get you this within 3 days of having some general idea of the figures."

David Russell did not take Tudor Pole up on his offer, though the current figures were not promising. Usually by the end of September mills were busy with autumn orders, but the returns from 19 mills showed a drop from the previous year's figures. In October alterations were made to machines at Rothes, to increase output and quality. "Of course, a paper mill is never complete, and alterations are always going on—at least that is our experience," David Russell told Tudor Pole.

Tudor Pole had another proposition. Tullis Russell supplied paper for the Cassell encyclopaedia. One of the directors, Thomas Young, indicated that his company wanted to treble its account with the Fife firm and were willing to put up £200,000 of capital if necessary. This offer was not taken up, since David Russell did not wish the complications of outside investment after his experience with the Hatry combine.

By the autumn of 1923 paper mills throughout the country were shut down and others were operating on short time. David Russell kept hoping that the alterations to Rothes Mill would bring a full order book. Better news came, with the possibility of a transatlantic order for vulcanising papers for Rothes because they were superior to the papers being produced in the US company's own mills. A 1000 ton order per year for the Italian market was also being discussed. But orders did not materialise, and he wrote despondently to James Watt in October: "We had all hoped to see a revival in trade by the end of September. Instead of this the reports we had from London and the Midlands last week are the most pessimistic we have had for many months."

Then there was a sudden upturn. By mid November the mills were running late for three Saturdays to meet orders. David Russell was negotiating with the bank for the loan to take over the Tullis interest, but he did not want Robert on the board. Tudor Pole offered advice on the persons to have on the new board for publicity reasons, and urged him to push blotting paper and other proprietary brands. "I've been a sort of psychic director to TR & Co for some years and can continue to act in that capacity, board or no board!"

As Christmas approached the mills were working to capacity, with some clients wanting to book up the whole output of one machine. Robert was in a nursing home, and David Russell found that every half hour was precious. He was often working till 11 o'clock at night in his study at Aithernie, and felt guilty about not having more time to spend with his family.

But it was a crucial juncture in his business affairs. Sir Frederick Becker's bank was selling off his interests, including the esparto mill at Bullionfield near Dundee. David Russell was doing calculations. In 1913 a new machine had been installed at

A line-up of Rothes machinery and the men who kept it running in the 1920s.

Bullionfield. At current prices the value was about £30,000, yet the bank would probably let the whole mill go for around £10,000. Becker visited him, but David Russell did not commit himself. There were also opportunities to pick up other paper mills very cheaply, but he was occupied with the takeover of the Tullis interests.

Business was now booming, with Number 3 machine at Auchmuty breaking its own production record over two consecutive days. Tudor Pole's thought for 1924 was: "I often wonder as to the extent to which yours and my psychic lives run parallel." If there was a psychic influence, it was certainly benign: 204 tons of paper were made at Auchmuty in a week, when the average was just over 150 tons.

David Russell summed up his business faith: "I am afraid I am never satisfied if a day passes without some suggestion either for improving the quality, or increasing the output." Since 1917 he had been interested in a process patented by Dr A. L. Rinman of Stockholm. Black liquor was a by-product resulting from the digesting of esparto grass. Soda was recovered from this liquor, but the other chemical products in it were lost.

The Rinman method for the production of pulp and its by-products could be used for a number of raw materials, such as esparto, wood, straw, reeds and bamboo. The method made it possible not only to recover the soda from the black liquor, but at the same time to obtain chemical products, including acetone, light and heavy oils, turpentine and resin soap for which there was a lucrative ready market. Another benefit was that the manufacturing process was odourless.

A pulp factory at Ratisbon, Bavaria, was successfully using the Rinman process. But David Russell preferred to conduct painstaking experiments in the laboratory of his own mills, under Dr Macdonald the chief chemist, and with Principal James Irvine of St Andrews University as a consultant. The results were promising, and David Russell was considering the formation of a company to acquire the ownership and full rights to exploit the Rinman method in Britain and other countries.

By the end of 1923 old Mrs Russell had to have two nurses with her day and night at Silverburn. But her son George was now living at Muircambus, and his wife Bessie was very attentive to her mother-in-law, relieving the burden on David Russell, who was fully occupied at the mills. "Our question is not to find orders, but to know how to select orders, as we are having far more offered to us than we can accept," he told Tudor Pole. The administration of the mills was being reorganised, with the appointment of a secretary, John Black, who had joined the firm as cashier in 1906, and returned in 1924 after a short absence.

David Russell had long since learned that the papermaking business was subject to interruption. The dockers' strike of February 1924 caused anxiety, since the mills had two ships loaded with esparto at sea. They duly docked, but one deck cargo was badly damaged by water. However, there was good news at Aithernie, as David Russell proudly told Tudor Pole in a letter of 11th March: "A fine little girl arrived at 6.30 this morning. She and Alison are both very well indeed." She was christened Margaret Anne Oliphant, but would be known as Anne.

Like many businessmen of his time, David Russell liked to maintain a wide shares portfolio, and Tudor Pole was always ready with advice. Since David Russell already had a stake in the non-stop scenic railway at Wembley, would he care to invest in the giant switchback at the same place? Tudor Pole also had another proposition: Chalice Well, which he had visited in 1912 on his Glastonbury pilgrimage, was owned by Alice Buckton, but she was struggling. David Russell offered to subscribe debentures up to £100.

He was fascinated by wireless, and put £200 into the National Portable Wireless Set, invented by Brett Morgan. A small box without aerials or attachments, it required headphones, and would receive clearly, provided the user was within a 25 mile radius of a radio station. But David Russell wanted something bigger for his own home. At Aithernie in mid April a wireless aerial was erected, and after dark the Russell family crowded round the set, managing to get in touch with eight stations, including Glasgow, Aberdeen, Newcastle and London.

George Leavey, a London financier and associate of Tudor Pole's, was behind the formation of Textiles (Surplus) Limited, for the "distribution of the whole of the British Government's stock of surplus textiles". David Russell had written a cheque for £33,000 for part of the shareholding, and acting as a kind of broker, proceeded to sell interests in the enterprise to various acquaintants in Scotland, including his brother-in-law Ben Blyth, Charles Carlow the Fife coalmaster, and Principal Irvine of St Andrews. David Russell retained a holding of £9,500 in the company, which went into voluntary liquidation in 1924, having paid a net profit of around 11 per cent.

Though there were two Rolls-Royces in the garage at Rothes, one was put up for sale when the market improved. David Russell liked to drive himself, though it could be hazardous, even in those days of little traffic. In July 1924 he was driving home in heavy rain when a car swerved and went into his back mudguard. He duly noted its number—SB393, an Argyll registration—and reported the accident to the Royal Automobile Club.

Binnie the chauffeur also had his mishaps. He was driving the Russells to St Fillans in Perthshire with the two boys in the back when a baker's van emerged suddenly from a side road and collided with the Rolls-Royce. The van lost a front wheel. But there was an element of farce about an incident in Rothes garage. Binnie was repairing one of the Rolls-Royces when he inadvertently put it into gear, then pressed the starter button. The result of the collision of the two limousines was a crushed petrol tank, but the insurance company settled the £13 9s 9d claim.

David Russell delighted in his young family. Near Largo House Pat "saw" soldiers in strange uniforms marching along a road which no longer existed. David Russell spent a long time researching old documents, verifying that the old road had run where Pat

David Russell's first Rolls-Royce, outside Silverburn House.

One of a fleet of charabancs taking Tullis Russell workers for one of their annual outings in the early 1920s.

saw it. He was also able to work out from his son's description that he had "seen" Cromwell's men.

Another unexplained episode dates from the 1920s. Tudor Pole was staying at Aithernie, when he suddenly told David Russell that a man was drowning and needed help. They reached the shore to see the police arriving to pick up the body.

At Chalice Well, Glastonbury, Alice Buckton was running a training college for gentlewomen for "dedicated work." The mystical poet had started buying up surrounding properties to protect the well, where she staged masques which she wrote herself. Since he linked the site to his sapphire blue bowl, Tudor Pole was worried about the future of the well if she overreached herself. He wrote to David Russell:

> The fact is that Miss Buckton cannot work in conjunction with others. She will not brook any interference or supervision. Had the place been run on businesslike lines it could have paid its way to date, but as it is I am afraid that no amount of propping will keep the place going, and I do not think it is much good making the effort.

David Russell replied that he was willing to take up debentures to the value of £100. "I cannot support her to any great extent, as I feel that any money put into such a concern must be regarded as a gift." However, he spoke to his friend Principal Irvine, who was a trustee of the Carnegie Trust, about helping Chalice Well financially, but the matter would have to be put before the Trust as a business proposition, framed on sound lines.

Though he spent as much time as he could spare educating his children on all kinds of subjects, and could have afforded tutors for them, David Russell knew that they would benefit from going to school. On a morning in early May 1924 Binnie had the car waiting. David and Pat were going to pay a visit to Craigflower boys' preparatory school at Torryburn, Fife, to see if they would like it. The car was also needed the next day for one of the most heartbreaking journeys of David Russell's life. Catherine, the eldest daughter, was retarded because of her hydrocephalic condition. Though her family loved her, she needed specialised care, and was taken to a home at Larbert at the age of 11.

In the early hours of 21st May 1924 old Mrs Russell passed peacefully away at Silverburn. She made her son David her executor because he was the one who had been devoted to her, so attentive since her husband's death in 1906. Besides, he had been so patient with Robert. But he was disappointed to find that his mother had had most of her papers destroyed, a great loss to the family history he was so keen on. In June David Russell took Invergarry House at Blair Atholl for a family holiday while developments were proceeding at the mills. Two new rag boilers had arrived in Kirkcaldy Harbour to increase greatly the output at Rothes, and new buildings were being erected.

William Harrison, a London lawyer, controlled some of the chief paper mills in England and Scotland. He was chairman of the Inveresk Paper Company at Musselburgh, and in the summer of 1924 he tried to get control of Guard Bridge near St Andrews, which would have left Tullis Russell the only big mill out of the combine in its type of business.

But there were pleasant diversions from business. The Russells (as the Tullis family had been too) were paternalistic employers who liked to reward hard work and loyalty. On the day of the annual mills trip Rothes and Auchmuty were shut down. In July 1924 Stirling was the destination, and 1000 tickets had been issued for the excursion; wives and children hung out of the windows as train after train pulled out. But there were tragedies too. Working in a paper mill could be hazardous if a worker's attention strayed. A 19 year old youth got caught up in machinery. It was not thought to be a serious accident, but he died in hospital that same day.

In April 1925 David Russell had a conversation with his two sons.

Dadie asked if I wanted them to go to the Mills. I said: no, not at all, if they did not want to come; and he then asked what I would do with the Mills. I said I would sell them. Upon hearing this, Pat grunted out a very definite "No, you won't sell them." Dadie then appealed to Pat: "But who would run them?" and Pat said very definitely, while he tucked himself into bed: "I will."

Dadie had apparently changed his mind about going into the mills because he wanted to be a soldier.

In May young David went to Craigflower School. His departure elicited a long and alarming letter from Tudor Pole, relating his "hellish experiences" at Blundells School at the hands of a prefect who was "a brute a beast and a bully." David seemed happy at Craigflower, but Pat was left lonely, and David Russell was considering taking a flat for the family in Edinburgh for the winter. The mills were running well: in the last week of May there was a record out-turn of 213 tons from Auchmuty. A lime-burning furnace for waste lime, the first of its kind in Britain, was on order. David Russell mused: "There is always an unwillingness to venture upon new methods, but when one mill has taken the step others follow . . ." There was also the possibility of a contract for 500 tons of insulating papers from the Belgian Government.

George Leavey had apparently made £600,000 out of Textiles (Surplus) Limited. In early June he let it be known via Tudor Pole that he was prepared to underwrite and place a first mortgage debenture of £250,000 on the Tullis Russell mills. But the protracted negotiations with the Tullis family were at last drawing to a conclusion, and in July 1925 the Tullises were paid out completely. The transaction was masterminded by James Watt the lawyer, who had been made a director of Tullis Russell the previous March. The share capital was reduced from £355,000 to £133,000.

But there was still Robert Russell to contend with. As with the Hatry negotiations, he had impeded the Tullis negotiations with an obstinacy caused by his mental illness. He had even threatened legal action against his own family. Tudor Pole wrote to David Russell with advice in August 1925: "Sooner or later the problem of Robert must be met and I don't see why you should continue to sacrifice yourself in a way that harms you and does him no good."

But the country was facing a threat which could affect the mills. In the spring of 1925 Chancellor of the Exchequer Churchill had announced the return to the Gold Standard, despite the advice of eminent economists like J. M. Keynes. Unless costs could be cut by at least 10 per cent immediately, the export trade would be ruined.

In July 1925 Prime Minister Baldwin met the miners' executive and warned them that not only the wages of the miners, but of all workers, would have to come down. The coal owners proposed to cut wages drastically and to abolish the minimum wage. The miners were given a month's notice of a lock-out on 31st July unless they acquiesced.

They resisted, and on the night of 30th June the Trades Union Congress issued strike orders to railway and transport unions, placing an embargo on all movements of coal after midnight on 31st July. The Cabinet capitulated on "Red Friday," eight hours before the lock-out of all miners was due to begin. Baldwin announced that the coal owners had suspended their notices, and that the Government would give a subsidy to the owners for nine months up to 1st May 1926.

At his desk at Rothes David Russell was relieved, since the mills depended on coal. But he realised that only a breathing-space had been bought, and that the miners would make new demands in May. Meantime he turned for consolation and amusement to his family. Pat was going once weekly with a tutor to St Andrews, to learn first-hand about Scottish history. He was keenly interested in archaeology, and at the age of seven showed a sensitivity that delighted his father. "We walked along to Silverburn with Pat on Sunday morning. Alison wore a fur stole round her neck. Pat said: 'Mummy, I don't like you wearing fur.' Alison asked him why, and he said: because he did not like to think of animals being killed for that."

In November the irrepressible Tudor Pole was in the Vatican, where Cardinal Gasparri offered him "a wonderful Velasquez" for £15,000. David Russell had also become a picture collector. He paid £200 for "Maternity," by the young French painter Jean Despujols, which was shown in the exhibition of the International Society of Sculptors, Painters & Gravers in London.

That same month a proposal was put to David Russell about a concession to build a paper mill in Turkey to compete with German and Austrian mills. The Turkish Government was apparently prepared to grant a monopoly for the manufacture and sale of paper and to make available special facilities, including free land and no taxation. Furthermore, the Government would purchase £2 million Turkish worth of paper per annum. Considering David Russell's fascination with Constantinople, it was a tempting proposition, but Turkey was too far away for business purposes.

Instead he strengthened the firm's position at home. The London sales office was well established, and one in Manchester had been opened in 1923. In 1925 he appointed a salesman to work up Scottish trade. He also considered giving the company a new name. Russells Markinch Paper Mills Limited was suggested, but in the end the company remained as Tullis Russell. David Russell had got on well with the Tullis family and was genuinely sorry to see the business connection broken, though they remained friends. For the time being the situation at the mills was stable, but a new year was approaching.

8
The General Strike

The year 1926 began auspiciously, with a possibility of selling esparto to the mill producing the paper for the huge circulation US magazine the *Saturday Evening Post*. There was other interesting news from overseas. William Harrison and a group of British financiers had purchased the entire share capital of the Koholyt Company of Berlin, which owned a sulphite pulp mill in East Prussia, apparently the biggest of its type in the world, producing 120,000 tons of bleached sulphite pulp annually. The Berlin company also owned a large paper mill and chemical works on the Rhine.

Harrison's strategy was to secure supplies of pulp for his paper mills in this country. David Russell wrote to Tudor Pole: "It is reported that he is very anxious to secure our mill, but I have often thought that his interests have been purely financial, and that, after getting a certain number of mills under his control, he would await the opportunity of making a big flotation and coming out of it a wealthy man."

Meantime, David Russell considered the question of schooling his sons. In March the Bishop of Liverpool wrote a newspaper article on the public school spirit, and David Russell wondered if such schools were real training for leadership, in the running of the mills and the government of the country, a theme that was of much importance to him.

The two mills together had made a profit of £130,000 in the financial year to March 1926, and the buildings, including workers' houses and the telephone installation, were valued at £656,000, showing the massive investments there had been over the years. If not yet booming, business was picking up, as he informed Tudor Pole on the last day of April. "Everything is running well at the mills. Trade appears to be reviving, and I hope everything is not going to be upset again by a coal strike."

But since "Red Friday" the Government had been making extensive preparations to counter the strike that looked inevitable once the agreement with the miners ran out on 1st May 1926. Just before Christmas 1925 Chancellor of the Exchequer Churchill had announced that preparations were practically complete.

On the wireless at Aithernie on Friday 30th April 1926 David Russell heard the proclamation by the King, bringing into force the Emergency Powers Act of 1920, giving the Government and the authorities special powers of search, arrest and even imprisonment. The following day, when the girls at Aithernie celebrated May Day by washing their faces in the dew, the coal owners countrywide locked out the miners who refused to go into the pits to work on the owners' terms.

It was in effect a Government show-down with the entire trade union movement, and on Tuesday 4th May a General Strike in support of the miners began. Both the National Union of Printing, Bookbinding, Machine Ruling, and Paper Workers, and the Amalgamated Society of Paper Makers came out. But David Russell was counting the blessings of a good relationship with his workforce. "The Union men in our mills had a meeting, but agreed that they could do nothing and that it would not be in their interests to leave work."

But Fettykill Paper Mill at Leslie was closed by the workers, and pickets put on the roads to it. There were few trains running, and miners at Thornton and Gallatown were obstructing motorists and lorries, with police making a number of arrests at Gallatown for stone throwing and other disturbances. The men were arrested in their homes—some in their beds—and were brought before the sheriff and sent to Dundee.

At St Andrews University most of the 650 students, along with many members of staff, enrolled for voluntary work. The majority were detailed to work at the Dundee docks, or on the railway at Perth and Leuchars Junction. Principal Sir James Irvine had promised generous concessions in class work to all students who answered the call to keep the country running.

After the day's business John Black, the Tullis Russell secretary, liked nothing better than to relax at home, listening to the crystal wireless set he had rigged up. During the General Strike a relay of office girls with shorthand notebooks trooped to the company secretary's house, took down the news bulletins, typed them on stencils and ran off duplicated copies for circulation among the mill workers.

Despite the nationwide disruption David Russell was optimistic. "I cannot help feeling that the effect of the General Strike will on the whole be good and that it will ultimately lead to a better understanding." On 12th May the General Council of the TUC called off the strike, but railwaymen, printers, dockers and other workers who believed that their wages and conditions were under threat resolved to continue the industrial action.

Within a week all workers except the miners had decided to return to work. Coal supplies at Aithernie were running out, but in mid May David Russell was able to buy 1000 tons for the mills, though it was poor quality. In the seven months that the miners stayed out, many paper mills had to close down or go on short time, but by early July 1926 production for both Tullis Russell mills was at a record 315 tons per week. Twelve hours' overtime were worked at Rothes Mill, and paper sales in June were a record. The record was broken again, in mid July, with 342 tons, and employees received an extra day's pay.

Train after train crossed the Tay Bridge for the annual mill trip, that year to Dundee, where the bonus money was well spent. In 1917 Tudor Pole had recommended Miss Ilse Bell as a private secretary, and David Russell had engaged her without an interview. She was to become indispensable to him through her efficiency and

Miss Ilse Bell (left), David Russell's secretary, on the Larig Leachach in 1932. An intrepid mountaineer, she climbed the Matterhorn.

her understanding of his ways. She too had certainly earned a holiday, and in September the intrepid mountaineer "bagged" five peaks at Arolla in Switzerland, the highest 12,700 feet. She reported back to overcast Fife that she had been up among the snows in brilliant sunshine.

Determined that the mills would move with the times, David Russell had an oil-burning plant installed in October. However, the miners' action was affecting coal supplies, and oil was not obtainable. He was anxious to keep the mills running, even at a considerable loss, since the loss would be less than the cost of shutting down completely. In the event the mills stayed open because he was able to buy up all the coal being produced from an open cast mine at Balbirnie.

Both coal and oil became available again in mid November. Later that month when the miners called off their action, with no gain, output at Auchmuty was a record 226 tons per week, exceeded again the following week at 235 tons.

By December coal prices were dropping, and David Russell could turn his attention to augmenting his library by trying to get a copy of the limited edition of T. E. Lawrence's *Seven Pillars of Wisdom*. But the problematic year of 1926 had threatened his health as well as the mills. Ill in bed, he meditated on the aims of education, a subject close to his heart, since he had children to educate and was involved with St Andrews University. A letter from this time explains:

Our schools and universities are all so busy teaching systems of philosophy and so-called facts about matter and methods of acquiring knowledge, there seems little time left for the consideration of what it all leads to. What might come of suggesting to the man of deepest wisdom of our day, whoever he may be, a lecture at St Andrews on the idea of the basis of knowledge, although that does not cover the whole idea?

As a result of an agreement between several Scottish mills, paper prices were being maintained, making the Tullis Russell situation better than before the General Strike. But David Russell feared that this business co-operation would disappear, with mills anxious to return to pre-strike prices.

Young David was at Craigflower School, but early in 1927 his parents were considering removing him. David Russell complained to Tudor Pole that in some subjects there were no corrections done, nor comments made on work. In music the teaching was "worse than useless, because they are allowed to get into bad habits." The place was not healthy, since the boys had colds most of the time. Young David was taken away, to be tutored by a Miss Pilcher at home. David Russell wanted to send him to a school at Dunbar, but it had no vacancies till 1931. In February the Russells crowded round the wireless at Aithernie to participate in Sir Oliver Lodge's radio telepathy experiment, but the results were inconclusive. The family took their usual continental holiday, in France and Italy, in March. Tudor Pole was in Italy in April, and sent an account of his adventures from Genoa. Walking to Camogli, he had climbed up to a semaphore station. His clothes were in tatters, and he could not get a bath in the hotel the Russells had stayed in, so he went back to his own hotel and asked the old couple who ran it if he could have a bath. After a family confab they promised him that he would be relaxing in hot water in a few minutes. But first wood had to be chopped. Two and a half hours later Tudor Pole could take off his clothes.

But the basement had no curtains to the windows and just as I was getting into the bath I discovered that I was an object of great interest to the proprietor and his wife and staff and several villagers who leaned over the railings for a better view of the mad Englishman taking a hot bath at 6pm on Good Friday.

Young David returned to Craigflower, after his parents were satisfied that the teaching and living conditions would improve. The mills began a period of expansion, with the largest paper machine—104 inches in width—started at Rothes Mill in the first week of May 1927. The range of products was wide, including ammunition and emery papers; insulating papers for power and telephone cables; and the "Scottish Heroes" covers. "Scottish Heroes" was the brand name applied to the range of Cover papers manufactured in various colours and a range of sizes and finishes. The papers were thick, strong and used for the covering of books.

The gardener at Aithernie had an obsession about keeping the flowers for Mrs Russell. When a maid innocently picked some he went into a depression and committed suicide. Alison Russell felt that the sunlight had left Aithernie, so the family removed to Silverburn.

When he was leaving for a holiday, David Russell was always late. But the family arrived safely at Kincraig, Strathspey, in June 1927, and watched the eclipse on the 29th. David Russell wrote to Tudor Pole: "The cloud effects were wonderfully beautiful. At times they were sufficiently thin to enable us to see the eclipse beautifully without darkened glasses, and the opalescent lights were like many rainbows."

Ever since his boyhood David Russell had been fascinated by photography, and loads of cameras, film and tripod had to be taken on holiday. Turning his cap back to front so that it would not interfere with his view, he would line up his family for the photograph. After much fiddling with knobs they would hear "Oh dear, wait a moment," and another adjustment would have to be made. Every subject was taken in triplicate, each with a slightly different aperture, and meticulously recorded in a little notebook.

Like Aithernie, Silverburn was a wonderful place for young ones. The children bathed, and ran barefooted through the woods. Anne searched for "a little echo" so that she could take it to bed with her and fall asleep to the sounds of summer. Sheila remembered the magic of being invited into her father's study, the loose covers on the chairs soft shades with branches of fruit and pheasants. He would put the earphones of the crystal set on her, telling her that the voice or the music was coming from miles away.

Edward Erdal arrived at Silverburn as tutor to the boys, partic-

Camels in Algeria carrying esparto grass destined for the Fife paper mills.

ularly Pat. He had an exotic background: his mother, who was Danish, lived in Paris. Her Norwegian, naturalised British husband had died from blood poisoning resulting from a graze on his head caused by a stone falling in an unguarded mine shaft. Since it was a Sunday, he had not worn a helmet while inspecting the mine.

At the mills a diesel oil engine from South America, formerly in a German submarine ("rather a doubtful record!" as David Russell told Tudor Pole) was started up as stand-by plant. David Russell had low blood pressure and went to London for treatment from Dr [Carl] Johan Swanberg, a former Kellgren employee who had set up on his own, using the same treatment methods. In November David Russell relaxed at Biarritz.

The Russells watched a Movietone newsreel at the New Gallery Cinema, London. "We saw a review of Italian troops, hearing the words of command and horses' hooves on the pavement, etc., and then Mussolini spoke. It is quite extraordinary how it seems to bring you into touch with the actions recorded on the film," he wrote in a letter. David Russell was interested in the medium and had considered having the mills filmed from the air for advertising purposes.

Nigel, the Irvines' son, was going to Stowe, and David Russell thought about sending his sons there also. "It is the only school we have heard nothing but good about. I would much rather keep them in Scotland, but Scottish schools do not seem to be at their best just now," he told Tudor Pole.

On Pat's tenth birthday in April there was a family picnic in the Lomond Hills. David Russell played with his children, but he was not well. Dr Swanberg recommended treatment at Vichy; instead David Russell went to the South of France, lying on the beach at Hendaye on the Bay of Biscay. But he was homesick: "If only I could walk with more ease, the Highlands would be much more bracing and invigorating than the South."

Back home, David Russell found his peace and privacy disturbed by the increasing traffic of the 1920s. "On our quiet Sunday, line excursion trains from Edinburgh and Glasgow and elsewhere now pour out their holidaymakers all day long—possibly good for the holidaymakers who are shut up in towns all through the week, but it destroys the quiet and seclusion of our sea shore."

Tudor Pole could always be relied on to provide spiritual edification. In Italy on business, he had set out from Rome, accompanied by a famous Italian general and a Venetian friend. Their destination was the Gargano peninsula on the southern Adriatic, an unspoilt region of lemon gardens and Greek ruins. They drove up the hill to the medieval town of San Giovanni di Rotondo. Perched even higher in the hills was the Capuchin monastery of San Giovanni.

The travellers were looking for Padre Pio da Pietralcini, the name in religion of Francesco Forgione, an Italian Capuchin friar. In September 1918, while praying in the chapel of the San Giovanni monastery, Padre Pio had fallen into ecstasy, and had been found next morning lying unconscious on the altar steps. The signs of the stigmata showed upon his hands, feet and side, and the flow of blood had been stopped with difficulty. Padre Pio had become famous throughout Italy and beyond for his saintly character and healing power, though the Vatican authorities discouraged pilgrims.

Tudor Pole described the scene in the San Giovanni chapel that Sunday noon.

Mass was being sung, and the chapel was filled with peasants from the surrounding country. We were told that Padre Pio was hearing confessions, and that he had been in the confessional box since 5am without a break. It was fascinating to watch the crowd of peasants and farmers awaiting their turn to approach the confessional box. As each man or woman rose from his or her knees and walked towards the altar of the little church to receive Mass after confession, their faces seemed to be illuminated by an inner light.

But eventually the bearded Padre Pio emerged from the confession box, and, wearing mittens to cover the marks of the stigmata on his hands, he blessed work that Tudor Pole was undertaking in southern Italy. Tudor Pole noticed that he walked with difficulty because of the wounds on his feet.

David Russell was also having difficulty walking, and Pat needed his tonsils out, though his father was "always opposed to operations." At the mills there was the possibility of an annual order for 500 tons of ammunition cartridge papers for Kynochs via ICI. It looked as if the St James's Literary Agency in which he had an interest was going to be amalgamated with a flourishing one in Regent Street.

The office car was stolen in London, but better news followed: in October 1928 sales at the mills passed all previous records. On 20th November they were struck by lightning in a severe thunderstorm. Evidently a flash had discharged down the conductor on the high chimney, coming into contact with the electric cables. Switches were blown, one of the turbine armatures was destroyed, but only half an hour's production was lost.

There were family excursions to Edinburgh. After the Russian ballet in December the little girls clamoured for dancing shoes. Young David was poorly at school with a quinsy throat, and David Russell himself was ill. It was his appendix, and it would have to be removed when he was better. He had to lie on his back in his bed at Silverburn, hardly moving, till the inflammation subsided. "I am a complete prisoner, but I hope only for a few days longer," he complained to Tudor Pole. The hammers of the workmen altering Silverburn did not help. He took Ox Bile remedy which did not agree with him. "The further one goes away from natural remedies the greater the risk," Tudor Pole warned him.

David Russell had lent the "Maternity" painting by Jean Despujols for the Society of Scottish Artists' Exhibition in Edinburgh. The evocative picture of the mother breast-feeding her child was reproduced in the *Scotsman* in mid December.

Tudor Pole was living in a houseboat with his family on the Thames at Hampton Court. The King was ill, and there was a general slump in the country. As Christmas 1928 approached the shops were half empty, and people had cancelled holidays to Switzerland and the Riviera.

David Russell was meticulous about his Christmas-present lists, and liked to give books and shortbread to his friends. Would Mussolini's autobiography interest Tudor Pole, he wrote to ask, knowing that his friend had close business connections with Italy. As he rested, he looked out on a cloudless blue sky and a calm sea. He was expecting an esparto ship before Christmas Day.

9
The Romance of Esparto

Up to the nineteenth century linen and cotton rags were the traditional materials for papermaking, but there had been experiments with other substances, including the down of catkins and thistles, bamboo, potatoes, nettles, and even wasps' nests. The dislocation of the supply of cotton through the American Civil War and the duties imposed on the import of rags by countries like Germany, France and Belgium made the search for a substitute even more urgent. In 1854 *The Times* offered a prize of £1000 for a satisfactory material.

The prize was never claimed, though samples of esparto grass had been shown in the Great Exhibition of 1851. Esparto had long been known to man. The historian Pliny the Elder (23–79 AD) gave an accurate description of it in his *Historia Naturalis*, and his interest in the plant is reflected in its first botanical name *Granum Spartium Plinii*.

In 1857 esparto was tried commercially in Thomas Routledge's mill at Eynsham, and Scottish papermakers soon began to specialise in the material. The Tullis mill owners were pioneers, since their notes of esparto imports start in 1863. The following year they were experimenting in boiling esparto with caustic soda. In January 1865 William Tullis went to Spain to escape the Scottish weather and to do some business. His native heath was on his mind on the journey, for he saw the resemblance between a bay at Perpignan and Largo Bay in the way the sparkling waves came tumbling in. Furthermore, "just as at Largo too, I noticed the esparto . . . growing in the sandy hillock which framed a narrow strip by the edge of the sea."

He made enquiries about esparto as he bought rags and sold yarn for the Rothes Bleachfield. Within a month of his return there was an entry in a mill memorandum book for April 1865: "from 73 tons 16 cwts. esparto of fair quality, 13 cwts. of *roots* were taken. Storage charge at Tyne Docks for grass, rent per week, 2d. per ton, delivering 9d. per ton."

However, that same year William Tullis saw that the location of esparto sources could bring problems. "I hear of some merchants closing their accounts with Spain on account of its unsettled state. Let this be kept in mind." The situation worsened with the revolution of 1868. But by 1870 esparto had become the main raw material at Auchmuty, with 925 tons of the grass used as against 570 tons of rags.

When David Russell took over from his father in 1906 the mills needed thousands of tons of esparto annually, and used agents in Britain to bring in supplies from North Africa. But David Russell was not impressed by their efficiency, and in 1920 he arranged to do business direct with North Africa for esparto grass. Tudor Pole was associated with this venture, and would in effect become a roving Tullis Russell agent for esparto.

The vast esparto grass concessions stretching from the Tunisian border right across Algeria were subject to a bidding system of allocation. The main Algerian agency David Russell dealt with was called Basiaux Frères, run by two brothers of Belgian origin, Carl and Ivan Basiaux, who had become naturalised Frenchmen. Basiaux Frères had been founded as a French *Industrie Nationale* to supply esparto grass to Papeteries Navarre and other French companies.

David Russell wrote to Tudor Pole in August 1921:

We have heard this morning that the concession in Algeria for which we were willing to pay as high as 55,000 francs for three years has been secured for 10,000 francs. We think we have done well and we hope the venture will prove a success. Of course the whole transaction will be carried through by Messrs Basiaux, as only a Frenchman can hold the concession. We are merely supporting them with a view to securing our grass supplies.

But the negotiations with Clarence Hatry and Sir Frederick Becker over the Scottish esparto combine had raised doubts in David Russell's mind about security of supplies. Becker had spoken to David Russell about cornering the esparto trade and so making it very difficult for mills not in the proposed combine to obtain supplies. In the autumn of 1925 the USA began buying up supplies of esparto grass, and David Russell had to move to ensure that his mills would have this vital raw material.

The solution was to form a syndicate in which Tullis Russell would have a principal stake, thus ensuring supplies, and at the same time being allowed to sell surplus grass to other mills, including Scottish ones. Exploitation Alfatieres de L'Afrique Du Nord was set up at the end of 1925. EAAN had on its board David Russell, Tudor Pole and the Basiaux brothers.

David Russell believed in delegating responsibility. He also believed that his key men should leave their desks and go out to meet suppliers and customers. Mill managers crossed the Atlantic to tour the USA, noting new methods and new machines. For years company secretary John Black had listed cargoes of esparto in the firm's ledgers, and in 1928 he was despatched on a tour of Algeria and Tunisia with Tudor Pole to see how the grass was collected and shipped.

As their ship approached the quay in Algiers on a Sunday afternoon, John Black joined the other passengers by holding up a coin and throwing it overboard. He watched one of a shoal of native boys diving 20 feet into the clear waters retrieve the coin. It was a vivid reminder of how much Algeria depended on foreign currency, including the revenue from the sale of esparto grass.

The map of the world was different in those days. The Algeria John Black landed in was a French possession. Between the Sahara Desert and the Tell, a region of forests and arable land, was the High Plateau, from 3000 to 4000 feet above sea level, where most of the esparto grass was found.

For his tour of the esparto concessions, written up for the Mill magazine, Black travelled south from Algiers in a well-sprung Panhard car. He sampled *kous kous*, semolina mixed with chopped vegetables and boiled mutton—not unlike haggis in flavour, he noted approvingly. He was told that Arab girls of marriageable age were stuffed with the dish, since prospective husbands liked plump wives.

The Panhard passed esparto-laden camels en route to the collection posts. The grass was pulled, not cut, by natives in national dress, and carried in 600 lb loads by the camels which would not eat esparto and which required no water, and very little scrub for sustenance. In his article the company secretary noted that at £8 a camel was a real bargain, far more dependable than a motor in the desert.

There were two broad divisions of peoples, the Arabs, including the Moors, and the Berbers, including the Kabyles. The Arab of the Plain wore a gown of white woollen material striped with silk and a wide coloured silk sash at the waist. The next garment was a white woollen burnous, a type of hooded cloak. The haick, a long strip of woollen gauze covering the white felt cap on the head, hung flat at the back to cover the shoulders and neck. It was kept on the head by a long string of twisted camel hair rolled round the cap a number of times, and came forward on the forehead just enough to shade the eyes.

Women also gathered esparto. John Black saw figures wrapped from head to foot in white haicks and muslin, walking like ghosts beside laden camels in the dust clouds. But when he asked the driver to stop so that he could take a photograph, he found that the tribeswoman he had seen had disappeared behind her camel, since the Koran forbid reproductions of the human figure. But in the privacy of their homes the same women perpetuated the Arabian Nights image, wearing gorgeous silk trousers of China crepe reaching to mid leg, their feet in velvet slippers embroidered with gold. Their hair, plaited in long tresses, knotted behind the head and descending almost to the ground, was crowned with a skull-cap of velvet, encrusted with gold and seed-pearls, or trimmed with gold coins.

On still evenings those at the esparto weighing posts knew that Kabyle women were coming because of the tinkling of the bracelets and bangles at their necks, wrists and ankles. But the *chef de*

Silverburn House, Leven, Fife, the Russell home for many years.

THE ROMANCE OF ESPARTO

chantier, or manager, concentrated on the scales and not their beauty, since stones among the camel's load was a common trick. Collecting the grass was hard work for the natives, and the pay at the end of the long trek was small, but better than nothing.

The esparto was baled in a wooden press, the motive power supplied by a horse walking round it. The bales were then dispatched to the docks in basic lorries, easy to repair with a length of wire when they broke down on the crude roads, as they frequently did.

John Black was driven 200 miles from Bou Saada ("the place of happiness" in Arabic) to Constantine. Mules were still a hazard for the motor on the road, especially at night, but in the daytime he saw dozens of Fordson tractors ploughing as mechanisation made its mark in North Africa.

David Russell was interested in his secretary's description of Constantine, through his own fascination with Constantinople. He was also interested in how Tullis Russell's investment in Tebessa esparto was being looked after.

Founded by the Romans in the first century, Tebessa stood at the junction of nine roads, and was surrounded by thousands of acres of esparto lands. In the second century it had been the richest city in Africa next to Carthage. The triumphal Arch of Caracalla (erected circa AD 214) contrasted with the nomads' tents on the upper plateaux, and a short distance from the modern town was the magnificent ruins of the basilica of a vast monastery built some 1500 years before. The entire ruins had been unearthed.

From Tebessa to Sfax on the coast of Tunisia was about 240 miles south-east. A city of Phoenician origin, Sfax was said to have derived its name from the Arabic word *fakous* (cucumber) because of the local abundance of the vegetable. When John Black arrived there it had a population of 135,000, and was a busy port for shipping out esparto. Commerce was causing change, with mud houses replacing the nomads' traditional tents. But some people maintained their ancient way of life, like the tribes of the Touareg, who drove their flocks northwards from their southern homes as the summer heat approached. John Black met slow-moving caravans of these tribespeople and their animals on the long trek homewards to the new feeding grounds sprouting in the Sahara in the autumn rains. He noted with wonder that it was the men instead of the women who were veiled.

Black proceeded to the walled city of Susa, Tunisia, where ships that had brought coal and other commodities from Britain were washed down before being loaded with esparto. In the bazaars and narrow streets Arabs rubbed shoulders with other races. There was a hint of menace in the depot of the French Foreign Legion, and stowaways among the esparto grass were a problem.

Abdullah, the foreman of the Arab labour gang, was a character, a war veteran from a German prison camp who preferred European working dress. On the side he ran an olive grove and a fleet of camel carts. His labour squad were his relatives, busy transferring the bales of esparto to the ship by one "mule power" *arabats*, or native carts.

The *Maindy Hill*, a 1900 ton ship registered at the Fife port of Methil, had loaded 550 tons of esparto at Bona, over 300 at Sfax, and more at Arzew, and hoped for a good passage home before Christmas 1928. From the North African coast the ship runs along the Spanish coast. At night the Morse lamp tells the Rock of Gibralter that the *Maindy Hill* is passing. The ship runs the Straits. For the Atlantic the lashings on the 40 deck tarpaulins are tightened, because the cargo is settling.

Cape Trafalgar, where Nelson's guns triumphed; Bay of Cadiz; Cape St Vincent, from the eastward bay of which Columbus and Magellan had set out on their voyages of discovery. Then along the

A full cargo of esparto, bound for Britain.

Portuguese coast past Cape da Roca, the most westerly mainland point of Europe, a palace of one of Portugal's departed kings provides a landmark, like a seaboard Scottish castle.

Past Cape Finisterre and the Bay of Biscay; the "grasshopper," as an esparto boat is called, heels over, and when the wind direction changes there is relief. The Thames estuary; the sandbanks of the Suffolk and Norfolk coasts. It is the home stretch, but the North Sea is a busy traffic zone with continental express packets, trawlers and steamers. The ship rounds the Bass Rock with its noisy gannet colony. As it follows the Fife coast the empty Markinch railway wagons are clattering towards Methil, to be loaded with the bales in the morning and hauled to the mills.

As he lay ill in bed at Silverburn at the end of 1928 David Russell heard the *Maindy Hill*'s horn announcing its arrival. He could relax, knowing the mills had adequate supplies of esparto.

The process of turning esparto grass into paper was a laborious and careful one, controlled by constant scientific testing. After arriving at the mill in bales, the esparto was forked manually into dusters where sand and other impurities adhering to the grass blades were removed. The cleaned esparto was then fed in seven-ton batches into Boving pressure boilers together with an 8 per cent caustic soda solution and cooked at high temperature with the spent caustic soda subsequently run off for recovery.

The brownish green cooked esparto fibre, virtually pure cellulose, was then thoroughly washed with water to remove all traces of the cooking liquor, passed over sand traps where heavy foreign material including sand and grit settled out, and finally treated with a bleaching solution.

At this point chemical wood pulp could be added and the fibrous mass prepared for papermaking in beaters which cut and fibrillated the fibres, enabling them to absorb water and become "slimy" to the touch. This "stuff", as the wet beaten pulp was called, was then passed to a large cylindrical tank ready for making into paper.

At this stage, materials which determined the eventual quality of the paper were added, such as size, colouring matter and china clay which helped to produce a better printing surface. After further cleaning, the pulp was fed to the "wet end" of the paper machine and spread evenly on to a moving, finely woven wire cloth. This wire cloth was supported by closely spread rollers, the rotation of which under the moving cloth extracted a large amount of the water in which the pulp mix had been suspended, leaving a "fibre mat" lying on the wire cloth. More water was removed during

Handling bales of esparto grass from North Africa.

passage over vacuum boxes and just before leaving the "wet end", a dandy roll could, if required, be used to apply a watermark design to the surface of the fibre mat. At this point the fibre mat or sheet was strong enough to support its own weight; it was then pressed and passed round steam-heated cylinders and through smoothing rollers and machine calendar stacks to produce the surface finish required on the paper.

One of the unique characteristics of esparto was that it could be made with a very smooth surface and also retain a high degree of bulk for any given weight.

Tullis Russell was the first mill in the world to build a twin wire machine for printing papers. The problem was that the underside of a sheet of paper—the side next to the machine wire—was always marked by the mesh. In printing a single ply sheet, the top was smoother than the bottom. But in the twin wire system, introduced at the mills in the 1920s, two separate webs of paper are made on two machine wires, one of which is reversed. The undersides of these two separate webs are then joined together while still wet at the first press, before being passed to the drying cylinder as a single sheet of paper. The final sheet therefore has two "top" sides which are equal in every respect, the "wire" or underside being totally enclosed.

In the days when the Tullis Russell mills were lighted by gas there was sometimes a grand finale to the process from grass to paper. From the friction of passing over the drying cylinders new paper became heavily charged with static electricity, and if there were visitors in the mill, a boy would jump up on to the framework and touch the revolving roll with a toe. He then held a finger to the gas jet and it would light up with a whoosh.

The esparto story has a fascinating sideline. Walking through the shed in the early part of the century, the inventive Robert Russell noted the dust clinging to his boots. It was full of wax. Why not recover it? A wax extraction plant to Robert Russell's design was set up in 1910, the first of its kind in the esparto paper industry. To make the scale of the process profitable, esparto dust was sent from other mills. The wax was used in various types of polish, and its outstanding properties were its hardness and high melting point.

David Russell had written to Tudor Pole in April 1924: "We have a patent for the extraction of esparto wax, but we know perfectly well that in itself the patent is of no value. What is of value is the experience we have and the skill in working the process."

As the esparto came in and went out as paper, David Russell was pleased with the smooth operation. But he was always looking for ways to consolidate the firm's position in the esparto concessions and ensure the annual requirement of some 10,000 tons. In 1928 he bought out Carl Basiaux's share in EANN and then transferred this holding to Tullis Russell.

John Black had enjoyed his tour of the esparto concessions in Algeria and Tunisia, but Tudor Pole was to go out several times annually for over 30 years, and to him there was little romance in esparto gathering and shipping. He wrote to David Russell in late November 1928, after the tour of EANN concessions in the Djelfa area of Algeria with John Black: "I cannot get used to a diet of sour bread and sheep entrails which seems to be the Arab standard of luxury." The nights were freezing in the hovels in which he usually stayed. Though the new grass was excellent in quality, the quantities would be small, he warned, and the mills outside the syndicate would have to "scrabble" for supplies.

As David Russell recovered his strength at Aithernie at Christmas with his family, he was thinking of the work that was awaiting him at the mills in the new year. Through Miss Bell's swift shorthand and typing, on paper made from esparto, he maintained a large correspondence, covering all aspects of the mills, family matters and domestic arrangements. No detail was too small for his attention. In addition, he always made time to attend to his ongoing concern with the affairs of St Andrews University.

10
St Andrews Benefactor

Though he did not go to St Andrews University after his early schooling in the town, David Russell was to have a long association with the institution, and there was a family connection that went far back. The Reverend George Walker, minister of Kinnell from 1813 to 1868, had attended St Andrews University at the end of the eighteenth century. He was described in his funeral oration as "a good and guileless man, temperate in his enjoyments, simple in his tastes, modest in his manners, shrinking from anything like public display, quiet and retiring, single-hearted in his purpose, devoted to his duty, self-sacrificing in the cause of Christ."

In memory of his brother George, John Walker of Homelands near Largo founded the Walker Trust in 1881. Its prime purpose was for "furthering the usefulness or relieving the needs of the University of St Andrews in such a way as the said Trustees shall deem proper."

One of the trust founder's nephews was David Russell senior, and he appointed his son David as a trustee. The original capital was £7500, but over the many years of his association, up until 1956, David Russell was to make many thousands of pounds of personal donations to the Trust and to utilise it as a medium for making substantial benefactions to St Andrews University. The money was used for general university purposes and for supplementing the stipends of professors, as well as assisting academic staff with grants for special work. Needy students were also helped.

David Russell became deeply involved in the affairs of St Andrews University in 1911, as a member of the quincentenary planning committee. In May 1916 the Walker Trust publicised a competition for essays on prayer; 1667 entries in 19 languages were received. In 1919, following the First World War, David Russell had an even more ambitious scheme for the Walker Trust.

The Trustees, believing that the strife of nations is but the effect of continuous conflict arising from the domination of egotism, whether national or individual, consider the moment opportune for directing attention to the study of world "reconstruction" on spiritual lines. With this end in view they have decided to offer prizes for essays dealing with this subject.

The prizes were generous. There were four students' prizes of £25 each, open on a worldwide basis; the same number and value of prizes were also open to all workers, including men on naval or military service. The open prize was £200, to anyone in any part of the world.

Entries arrived from many countries and regions for the deadline of 1st March 1920. From Punjab came an essay by Dinanath Sharma Shastri, who had gone to the trouble of having it printed. He was a "gold and silver medallist, son of Viprarsh Hrishi Kesh, Firozpur City." He sent 25 copies of "Light on the Spiritual Regeneration," written in a mixture of English and Punjabi. Frustrated at not winning the open prize after his effort, he accused the judges of being "partial" to essays written in English, and argued that a rich country like Scotland should help a poor country like India. David Russell replied: "It would probably surprise you to know how much the Scottish universities are in need of money, how poor are many of the professors and lecturers and how small their incomes are."

In 1920 a selection of Walker Trust essays from the first competition was published under the title *The Power of Prayer*, edited by the Right Reverend William Paterson, Professor of Divinity at Edinburgh, and by David Russell. Dr Henry Hodgkin won the £200 open prize in the Reconstruction competition, but his effort and the other winning essays were not published in book form, nor was the competition repeated. Though David Russell regarded the competition as having been eminently worthwhile, he did not want to lose sight of the fact that the Walker Trust was principally for the benefit of St Andrews University.

His closest friend next to Wellesley Tudor Pole was James Colquhoun Irvine. After the Royal Technical College, Glasgow, Irvine went to St Andrews University. While working as a technician in the laboratory of Thomas Purdie, Professor of Chemistry, he studied for his BSc, which he took in 1898. Irvine proceeded to further studies and research, graduating PhD in 1901 from Leipzig and DSc from St Andrews in 1903.

James Irvine succeeded Purdie in the chair of chemistry in the United College in 1909. When Purdie died in December 1916 Irvine confided to David Russell: "He was my scientific father and the inspiration for all I have done."

As his own studies in Edinburgh showed, David Russell had always been fascinated by science. He was aware of the importance, not only of keeping up with developments, but in actually creating them. In 1908–9 he had appointed a chemist and the following year installed a laboratory at the mills. During the First World War Professor Irvine and several of his research assistants worked closely with the Tullis Russell mills on the chemistry of paper production, and in particular on the Rinman method. Irvine encouraged his best graduates to make their careers in the laboratory at the mills, most notably Dr James Macdonald, chief chemist from 1919 to 1952.

Irvine's energy seemed inexhaustible. As well as his wartime teaching and research at the mills, he devised special processes for the production of bacteriological sugars such as dulcitol to maintain the health of British and allied soldiers. He also worked on the production of synthetic drugs including the local anaesthetic novocaine, vital for the war wounded.

In the temporary chemistry laboratory on the tennis lawn of the United College, a German shell was opened one Sunday morning as the church bells of St Andrews were sounding. It was a hazardous undertaking, since the shell contained the deadly new mustard gas. The authorities pressed Irvine not only to make a chemical analysis of the shell's contents, but to reproduce the gas as a counter-measure. After his work on life-preserving sugars and drugs, Irvine felt that his position as a chemist was being compromised. Fortunately, he was able to share his frustrations and anxieties with his close friend David Russell. Irvine's wife, Mabel, was deeply grateful for this friendship and summed up David Russell's character in a sentence: "You have a helping hand for everybody."

But in January 1918 Irvine, a long-distance runner and keen tennis player who believed in physical as well as mental fitness, wrote despondently to David Russell: "No day brings the leisure to think of anything but the work in hand, and the solitude without which no man can know himself is hard to find." But that summer the St Andrews chemist found some respite from the production of cordite and aeroplane "dope" by taking a house in Inverness-shire, close to Loch Meiklie. The Russells were guests, and every morning before breakfast David Russell and the Professor rowed across the loch to swim in a little sandy bay.

A 4 lb pike was landed, and there were long walks and earnest discussions on the world situation. Alison Russell and Mabel Irvine were also close friends. Mabel wrote songs, poems and plays which were performed in the drawing-room after dinner.

Irvine returned to his St Andrews laboratory. But the long war ended, and the chemical production team was dispersed. For his services to victory the greatest living authority on carbohydrates was made a Commander of the Order of the British Empire.

In 1920 Sir John Herkless, Principal of St Andrews University, died after a short period in office. The ambitious Irvine considered that he had sufficient experience for the post. Purdie's protégé had become dean of the faculty of science in 1911, and his responsibilities included control of science teaching at University College, Dundee. In 1913 he had been made an assessor on the University Court, and his experience of the financial and business management of the university included the difficult war years. He could also claim that the chemistry research school which he had been instrumental in creating was the largest in Scotland.

Irvine turned to David Russell for support, sending him his letter of application with the injunction:

Use the document as fully as you think fit by sending copies to friends who may help. Munro, the Secretary of State for Scotland and Balfour of Burleigh I should think the most important. Any connection with the Premier would not be amiss. Haldane likewise. As for others, the Lord Lieutenant of Fife is officially connected with the university and might be enlisted. Mr Younger is working the M.P. influence, I think pretty thoroughly, but it occurs to me that the university members might be approached if you saw any avenue. They could perhaps be neutralised if not enlisted.

David Russell wrote to Tudor Pole in June 1920:

I am most anxious to put forward the name of Professor J.C. Irvine as one eminently qualified to be Principal of the University. The appointment, I believe, lies with the Prime Minister, and the Rt. Hon. Robert Munro, Secretary for Scotland, and Lord Balfour of Burleigh may have a considerable influence in the appointment.

I shall be very glad to know if you can put me in touch with anyone who could introduce the matter to any of these gentlemen. I believe Professor Irvine to have all the qualities to fulfil the duties of Principal to the great advantage of the University and of the students . . .'

But in reply Tudor Pole warned:

It is rather a delicate matter because if it leaks out afterwards that a certain candidate was being pushed it causes difficulty in the university itself. I fancy you will be able to ensure that JCI is placed on the list from which the selections are being made but I do not think you would be wise to do more than this. I am not sure that this would be the best choice either from the university's or from JCI's standpoint. He is a chemist and a physicist and his theological and religious views are still nebulous in many ways. He has not found peace within himself and is hardly ready (do you think?) to become Principal of a university that is mainly theological.

David Russell rebuked Tudor Pole for this assessment of his friend's character. But in September Tudor Pole wrote: "I hear Prof Irvine is not to get the St A's post and that an appointment has been approved tentatively of an outsider whose name has not been divulged."

The "outsider" was apparently Dr Andrew Wallace Williamson, minister of St Giles' Cathedral, Edinburgh. A former lecturer in pastoral theology at Edinburgh University and Moderator of the General Assembly in 1913, Williamson was Dean of the Order of the Thistle and of the Chapel Royal. Sir John Herkless had also been a theologian, and St Mary's College, the theology school at St Andrews needed support and public prominence to maintain its student numbers. But Williamson is said to have decided against the post because of poor health. Irvine was the second choice.

In mid December David Russell wrote to Tudor Pole: "Everyone here is pleased to hear of the appointment to the Principalship of St Andrews. It will undoubtedly be a very popular appointment among the students, and I think generally at St Andrews and Dundee. With one exception all the professors and lecturers at Dundee signed a memorandum in his favour."

David Russell knew what he expected from the new Principal. "The important thing is not that our universities should produce scientists and learned men, but that these scientists and learned men should carry light of a deeper order to lighten the world."

Irvine saw himself getting no peace in St Andrews to write his inaugural address, and planned to spend a couple of days with the Russells in the quiet and inspiration of Aithernie. His inauguration on 11th January 1921 was rather rowdy, but the students settled down to listen to their new Principal's predictions.

I see before me the Universities of the future becoming more sharply divided into two utterly divergent types. The one is a large University offering instruction and degrees essentially designed to meet the requirements of industrial and commercial life. No doubt it will provide trained workers for the community, and will, deservedly, be deemed successful.

On the other hand, I see a University, inevitably smaller, equally alive to the necessities of the times, but pledged primarily to the advancement of learning. From it will proceed the trained thinkers—those who in time will lead the trained workers. It will remain a small University, but the limitation will be deliberate and necessary. Students will clamour for admission, not because other Universities are full, but because they wish to get in.

Under Principal James Irvine students were to "clamour" to get into St Andrews. He developed the residential system by building halls like St Salvator's, to which David Russell contributed. In 1924–25 there were 655 students at St Andrews: by 1950–51, towards the close of his principalship, there were 2062. The partnership between David Russell and Principal Irvine benefited both the university and the paper mills. Between them they selected applications for support from the Walker Trust, and at the mills the Principal supervised experiments in esparto wax.

The Walker Trust put up the money for a series of speakers at the university. In January 1922 Professor Emilio Marcault the theosophist lectured on "The Evolution of Intuition," but the sceptical Principal would not allow notices to be posted on the university boards. It irritated David Russell, but their close friendship endured.

Field Marshal Douglas Haig, who had been schooled in St Andrews, had been Rector of the university from 1916 to 1919. In May 1922 the Earl was installed as Chancellor. At the same ceremony James Barrie delivered his rectorial address on the theme of Courage. The hall was hushed, and David Russell had never heard a finer oration.

"We met Barrie, Ellen Terry and others at a reception in University House," he told Tudor Pole. "Barrie is very much aged and is in a sense a pathetic figure. It appears that he has never got over the death of his adopted boy at Oxford just a year ago." Haig unveiled the war memorial in the College Chapel, which had been partly refurbished. There were five mosaics by Douglas Strachan, and some small stones from Constantine's tomb in Constantinople, supplied by Professor Kay, had been worked into one of them. But

David Russell found the three stained glass windows above the mosaics "very crude," and wanted to have them replaced.

Tudor Pole had a psychic message for Irvine through David Russell. He was "close to a big achievement, much greater than he realises. That depends upon himself, his self-control, faith and mental attitude."

In July 1922 David Russell received an honorary doctorate from St Andrews. The oration stated that "By prompt and practical interest in our corporate life, by wise provision of lectures and musical recitals, and by the international essay scheme, he has done much to enlarge our outlook and humanise our intercourse."

In September the Prince of Wales came to St Andrews to be installed as Captain of the Royal & Ancient, and to receive an honorary degree from the university. The Russells stayed in St Andrews for several days for the festivities. On the evening of his arrival the Prince asked Principal Irvine to sit on the arm of his chair in the Royal & Ancient clubhouse and talked to him about the university; the Prince was informal and friendly. Next morning, Wednesday, was dull and rainy, and about 4000 watched him play himself in as Captain. Royal & Ancient ceremonial decreed that members of the

James Irvine, Principal, St Andrews University and his wife Mabel relax with Alison Russell (left), Loch Rannoch, 1922.

famous club were not fully initiated until they had kissed the golf balls on the silver putter which had as many balls attached as there had been captains of the club. The Prince held the putter for the initiation ceremony.

Irvine read his address for the royal graduation ceremony to the Russells and other friends for their approval. The Russell car and chauffeur were used to take the Prince to the ceremony on Thursday evening. But David Russell was critical of Haig, who as Chancellor conferred the degrees.

He is very formal and gave one the impression when speaking during the graduation of being almost in a bad temper. He brought no warmth or good feelings into the proceedings. They say too that when he is present with the Prince, he makes you feel that you are in the presence of the Prince, and have to be on your best behaviour. When Haig is not present, people apparently get on perfectly easily with the Prince, without feeling that he is in any way in a superior position.

The Russells and Irvines formed a foursome at the Royal & Ancient Ball that evening. There had been many applications for tickets, and many new dresses had been bought, so there was much disappointment when the Prince did not attend the ball, having in fact left St Andrews. The foursome went back to University House at 2.30 a.m. After three days of rain the streets were dry, the stars shining bright. But Mabel Irvine was feeling run down because of so much entertaining, and had been ordered by her doctor to go away for a month's rest.

Stanley Baldwin left the Imperial Conference in London to go to St Andrews in October 1923 for an honorary degree. David Russell told Tudor Pole: "The Premier's absence from London has caused some bitter comment. People in high places have been asking whether St Andrews University considers its affairs more important than the affairs of the Empire and of the world."

It was a time of crisis, with France having occupied the Ruhr because it believed that Germany had not fulfilled its obligations under the peace treaty. At a private conversation in University House, Baldwin said that Britain had no alternative but to follow France, for the simple reason that we had disarmed and were powerless to do otherwise. Baldwin's cousin Rudyard Kipling also received an honorary degree, but David Russell found his address without volume or inspiration.

The residence of the St Andrews Principal has a magnificent situation on the Scores, overlooking the sea and the West Sands. In the "gay twenties" in St Andrews the Russell Rolls-Royce was often parked outside University House. The Principal and his wife were "uncle Jim and aunt Mabel" to the Russell children. There were cream teas at the University Café, golf on the Old Course, and soirées in the drawing-room when Mabel Irvine played sonatas on the grand piano while the Russells watched the moon on the North Sea.

Irvine was knighted in 1925, and in 1948 was made a KBE. Famous men and women continued to come to receive honorary degrees. The ceremony for the explorer, statesman and humanitarian Fridtjof Nansen had to be cancelled in May 1926 owing to the General Strike, but it took place in November. The Walker Trust continued to contribute to the development of the university, and from session 1928–29 David Russell made available residential scholarships for men to the value of £100.

11
Alexis Aladin

David Russell might have made the acquaintance of Alexis Aladin through the Kellgrens. Born in the Volga region of Russia in 1873, Aladin was at the same school as Lenin, but was expelled from school and from Kazan University for subversive political activity. He was sentenced to three years' exile to the extreme north of Russia.

Aladin escaped abroad, to France, then Belgium. In 1900 he moved to London and worked as a translator. The year 1905 was a turbulent one for Russia, with a general strike in Moscow, the *Potemkin* mutiny, and the Tsar's October Manifesto conceding the principles of freedom of speech. Aladin used an amnesty to return to his Volga homeland. His leadership of the Labour Group in the First Duma in 1906 allowed him to develop his undoubted powers as an orator.

But the Russian Government dissolved the Duma after four months. The leaders of the major parties fled to Finland, where they signed a manifesto urging the Russian people to defy the Government. On their return to Russia they were imprisoned and disqualified from election to the Second Duma. Aladin, however, was in London at a conference. He liked to wear yellow gloves and spoke out of the corner of his mouth "like the most pure-blooded Britishers," his friend Bogoraz-Tan recalled. In his book *What I Saw in Russia* Maurice Baring described him as "a dark, shortish man, with a small moustache and grey serious eyes, short hair and a command of incisive language" with an oratory "English in style."

After an abortive attempt to return to Russia, Aladin lectured in England and the USA on the political situation in Russia. In March 1907 the *New York Times* reported him as pleading: "Our object in coming here was to cut our country off from the money market of America. What we ask is that if you do *not* help us, do not help our government, do not give them guns to shoot us."

There was now no question of Aladin being able to return to Russia. Back in London, he earned a living as a journalist and translator. He was willing to try his hand at anything, and was put in charge of a laboratory for the preparation of sour milk and cheese. He then moved to Southampton, where he worked in a motor boat and engine building works.

Aladin took a deep interest in Russian exiles in England and North America, including mutineers from the battleship *Potemkin*. He was also involved in raising funds to defend some of the accused in the notorious Siege of Sidney Street in which Winston Churchill the Home Secretary took a prominent part.

With the outbreak of war in 1914 Aladin offered his services to the Russian Embassy in London, but was refused free entry to his motherland. On his own initiative he became a liaison officer between Russia and Britain. He was apparently sent to Dublin in 1916 to investigate the Easter Uprising by applying his revolutionary experience to the situation. As a journalist he visited the British troops in France, and evidently the French Government invited him to enter enemy-occupied territory. He might have been involved in intelligence work, as Tudor Pole was.

In 1916 Alexis Aladin met David Russell, who was to supply him with money and encouragement for the rest of his life. A common

Alexis Aladin in 1915, ex-Duma member and a dandy.

bond was their interest in mysticism, with Aladin claiming that he had had visions during his childhood. In fact he suggested to his patron that a chair in mysticism, and also a degree in Russian should be established at St Andrews University, but nothing came of either scheme. In February 1917 Alison Russell recorded in her diary in London: "Mr Aladin for lunch. Liked him very much." That same month Aladin lectured at St Andrews University, and also to the Edinburgh section of the Russo-Scottish Society on the theme "Necessary Elements for a Lasting Alliance with Russia."

But after the Russian Revolution in February 1917 and the abdication of the Tsar Aladin set off for Russia, in a British lieutenant's uniform. He met General Kornilov, who had been appointed Supreme Commander-in-Chief in July 1917 by the Provisional Government headed by Kerensky. Kornilov was suspicious of Aladin, and Trotsky was contemptuous, dismissing him as "a seeker of adventure . . . who had spent some years abroad, who never removed an English pipe from his mouth and therefore considered himself a specialist on international affairs."

In the Civil War Aladin was with the Southern Group of the Army of the Don in May 1918, and in November was promoted to staff captain. In February 1919 he wrote to David Russell in his usual ebullient style: "Greetings from your roving friend,—greetings as warm as summer noon in the steppes, as true and bright as the glimmer of a friendly covering blade—greetings to your Lady, your baby and yourselves . . . Greetings . . ." He had a request: "I am in need of everything—my clothes are in rags, my underwear does not exist, my boots are gone, my cap and the rest are equally deficient." But he assured David Russell that his soul was in better order. He was becoming "more Christian and less pagan," reading the New Testament daily and thinking about his early interests in the religions of India, Greece and Egypt.

In April 1920 Aladin moved to Sevastopol where he assumed control of the Political Division of the General Staff under General Vrangel, leader of the White Armies of the South. That summer Aladin was sent abroad on information-spreading missions. He was heading for London on the Orient Express when the train was rerouted owing to damage to the track, leading to a meeting with Miss E. Constance Nightingale, a schoolmistress who was to become one of his closest friends and supporters.

Back in London the elegant Aladin, now a major in the British army, held forth on his beloved Russia in the National Liberal Club. At the same time he was appealing to David Russell for financial help to support his lifestyle. There was mutual dislike between Aladin and Tudor Pole, but the Russian wanted Tudor Pole to become the representative of the Vrangel government in Britain. Aladin wrote to him:

I am in full accord with General Vrangel's action, and would join his forces tomorrow for the cause (in my opinion of right and justice) were I free and, by doing so I could at least counteract this bad, rotten Bolshevist regime, as it exists today. I hope you will do your best to help on the good cause so ably defended by General Vrangel and his valiant small but loyal army.

But Tudor Pole expressed his doubts about Aladin to David Russell: "I feel confidence in 90% of all A.A. says, feels and does; somehow there remains 10% doubt of certain elements in him which I do not understand or cannot fathom." David Russell replied: "I have always felt that I could trust Aladin as a man, but I also feel that his methods of attaining his ideals might lead to criticisms and misunderstandings, and I am inclined to think that the jealousy and criticism against him are largely due to his independence and to his carelessness about the opinion of others."

David Russell was involved with several organisations dedicated to bringing relief to the victims of the Revolution. Mrs Winston Churchill and Lady Cunard were on the executive committee of the Russian Relief and Reconstruction Fund. The principle of the Fund was that all relief should be distributed by British agents. Work began in the Crimea in 1920, when a small children's home was opened at Balaclava.

In mid November Vrangel's defence collapsed, and David Russell urged Tudor Pole: "There seems more urgent need than ever to provide funds for the relief of the suffering of the refugees from the Crimea. If Aladin knows of any means of using funds for the relief of the sufferers, I shall send a cheque immediately upon hearing from you or from him."

Aladin was depressed and disorientated. Should he remain in Britain, return east or go to the USA? Tudor Pole gave him "cogent reasons" for staying. But Aladin planned to go to the States, and perhaps also to Australia and New Zealand on a political campaign to encourage support for White Russian ideals. He believed that if the world did not take active steps to counteract the Bolshevist crusade, "Red" Russia would join with Germany to spread east and dominate China, threatening if not destroying the fabric of the civilised world.

SIR DAVID RUSSELL

Tudor Pole wrote to David Russell in January 1921:

I feel that we ought to make a special effort to arrange help for these high-minded cultured Russian intellectuals, who have lost everything, and are not touched by ordinary charities and who have a certain definite mission in this country in explaining and enlightening people here on the actual Russian situation, not simply of the moment but, from the viewpoint of history, past and future.

David Russell was interested in the idea of setting up a house in Britain for them. He wondered if it should be in London or in the country, and offered to collect some funds. Walburga, Lady Paget, daughter of a Saxony noble and wife of a British ambassador who had served in Rome and Vienna, suggested the setting up of a colony. Lady Egerton, the Duchess of Somerset, Lady Plymouth, and the Bishop of Exeter were interested in helping to establish such a colony. The post of hostess-cum-housekeeper was provisionally offered to the Countess Sofia Panin, who became one of David Russell's correspondents.

This remarkable woman had lent her estate in the Crimea to Leo Tolstoy in 1901. A well-known social worker, Countess Panin had established a People's Palace, where many Russian workers learned to read and write and received an education. She had been imprisoned by the Bolsheviks, but friends procured her release, and she became a refugee in France and Switzerland.

But David Russell came to believe that money should be distributed to needy Russians, instead of setting up a Russian communal house.

In February 1921 Tudor Pole wrote to him: "A.A. seemed cheerful and had a 'romantic' experience with 'une jeune Americaine' going over on the boat, which he says has resulted in his being 'in love' for the first time in his life. His plans are undecided and his visions are very far removed from daily events."

The "jeune Americaine" was a 17 year old beauty, Clare Boothe Luce. The crossing to France was stormy and the future playwright of social satire (as Clare Boothe Luce) would later recall how the "Colonel" hypnotised her with his voice and eyes to cure her of seasickness. The romantic Aladin presented himself at her Paris pension and, having showed her his cigarette case with the signature of Nicholas II, claimed that he had rescued the Tsar's eldest daughter, Grand Duchess Olga, and helped her to escape abroad. Aladin sent David Russell a press cutting about Miss Boothe, "voted the most beautiful girl on the Riviera in the recent contest held here at Nice."

In late March Aladin asked Tudor Pole for office space so that he could develop his "economic political" plan, but Tudor Pole did not want to be identified with his "somewhat mysterious propaganda work." The following month Aladin was arranging a scheme for the creation of a central committee in London for dealing with the various Russian famine organisations. But he was dejected. "My girl—she is mine in many senses, so let me call her that—has gone to America," he told David Russell.

But Aladin's condition was more than lovesickness, and Tudor Pole supplied the diagnosis:

he seems to be extraordinarily bitter towards certain of his friends—whether Russian or English I do not know—who are no longer supporting him financially, and seem in a mysterious way to be associated with the Masonic Movement. Whether the possibility of a return to Russia next month is creating a certain amount of excitement in his mind, or whether there are other reasons for it, I do not know.

In mid May Tudor Pole reported:

A.A. is inclined to be obsessed by the idea that he is being persecuted and followed round by both friends and enemies. I don't think it's true but he believes it and his nerves are anywhere. All this talk about the evil magic employed by Masons is really baseless. I think he is misunderstood by his fellow refugees and is sometimes accused of leaving Vrangel at the critical moment and flirting with the Bolos; but these charges, if they exist, are unfair to A.A.

It is because of his interviews with Krassin and offers to go to Moscow that he is no longer helped financially by certain Russian friends and in this I think he is unfairly treated; but one must remember he brings a good deal on his own head by his secrecy and wild accusations. It is not easy to know how to help him while he remains in this hysterical condition but it's evident that he's hard up, like so many thousands of Russians over here and I'm not quite clear whether he takes any steps to find work, but rather continues to attempt very obscure and illusory political negotiations which can lead nowhere.

Tudor Pole warned David Russell bluntly in mid October 1921: "If you finance A.A. further, let it be for some work actually done, or lectures given, and not for staying on at the National Liberal Club (where he is regarded as a useless limpet, which is unkind and only partly true)."

In January 1922 Tudor Pole allowed Aladin to use his office

while he was absent on business, but was apprehensive that he would stay. The Russian exile was philosophical. "The National Liberal Club has blackballed his re-election (Jewish influence he says). He seems fairly cheerful," Tudor Pole reported.

That summer Aladin sent David Russell an article, asking him to secure journalistic work for him with the *Scotsman*. David Russell approached the editor without success. Meantime, Tudor Pole had had a strong psychic message, requesting help in the form of clothing, goods and books for imprisoned Russian patriarch bishops and priests. He complained about the "scandal" of the church authorities in Britain not doing enough and asked the American Red Cross to help to get comfort through to the Russians.

In August the *Glasgow Herald* also rejected Aladin's article. But he was preoccupied with another scheme, and asked Tudor Pole for introductions to the Foreign Office and the War Office for a proposed visit to the East.

David Russell became Aladin's confidant in his depression at not being able to find remunerative work in Britain. There was a bizarre suggestion of undertaking an expedition in mufti to the Baltic States, Poland and Czechoslovakia. The intrepid Aladin even asked John Buchan for his support.

But Aladin was lucky in his contacts. He met the art collector and philanthropist Chester Beatty and lived for several months in 1922 in his luxurious homes in London and Kent. Aladin helped Beatty to search for rare manuscripts, but the two men parted company.

Aladin became a denizen of bed-sitters, living on assistance from David Russell and Miss Nightingale. He became preoccupied with spiritual matters and joined a religious and spiritual society called The Quest (which had no connection with Tudor Pole's Quest).

Yet another relief organisation, the Appeal for the Russian Clergy, was started in 1922–23, with the Archbishop of Canterbury as patron, David Russell on the executive committee, and Tudor Pole as joint honorary treasurer.

In September 1923 a sceptical Tudor Pole wrote to David Russell:

A.A. tells me that his adopted son, who is now a general in the Czech army has asked him to go to Prague to edit a peasant paper. A.A. is anxious to combine commercial work with this venture and to develop trade between London and Prague. Candidly I don't think such schemes will bear fruit because A.A. doesn't understand business in the concrete and would make a better journalist than a business man.

Aladin asked David Russell if he could represent Tullis Russell interests in Czechoslovakia, Bulgaria and Yugoslavia. David Russell concurred, but the necessary visa did not arrive. What did arrive in December 1923 was a child fathered by Aladin, born to a housemaid, "a brave soul by her nature," as he told David Russell. It was an awkward situation. Aladin had a wife in Russia, but he did not know if she was still alive, and he was frightened of being accused of bigamy if he married the mother of his child.

In the autumn of 1924 Aladin prepared for his trip to Prague. He told David Russell: "I am taking a little of British soil; it would be mixed with a little of Russian soil, which I am taking from Russia. Both would be wrapped up into a hand-written text of the Psalm 91 and sewn in a piece of silk."

During Aladin's two month sojourn in Prague David Russell sent money, and also a letter saying that the Department of Overseas Trade believed that there were prospects of doing business in Bulgaria in blotting papers, and enclosing a list of prospective buyers. Aladin wanted to travel home via Sofia and Belgrade to establish permanent contacts in Bulgaria and Yugoslavia for Tullis Russell. He received the hotel and travelling expenses he asked for, but his report was not promising. Stranded in Paris in the last week of the year with no money, he appealed to David Russell and Miss Nightingale for his fare home.

His next scheme was a transatlantic trip to put Russian and US farmers in touch with each other, but it fell through. He remained in "the wilderness of London." Though there were holes in his clothes, his headed notepaper proclaimed: Alexis Aladin, Ex-Member, The Duma, Russia. He struggled to earn a living as a journalist, though his style was too stilted. A heavy smoker, he also had a brief spell in the tobacco industry. "Caged up in Hampstead," existing on one orange and a cigarette per day, he continued to believe that his work would lead to the establishment of a peasant-based economy in his beloved Russia. He slept with a loaded revolver under his pillow in case the Bolsheviks called. In January 1927 the Foreign Office regretted that there was "no opportunity at present of utilising your services."

In May 1927 Aladin consulted Carl Swanberg on David Russell's recommendation. He had prostate cancer, and spent the last harrowing six weeks of his life in St Thomas' Hospital, London, undergoing surgery, and trying to fit into the life of the ward. David Russell went to London to visit him. Aladin was touched. "David came today, brought lilies of the valley and blue sweet peas."

Alexis Aladin died on 30th July 1927, aged 54, and was buried at Brookwood Cemetery, London, in his British army officer's uniform. David and Robert Russell started an appeal to secure the future of Aladin's son Alexis. David Russell wrote to Mrs Chester Beatty: "I am prepared to do all I can to give the boy a sound foundation for a good start in life and will give him what personal supervision and help I can." Chester Beatty gave £75 for the first year, and £50 for the second. David and Robert Russell settled a generous annuity on young Alexis, and Miss Nightingale took him to bring him up as if he were her own child, freeing his mother to fulfil her ambition to train as a nurse.

For his Russian friend David Russell commissioned a rough red granite stone based on the design of the war memorial at Kinnesswood, on the shores of Loch Leven, a carved cross inside a circle. It was fitting, since Aladin had once told Mabel Irvine: "I have smelt the heather and heard the cry of the curlew."

12
Iona

In the summer of 1881 a nine year old boy was helped from the steamer that made the daily round from Oban to Iona. He went round the ruins of the cathedral and monastic buildings, but when he got aboard the boat again, he curled up on a coiled rope and slept all the way back to Oban.

But David Russell did not forget Iona. He went back in 1886, when he was 14. In 1897 or 1898 he photographed the sacred ruins he had wandered as a boy. In 1917 he motored through from St Fillans and had "interesting experiences" in the restored cathedral. Tudor Pole had also been there. In 1907 the psychic and three "custodians" had taken the sapphire blue Glastonbury Bowl to Iona, on a pilgrimage of important spiritual centres.

David Russell's first photograph of the Iona monastic buildings in ruins, 1898.

Iona inspired David Russell with an idea which he took to Professor Paterson, Moderator of the General Assembly of the Church of Scotland, as he explained to Tudor Pole in October 1919. "Professor Paterson proposes if possible to arrange to invite all the divinity graduates in April next to spend ten days in Iona under the guidance of two or three of the most spiritually minded men of the Church, and he hopes to spend at least part of the time there himself."

David Russell arranged the Iona Retreat under the auspices of the Walker Trust. In April 1920 the specially chartered SS *Princess Louise* sailed from Oban with 24 students from the four divinity halls of the Scottish universities. Each had a copy of Adamnan's *Life of Columba*. They were accommodated at the Argyll Hotel, Iona, at £3 for the week. The communion wine cost 9s. The bill, which totalled £132 18s 5d was settled by David Russell. The students put their names to a letter to the Very Reverend Professor William Paterson, to be passed to their benefactor. "We have enjoyed a week of Christian fellowship and communion which will ever remain an inspiring and enriching memory, especially in conjunction with the unique, hallowed association of the Isle of Columba."

The Retreat became an annual event, based at the St Columba Hotel. The divinity students played an annual game of golf against the locals on the machair course, and staged a hilarious concert in which they impersonated Tommy Lorne and other comedians. There was a proposal to make the Retreat an essential part of the training of every divinity student of the Church of Scotland, and the possibility of a permanent community on Iona was also considered.

David Russell and his family went regularly to Iona for holidays in the 1920s, staying at the St Columba Hotel and at a house in the village. They made friends among the islanders and the many visitors, notably F.C.B. Cadell. Kilted, larger than life, the Scottish artist landed each summer to catch the clarity of light, the brilliant colours of Iona in paintings that now fetch six figures.

Cadell paid for his board and lodging on Iona with paintings, but it was not so easy to dispose of his work through the galleries of Edinburgh. He wrote to David Russell in February 1926: "The picture market is so bad just now that I have determined to write privately to people interested in my pictures offering them this opportunity of buying my work at half its original price. The small Ionas, 18 × 15 thus work out at £12. 10/- each and the large ones in proportion."

IONA

In August 1928 David Russell looked forward to his holiday on Iona. "For myself at least, to lie for hours on the sands in the sunshine with a cool breeze blowing upon the naked body, is a most excellent tonic, far better than artificial sunlight." But there might be a problem getting there, as he told Tudor Pole. "I am wondering if Coll, the ferryman at Iona ferry, will make difficulties about taking us across the Sound if there is any wind blowing! Last time we went he suggested that we would have to go back to Salen, 36 miles off, and come back next morning!"

David Russell was deeply interested in the flora and fauna of Iona. He discovered in the Nunnery ruins a particular type of acanthus which, he assumed, had survived there from the thirteenth century. For Christmas 1928 Angus MacPhail the Iona postmaster sent him a "taste of Coll cheese" to show that he was accepted as an islander.

MacPhail found he got relief from his sciatica by bathing with hot salt water. While he lay on the white sands, having what he called "sun baths," David Russell thought of reviving the Iona Press, founded in 1887 by William Muir, former manager of the Tormor granite quarry on Mull, and John MacCormick, eldest son of the quarry foreman. For five or six years the Iona Press, housed behind the St Columba Hotel in a former bothy, had produced a dozen small pamphlets based on Gaelic lore and legend. David Russell had heard that William Muir was still alive in London.

Alexander Ritchie, who lived at Shuna Cottage, was another Iona artist, a distinguished silversmith specialising in Celtic designs, some taken from old stones. In his spare time he showed visitors round the abbey ruins. Ritchie and his wife Euphemia became close friends of the Russell family.

James Richardson, Inspector of Ancient Monuments for Scotland, was one of the foremost figures in Scottish antiquity, admired for the style and technique of his ideas for conservation and display. Richardson, who was in charge of the monastic ruins on Iona, was also a close friend of the artist Cadell. David Russell was interested in restoring part of the ruins as a permanent centre for the annual Iona Retreat. An alternative idea was to build a residence for the divinity students beside the ruins.

In 1929 he had a meeting with Richardson, who had drawn up a plan to convert the Chapter House and vestibule into a museum for the preservation of the monuments. David Russell asked about the feasibility of covering part of the cloisters as a museum for the same purpose.

Alex Ritchie, the Iona silversmith and his wife Euphemia, evidently wearing one of his creations on her scarf.

David Russell's camera catches the Reverend George MacLeod, relaxing on the sacred isle with a canine acquaintance.

Alexander Ritchie wrote anxiously: "If anything in future is done to adapt the monastic buildings into a retreat for clergymen, would the conversion of that particular part into a museum not interfere with a general scheme for utilizing the existing buildings?"

To soothe his agitated friend David Russell sent a record of the Tchaikovsky *Andante Cantabile*, and the book *The Fellowship of Silence*. In return Ritchie engraved a cross on a pebble from Port a' Churaich, the Port of the Coracle, as a memory of Anne and Sheila Russell's childhood on Iona. "I missed those children more than all the friends who come here during the year," Ritchie later told their father.

In June 1929 David Russell had been asked by the Very Reverend Professor Paterson to meet the Reverend George MacLeod, minister of St Cuthbert's Church, Edinburgh, to discuss developments along the lines of retreats in Scotland, since MacLeod was interested in securing a place on Iona for that purpose. That September an Iona Fellowship was instituted, consisting of those "who had taken part, or shall take part, in any of the retreats organised for students in the Church of Scotland and the United Free Church Halls and in the Halls of the United Church, and others who may wish to be identified with the Fellowship." George MacLeod and David Russell were appointed to the committee of the Fellowship, which it was hoped, would have "a national character and an historic setting." But the "vital importance" of the association with Iona was stressed.

George MacLeod's fascination with Iona was growing. He spoke to the students on the 1930 Retreat, and in May a meeting of the Iona Fellowship considered the development of the retreat concept, for lay people as well as the clergy in Scotland. A committee was appointed to consider the matter and to organise retreats at Dunkeld, in the partially restored old cathedral and the grounds of Dunkeld House.

In June 1930 "your affectionate friend Alec Ritchie" wrote to little Anne from idyllic Iona:

It is now over a month since we returned home and it passed away just like a dream—we had much to do to prepare for the summer. The weather was beautiful—no rain for weeks, the cuckoo woke us in the morning and also some starlings in our chimney. Last year I put netting all over the opening but they found some place to get in and begin chattering to each other at dawn. What can I do?

Tell Pat and David that I was fishing several times and only got one large lythe. Many visitors are now here, and a nice man all the way from New Zealand told us how we could get water by digging where a rod he held began to bend. But I can tell you all about that and other things when you come in August.

At Silverburn there were evocative mementoes of summer in Iona. David Russell wrote to Cadell in October 1930: "Your oil painting of *Traigh Geal* was set up on the mantelpiece in my bedroom beside a standard lamp with a shade in warm, glowing colours, and in its light by day or by night your picture seemed flooded with golden sunshine and was a great joy."

Iona also featured in David Russell's photographic album and in his constant thoughts. He still wanted a permanent building for the Iona Fellowship, and in mid January 1931 he wrote to the Very Reverend Charles Warr, minister of St Giles' Cathedral, Edinburgh, a trustee of the Iona Cathedral Trust, established in 1899 to maintain and interpret the buildings and associated memorials of Iona Abbey, Nunnery, and the royal burial ground.

I have given a good deal of thought to the question of the preservation of the Cathedral and to the possibilities of the restoration of the Chapter House and other ancient buildings at Iona, and to the provision of protection for the carved stones now exposed to weather erosion.

My object in writing to you now is to ask if the Trustees would, without any obligation on their part, allow me to submit for their consideration a statement indicating what might be done, and, if as a result of this it should be decided to make a public appeal for funds, I would very gladly give any assistance I could.

The architect Reginald Fairlie had recently completed additions and alterations to Silverburn. He was also a distinguished church architect, and asked for his client's support in getting him the contract to restore the Collegiate Church of St Salvator, the chapel of St Andrews University, which he carried out in 1931. That same year David Russell commissioned him to see what could be done with the Iona ruins. Alexander Ritchie informed David Russell in early May:

Mr Ian Lindsay [of Fairlie's firm] arrived on Iona on Saturday, and is now busy making plans of the old monastic foundations. The Cathedral bell is expected tomorrow, and the advent of the new steamer the *Loch Fyne* is looked forward to with much interest. I saw the superintendent in Glasgow, and from his account the vessel is a miniature liner fitted up with all modern conveniences, even a huge gramophone. I begged of him to ban all those most objectionable American 'discords,' and that he promised me.

On 10th June 1931 David Russell attended the dedication of the cathedral bell, which, as Ritchie reported, had a "massive amount of sound." At David Russell's instigation Cadell surveyed the parish church on Iona, recommending that the pulpit and seating remain, but that the wall in front should be removed. Meantime, Ritchie was fashioning Celtic cloak clasps for the Russell girls.

Fairlie sent his client his Iona drawings in mid July 1931, explaining:

In working out the scheme my endeavour has been to provide the accommodation needed without destroying or altering any fragment of the existing medieval masonry.

At the North East corner the walls have perished to within three feet of the ground. In rebuilding these walls it would be possible to insert windows large enough for a habitable house without destruction of old material: I therefore propose that this should be the position for the caretaker's house and for the accommodation of visiting ministers.

As the windows in the Dormitory are so small, I cannot suggest any use to which this could be put. I propose that the whole of this portion of the building including the chapter house should be merely floored and roofed.

There seems little doubt that in its later form the Refectory was approached by a stair at the west end and that a portion at this end was screened off to form a Servery. At the East end was the dais with the Abbot's door giving on to it.

For use as a hall for meeting I propose to restore this as far as possible in its original form, except that I would finish the West end with a gable in place of the Kitchen buildings which must have abutted here.

The Cloister I propose to restore to its original form so far as the evidence permits. This I suggest should house any of the old carved grave slabs and crosses which are no longer in their original positions and which should be protected from the weather.

Owing to the unusual nature of the work it is difficult to find a basis for an estimate of the probable cost, but as a rough guide I think we may take the probable cost of the scheme at about £47,000.

David Russell settled Fairlie's £150 account for a survey of the monastery buildings, including a photographic survey; preparing sketch designs for proposed restoration; and a complete survey of the Nunnery buildings, since their reconstruction was also a possibility. In August he wrote to Tudor Pole: "I arranged to see George MacLeod, but we only had about an hour and a half in Glasgow. He met us on arrival, and saw us away in our train. He is, I might say, enthusiastically pleased with the plans for the restoration of Iona."

On 16th September Ritchie reported: "This forenoon the island was in a turmoil of excitement over the arrival of the seaplane *Cloud of Iona*, which, to our amazement, after landing in the Sound, spun along and ran up on the sands at Martyrs Bay. Several people took advantage of a flight over the island."

But Cadell was not flying high. He wrote to David Russell from 30 Regent Terrace, Edinburgh, in February 1932:

> Getting into a new house, and things being what they are, I am selling my 18 × 15 oil pictures for £12. So if you want a cheap "Cadell" now is the time. The "Marigolds" you liked so much in Iona is still unsold, but in any case you can see all the pictures I have at present at the above address any afternoon.

David Russell could always find time for yet another good cause, particularly in connection with Iona. Both the Iona charges were vacant, and the two congregations had come together, prepared to elect a minister to the united parish of Iona and the Ross of Mull. But it was argued that the minister of Iona served an area wider than the parish, since thousands of visitors went to the sacred isle each year. Iona needed a minister of its own, and David Russell went on the executive committee of an appeal, to raise £1500 "to guarantee a sum which, with local resources, shall secure a stipend of £400 a year and Manse to the incoming Minister." He had drawn up a chronological table of the history of Iona which was sold on the Iona–Oban steamer to raise funds for the appeal.

David Russell had promoted the career of Marjory Kennedy-Fraser, the Gaelic song collector and performer, by subsidising concerts by her at St Andrews University and Sedbergh School, where young David was a pupil. She had been a guest at Silverburn, and had joined the Iona Fellowship. At the age of seven Sheila Russell was wakened "in the night" in the St Columba Hotel, Iona, dressed and then taken to the Abbey to hear Mrs Kennedy-Fraser singing to the clarsach as she sat on the crossing steps, a "magical" experience for a child.

The woman who adapted the Gaelic songs of the Hebrides for concert platforms all over the world died in November 1930. At

IONA

The artist F.C.B. Cadell in characteristically jovial form in 1932.

her own request her ashes were to be taken to Iona. David Russell was on the executive of the Marjory Kennedy-Fraser Memorial Committee and went to painstaking trouble to select a suitable gravestone. On 11th July 1932 Mrs Kennedy-Fraser's ashes were carried from the cathedral to the Reilig Oran, to lie among the dust of Scottish kings, under the granite stone with Celtic text and ornamentation designed by John Duncan, the artist who had introduced her to the Hebrides and Gaelic song.

Francis Cadell was painting on Iona that summer. McNally, a Glasgow musician, entertained tourists with a dulcimer in Oban and on the steamer to Iona. Cadell reported to David Russell:

By the way, there was a monstrous end to the Kennedy Fraser funeral here in McNally who after the Very Rev Warr's final prayer at the graveside, struck up *The Road to the Isles* on his dulcimer (this with Alec Ritchie's permission!) The bereaved relatives were horrified, and so was nearly everybody else. I could hardly believe my ears or eyes when it started. You know what a dreadful looking creature McNally is, which made it, if possible worse. The paper talked of the crowds that attended the funeral and came for it from near and far, but Mrs Maclean of the Manor House, Oban, told me there were only 6 on the boat—the rest being the ordinary tourists. They certainly all gathered at the grave and witnessed a real dulcimer Highland funeral, descriptions of which have doubtless found their way to the States by now.

In September 1932 David Russell bought three Cadell pictures, paying £37 for an oil of Clouds, Iona, and two watercolours, the interior and exterior of a cottage. That same month, at the end of their holidays, the Russell family watched Cadell departing. "I wonder if you saw us all waving from Cnoc Mor as you passed down the Sound? We did feel a little anxious about you with such a large company of sheep!" He asked Cadell to help to produce "a really striking advertisement" for Tullis Russell brand papers, Artine, Mellotex and Ivorex.

David Russell bought a house on Iona in 1933. It was for his children, because they shared his love of the island. He gave Tudor Pole a Gaelic lesson on its name: "'Cnoc' means a little hill or mound. 'Mor' means large, so that Cnocmor means the large little hill. The terms are not really contradictory."

Alexander Ritchie was delighted about Cnocmor: "Your having a second home here would be of benefit to the island in many ways. It lacks someone who can take detached views, and whose counsel and advice would all be for the common good; also one whose

Alison Russell picnics on Iona with two of her children, David and Anne. The gentleman in plus-fours is thought to be F. C. B. Cadell's brother-in-law.

interest in the historical buildings would restrain the Vandal and help to preserve our priceless relics."

Ritchie's brother, the Reverend Robert Lamont Ritchie of Creich, died in June 1933, leaving his estate to the Iona Cathedral Trustees for the foundation of a Celtic library. David Russell was thinking about the library at Schaffhausen which contained the oldest Scottish manuscript extant, that of Adamnan's *Life of Columba* in the handwriting of Dorbene, Abbot of Iona, who died in 713. In 1930 Dr Elias Lowe, reader in palaeography at Oxford and a foremost authority on early manuscripts, had suggested to Professor James Houston Baxter of the chair of Ecclesiastical History at St Andrews that the Dorbene manuscript should be reproduced in collotype facsimile, with a good introduction, historical and palaeographical. The American Iona Society would meet half of the £200 cost, with David Russell guaranteeing the other half.

Iona was a busy place in the summer of 1934. A water diviner was at work, reporting that "metal lay south of MacLeod's tomb, a sheet of silver in the form of a crypt." A favourable east wind brought the small sailing ship *Bernera* to the sacred isle. It anchored in the Sound on a beautiful evening, and the next

Cnocmor, the Russells' home on Iona, place of many happy holidays. It later burnt down and was replaced by a modern house.

The furniture arrives for Cnocmor, summer 1934.

morning beached in Martyrs Bay. The Russells' furniture had arrived from Oban, and everything was unloaded at one tide with local help and carried up to Cnocmor.

But Tudor Pole was not so settled. He was getting impatient about the Quest.

13

The Quest Begins

The Quest is one of the great untold stories of the twentieth century. Its instigator was Wellesley Tudor Pole, and it had its origins in the discovery of the sapphire blue bowl at Glastonbury in 1904. This bowl was apparently used in psychometry sessions by Tudor Pole and his associates, during which it was indicated that a great treasure was buried in Constantinople.

Tudor Pole first visited that mysterious city in 1908, returning in 1911 and 1913. He was interested in the emperor Justinian the Great, who ruled from 527 to 565 AD. He was said to have constructed more than 30 churches in Constantinople alone, and above all, Hagia Sophia. Legend insisted that an angel revealed the plan of this church to Justinian in a dream, and a ninth or tenth century mosaic in St Sophia shows the bearded emperor presenting his foundation to the Virgin.

The fabulous treasures of Byzantium increased under an emperor of such grand designs. The Great Palace of the emperor, founded by Constantine after the defeat of Licinius in 324, has been described by the Byzantine scholar Eugenia Recchi Franceschini as belonging among "the famous lost monuments of archaeology and art history." She explains:

It was situated on the side of the hill which runs down from the Hippodrome (now the great area of At Meydan), to the shore of the Sea of Marmara, within a vast area bordered to the north by the cathedral of Hagia Sophia and to the south by the church of Sts Sergius and Bacchus. But its many rooms, churches, chapels and gardens no longer exist. Those who, searching through modern Istanbul for ancient Constantinople, walk down beside the Blue Mosque towards the sea, will find in the Museum of the Mosaics what seem to be the sole remains of that lost palace.

In 1912 a huge fire in the Great Palace area destroyed many of the modern buildings that had prevented investigation of the historic site, laying bare several Byzantine terraces, the entrances to a number of vaulted substructures and fragments of the Palace which had been incorporated into later buildings. The next twenty years saw much archaeological activity in the area. In 1918 Ernest Mamboury and Theodor Wiegand discovered two structures to the south of the Blue Mosque (the Mosque of Sultan Ahmed). There were also investigations and work in the area of the Hippodrome and the Baths of Zeuxippus by a British Academy team under Hugh Casson and David Talbot Rice in 1927–8.

It was the remains of the lower palace structures (now intersected by the railway line) known as the Bucoleon Palace or House of Justinian that interested Tudor Pole. They stood adjacent to the Bucoleon harbour on the coast of the Sea of Marmara, to the south of the Peristyle. An examination of them had been instigated by Mamboury and Wiegand (details of which would be published in their study of 1934), but Tudor Pole was already interested in the site two decades earlier: he was convinced through his psychic sessions with the sapphire blue Glastonbury Bowl and other artefacts that the library of the emperor Justinian, containing priceless manuscripts and other treasures, was buried under the House of Justinian in a specially prepared chamber. The search for the library became his lifetime's Quest.

After the 1917 Russian Revolution Tudor Pole had helped a number of Russian priests to escape from persecution. Among other Russian refugees he befriended at this time were Dmitry Sissoeff, Anatoly Bergengreen and Michael Pojidaiev, a former Tsarist officer turned sculptor who was married to Princess Kropotkin. Tudor Pole was joined in his Quest by these three Russians, together with Frederick Leveaux, an English coalmine owner and lawyer who practised in Egypt until 1919, and David Russell in Fife who would supply most of the financial support for the project.

Tudor Pole did not rely only on his own psychic powers in seeking guidance for the Quest. He sat with the three Russian refugees, putting questions through a planchette, a small heart-shaped board supported by two castors and a vertical pencil. When the operator's fingers rest lightly on the board it is believed to trace letters without conscious direction. The spiritual "control" announced himself as BB. The messages and drawings that were transmitted by BB indicated to those sitting round the planchette the rough location of the library of Justinian.

Tudor Pole's business interests made him an international traveller and he combined commerce with Quest work. The three

David Talbot Rice (right) poses at the Golden Gate, Istanbul, with Hugh Casson (left) and Macridy Bey of the Istanbul Museum, in the late 1920s when the two British archaeologists led British Academy sponsored excavations in the Hippodrome area.

Russian psychics had congregated in Paris and had to be supported there till the Quest could be accomplished, so Tudor Pole tried to find funds for them through a clothing deal with Poland.

In the spring of 1922 he returned to Cairo, where his *Private Dowding* had apparently run into five pirated editions of 5000 copies each. He wrote to David Russell:

I feel the strong vital urge to go on to Constantinople and continue the 15 year old research, the more so because I now have the absolute interior *certitude* that the [manuscripts and artefacts] I seek . . . are undamaged and . . . I know now their exact whereabouts to a question of inches.

One must follow the Light one sees. I feel unable to turn back now; you would feel the same were you in my shoes, also all the preparations have been made, some very complicated, and I only await the late April tides but expect to leave Egypt before 10th April. The expenses mount up (a motor boat will be necessary for none of the land entrances are safe) and I cannot go alone; there is too much to remove . . .

He wrote later:

I am not going to utilise any of the dangerous land entrances. I have a safe sea entry and a fairly safe sea exit. I have a complete plan to scale of the chambers . . . Next year Constantinople will not be under English dominance so I feel that next month when the tides suit I must make my third and I hope successful effort to bring these [manuscripts and artefacts] to light for the use of the world.

There are no tides as such in the Bosphorus, but the flows are complex. Surface Black Sea water goes out and deep saltier water comes in from the Sea of Marmara, with surface winds an added complication for mariners. David Russell must have thought Tudor Pole's attempt was feasible, because he sent £50 to help with expenses.

In early April 1922 Tudor Pole moved to Constantinople, conceding to David Russell that the research must look "full of moonshine" from a distance. He revealed that if the necessary equipment was ready, he was going to make "the big underground effort" before 15th May. It did not come off, but back in London in late May he wrote ecstatically: "the world nears the verge of the most wonderful series of discoveries . . . The direct, accurate and practical 'guidance' received has been the most extraordinary that I have ever known."

But there was a French archaeological team excavating in Constantinople, too close for comfort to the Quest site. Tudor Pole wrote to David Russell:

Today I got a letter from Guy Thomson, who is watching the situation on the spot for us. On 17.8.1922 (mark the date) he intercepted or censored a letter from a French engineer officer at Constantinople to Paris. This shows that the French have just penetrated into the catacombs and vaults near Saint Sophia and within 100 metres (but *above*) of our special spots, and are continuing their work secretly, for the Vatican. He urges me to come at once. I have cabled Cairo, guardedly, to discover what BB knows and whether he is able to get through yet.

The French have unearthed and found a wonderful marble statue of the Virgin Mary and from these foundations they have penetrated into the catacombs and vaults under Saint Sophia and the Hippodrome.

Tudor Pole wrote again: "I won't go into details but the news I have had concerning the progress and extent of the Franco Vatican excavations is somewhat disquieting owing to the proximity of our own 'region.'" But BB was contacted, and he advised that no immediate move was necessary by the Quest group.

Lord Dunraven offered the use of a yacht, but a visit to the Quest site was too dangerous, as Tudor Pole warned David Russell in a letter in September.

The situation at Constantinople is very critical owing to the fact that there are some 20,000 of the Turkish scum of the city who possess firearms, and who may at a given signal start a Christian massacre, with arson. Unless France is willing to support us more whole-heartedly than seems probable at present it looks as if we should be compelled to send very big reinforcements to the Near East, and in any case the outlook is very grave. I cannot help being greatly upset by the Near East crisis as the cries of the massacred rend the air. It may cause a postponement of our Quest plans.

But the Quest group continued to meet in psychic sessions, marking photographs showing the entrance to the treasure. In October 1922 Tudor Pole tried to get permission for the three Russian psychics to enter Britain, but the Home Office refused them three month residency visas. Meanwhile, the psychic message was that new technology was to help the Quest. "We are to use acetylene in one of the chambers where the air is good. The leader of the 6 carries a telephone and the last of the 6 in the underground queue a receiver, so that instructions may pass up and down the line."

The Home Office relented, no doubt through Tudor Pole's contacts, and the Russians reached London in mid December 1922. In January in his new home in Hampstead Garden suburb Tudor Pole conducted sittings with the Russians amidst packing cases full of his belongings. In early February David Russell's presence was requested, since BB was going to make drawings. On a more down-to-earth level there was a suggestion that Pojidaiev should do a bust of Pat Russell.

BB warned the group to be ready to move on the Quest "when the trumpet blows." Then came the psychic message that it had been postponed till 1924 "at the earliest." At Lundin Links cinema the Russell family had to make do with another Quest, the film about Antarctic exploration.

In late February 1924 Tudor Pole wrote to David Russell, assuring him that there was nothing to fear at Constantinople: "Poor Howard Carter does not seem able to divest himself of the 'Curse' that seems to hang over all who disturb Tutankhamen's repose! It could have been dealt with quite harmoniously but for that occult knowledge would have been necessary."

The three Russians, in Paris again after their British visit, had to be supported financially, and Frederick Leveaux began sending Tudor Pole £50 a month to remit to them. David Russell was also regularly sending money. In early April 1925 David Russell went to hear Professor James Baxter of Ecclesiastical History lecture on St Andrews manuscripts of the fifteenth century in a German university library. "A most interesting lecture. I should like you to meet him sometime. He is a young man of about 30 with a European fame," he reported to Tudor Pole.

But Tudor Pole was meeting someone else with a European reputation. Sir Arthur Conan Doyle warned him that the world was "on the eve of a gigantic cataclysm, a greater upheaval even than the Atlantean Deluge. Hundreds of millions of people are to disappear..." Tudor Pole was sceptical about these dire prophecies, though the creator of Sherlock Holmes paid him a compliment: "What a wonderful power you have!"

While the Quest awaited fulfilment there was spiritual work to be done at home through the medium of print. To his many activities David Russell had added that of publisher, creator of the Deeper Issue series of books. For the first in the series he had arranged the publication of Tudor Pole's *The Great War* through the London firm of Bell & Sons in 1915. *Private Dowding* and *Christ in You*, an anonymous "book of devotion," had been published under the imprint of John M. Watkins of Charing Cross Road, London. David Russell did the negotiations, put up money for the books, chose the binding and supervised the advertising, all without his name appearing anywhere.

In 1926 a new manuscript, "Cleophas," was brought to David Russell's attention. It was by Geraldine Cummins, the automatic writing medium. Miss Cummins claimed to be receiving an account of early Christian history dictated by a group of "Seven Messengers." Her powers had attracted the Irish poet W. B. Yeats and many other famous personalities.

David Russell read the manuscript of volume three of the Cleophas series and, like Tudor Pole, was convinced that Miss Cummins was receiving messages from "the other side." He was eager to arrange the publication of volumes one and two as well. They had not appeared in print because they were the subject of a legal dispute, with Frederick Bligh Bond claiming that since the messages of Cleophas had been addressed to him, and typed by him, he held the copyright, since a spirit could not.

But Miss Cummins got judgement with costs in a famous trial, leaving the way open for David Russell and Tudor Pole to arrange publication of part of her remarkable chronicle, which ran to over a million words. Miss Cummins needed the royalties, since she had no private means and lived with her widowed mother.

David Russell persuaded Professor James Baxter to write a scholarly introduction to volume three, but because he was apprehensive about damaging the interests of St Andrews University by associating it with a spiritualist publication, Baxter did not put his name to his introduction to *The Scripts of Cleophas*, published in 1928 by Rider & Co., London, with David Russell subsidising it.

Though he sat at the planchette together with the three Russians, Tudor Pole was not over-enthusiastic about mediumship. He told David Russell in April 1926:

Unless the spiritualist movement can be steered away from developing almost exclusively through the agency of trance mediums and automata, then it will strike the rocks and chaos and disillusionment will result. But there are no leaders with real vision and first-hand experience; people are hungry and will swallow almost anything that is sensational or seems to afford a short cut through to a wider world.

Despite encouraging messages from BB, the Quest languished. Tudor Pole wrote to David Russell from Genoa in April 1927 on the necessity for urgency:

The British mission have only been at work a week on the Hippodrome site at Stanbul and have already unearthed a box of Byzantine gold jewels and some statuary. They are at work about 1 kilometre from our centre but at least 100 metres higher up. These discoveries show that the whole area is probably untapped, and make one very restless at the Quest's continued delay.

Meantime the three Russians were "in some material distress" in Paris, as Tudor Pole informed David Russell in September 1928. Though he was in bed with a lung problem David Russell sent money. By June 1930 the Russian trio's position was "increasingly desperate." Sissoeff was in hospital with kidney trouble; the other two were out of work and depressed, believing that if Sissoeff died it would mean the end of the Quest group. Tudor Pole, however, held the opinion that the Quest was not dependent on individuals.

Sissoeff died in October 1930. But the Quest was at last moving towards fulfilment. In the 1920s the Russells had gone out to the Riveria in the springtime, and there were meetings with Tudor Pole and the Russians, with David Russell sitting in on the planchette sessions. Now Tudor Pole persuaded his closest friend to charter a yacht to sail to Constantinople for a surreptitious search of the treasure site.

There was competition to charter the Cannes-based yacht *Tyrant* in May 1931. Charlie Chaplin apparently wanted it, but E. W. Janson, a London-based mining engineer, secured it on behalf of David Russell, who provided the bulk of the £1200 charter fee through his Iona Trust (which had grown out of the Iona Fellowship). In his study at Silverburn he developed a code for the Quest, using words not likely to be used in ordinary communication. Thus the message, "Complete success, proceeding Cannes, expect arrive there 3rd," would come across as "Repaired sending rope expect see Anne third."

Tudor Pole wrote triumphantly to David Russell on May Day, 1931: "On the 8th May between noon and 3pm (Sun time) will take place the culmination of the drama and the work for which we have laboured, watched and prayed since 1903." He joined the *Tyrant* at Naples. The two remaining Russian psychics were also aboard, but the voyage of discovery turned into a fiasco, as an angry Janson reported to David Russell.

My first distrust of the script, apart from the route was when I saw the tools that had been made etc and left at a bank at Athens. Both Lovelock and I, when I saw these, came to the conclusion that the writers of the script had no practical knowledge whatever. Still I determined to do my best for the script. When Lovelock and I found what looked like the tunnel, which was impossible to enter, I came to the conclusion that the authors of the script were quite unreliable as to the present conditions.

He went on: "There were only two men, Lovelock and Bergengreen, who could have done any serious manual work. The fact also, that the shore was guarded night and day rendered any work inland impossible."

Since the month's charter had been extended to six weeks, Janson demanded an additional £638 from David Russell. But Tudor Pole was not daunted by the failure. In a secret report drawn up in December 1931 he revealed his 25 year old obsession with the House of Justinian,

beneath which excavation has never been permitted, although the ex Kaiser made various efforts to secure a concession in 1912 and 1913.

We have some reasons for believing that a chamber exists beneath these ruins, still sealed up, and containing manuscripts from the Library of Justinian the Great (Greek, Hebrew, Latin, etc and Indian tongues) and some relics of Christian saints and sacred vessels. The whole area under review is honeycombed with passages, tunnels, catacombs and chambers. A plan to scale of the more important of these is in the writer's possession and has to some extent been checked up; including traps, oubliettes, false passages and walled-in entries.

Investigations have taken place not only on the spot, but from records and other sources in London, Rome, Cairo and Kiev. Through Cardinal Gasquet the writer had the opportunity of hearing certain facts bearing upon the research, contained in documents in the Vatican Library.

At the Kiev Pechovskaja Monastery, documents existed from the time of Prince St Vladimir and among then MSS brought there from Byzantium by Imperial ambassadors and Patriarchal missioners and dating from the IX and X cent AD.

The Kiev Monastery in question has been converted into Soviet offices and flats, but in 1918 and 1919, the monks succeeded in hiding these and other treasures from their library in secret places where they still exist, it is believed. The actual secreting of the more important documents took place in September 1918 in the rocky catacombs near and beneath the Kiev Monastery in question.

The writer and those working with him have collected data from other sources and have been enabled by secret investigations on the spot at Stanbul to check the accuracy of much of the information and to satisfy themselves that apparently the depository has never been opened or tampered with.

Professor Baxter, who was writing a book on European history, was asked if he was interested in excavating a site in Constantinople. He told David Russell that he was in touch with two men who had experience of excavations, one a Turk, the other from Sofia. Baxter's advice was that if the matter was approached properly, the Turkish authorities would not be difficult to deal with as regarded excavation concessions.

But Baxter was not told about the Quest. Tudor Pole cautioned: "To have given Baxter to realise that virtually *all* is or was psychically received, would have resulted (as BB foresaw) in his refusing to help us, nevertheless as time goes on I want to gradually enlighten him on these questions."

David Russell decided to apply for a permit to excavate in Constantinople through the Walker Trust, since the connection with St Andrews University would give the application more authority than one coming from an individual. He wrote to Tudor Pole in September 1931: "I saw Jim [Principal Irvine] yesterday and discussed a number of things, among others the proposition of applying for a concession to excavate. I did not find him too willing to help. He seemed inclined to take the view that to ask for the support of the University would mean needless publicity."

Nevertheless careful plans went ahead to apply for permission to excavate. Draft after draft of an application letter was prepared; among other alterations the reference to "the remains of the library of Justinian the Great, containing many manuscripts (Greek, Hebrew, Latin, Indian), some relics of saints, sacred vessels, etc." was removed because it would have given too much away to the Turks.

Tudor Pole stressed the necessity for absolute secrecy with regard to diplomats and archaeologists of all nationalities. In particular he was worried that the Germans would forestall the Walker Trust team by asking to be allowed to survey the sea walls at the House of Justinian. He also advised that the application should be for a four to six month digging period, with a wide remit, using the form of concession the British Academy had used on the Hippodrome investigations.

Tudor Pole discussed the application in general terms with the eminent archaeologist Sir William Budge, who encouraged the group to proceed. But it was Professor Baxter's status as a scholar that was central to the success of the application. "It's for Baxter and not us to make the title of the book he proposes writing fit the sites or give an excuse for their inclusion," Tudor Pole had complained to David Russell. However, Tudor Pole liked the St Andrews professor. "I consider Baxter a most valuable ally and a very sane and level headed man, not too narrow in outlook.

Apparently he thinks he can get what is needed from Jim [Principal Irvine]; but *no money* from the University."

The Quest member Frederick Leveaux wrote to Baxter at the end of May 1932:

Soon after you left, on thinking matters over I wondered whether it would not be more advisable to apply for a concession to excavate rather than a mere licence or permit to investigate and explore which, as I gather, is what you contemplated. Whilst the latter might give you the right to dig, I take it such right would be limited to digging for the purpose of investigation and not excavation.

Leveaux had a family contact with a former secretary at the British Embassy in Turkey who promised to get the application "through the right channels."

The Walker Trust application was typed on carefully chosen blue-tinted paper, with the arms of the university used, because "these little things count," Tudor Pole insisted. The petition, dated 17th August 1932, and addressed to His Excellency, the Minister for Public Instruction of the Turkish Government, Ankara, sought permission to investigate certain sites "in pursuance of a plan to publish a work dealing with the topography and history of certain parts of the ancient capital of the Eastern Roman Empire during the reign of Justinian the Great and especially the Villa, so called House of Justinian on the Sea of Marmara . . ."

Professor Baxter and the Walker Trust wanted to examine, investigate, and explore parts of the sea walls in the area of the House of Justinian, and to make "minor excavations" in the foundations and lower parts of the sea wall "at spots to be decided upon during the said investigation." The petition also sought permission "to dig trenches in the south of the Ahmediye Garden, in the vicinity of the Sultan Ahmet Mosque [the Blue Mosque], on the Great Palace site." The application pledged that any objects found would become the "sole property" of the Turkish Government.

David Russell was about to leave for holiday on Iona when Tudor Pole asked if he could manage another cheque for the two Russian psychics, who were at "bedrock." He sent money as the application was being submitted through the Foreign Office, whose judgement was that it was "well put together." It went by King's Messenger on its week-long journey to Turkey, carrying a great deal of hope.

However, David Russell's mind was not only on Constantinople; he had his Italian affairs to think about.

14
Italian Affairs

With hindsight Benito Mussolini is recognised to have been an evil despot, but in the 1920s he looked a dynamic leader, determined to make Italy one of the most progressive countries in Europe by building highways and instigating a huge land reclamation scheme. David Russell began to invest in Italy, through Tudor Pole, but principally through Count Daniele Pecorini, Venetian businessman, former Commissioner of Customs in China, collector of jade, and inventor, or rather, reviver of Wei-chi, a 4000 year old Chinese game played with counters. He was also said to be "well up" in the paper trade.

Marshes were being drained in southern Italy, on the Gargano peninsula that juts out into the Adriatic, a beautiful place but one where malaria spread by the mosquito shortened the hard lives of the peasants. The concession for the Gargano work had been secured in the early 1920s by an Italian financial group with political as well as profit-making intentions, but Daniele Pecorini had worked out a better scheme, and the Italian Government had transferred the concession to his consortium.

The scheme was in several stages. First, the marshes round the lakes of Lesina and Varano were to be drained, with canals constructed to carry away the surplus water. Tudor Pole described lake Lesina as "a large sinister stagnant spectral stretch of shallow water surrounded by many miles of malarial swamps and marshes." Breakwaters were to be built round the lakes, and the sea let in by canals cut through to the Adriatic. Second, the Fortore river was to be dammed to generate electric power for domestic and industrial use throughout the Gargano peninsula and for irrigating wheat lands throughout the district. Third, a railway was to be built from Apricena to Rodi, then round the peninsula to Manfredonia, to join the existing railway. The scheme was to be followed by the construction of a plage, with hotels and other amenities facing the sea near Lesina, creating a "second Riviera," Tudor Pole promised.

The Gargano scheme was operated by Sindicato Agricolo Cooperativo Italiano (SACI). The board of directors included Anselmo Ciappi, said to be the foremost civil engineer in Italy; Bernardi Vincenti, professor of agricultural science at Rome University; Daniele Pecorini; and his cousin Alberto Pecorini. George Leavey, the London financier and developer, was a major investor in the Gargano enterprise, and his agent in Italy was Tudor Pole.

In April 1925 Count Pecorini visited David Russell in Fife to discuss investing in Italy and the marketing of Tullis Russell papers there. Tudor Pole wrote enthusiastically to Leavey in May: "Italy is prosperous, her Budget balances." The Italian Government was apparently prepared to invest between 80 and 100 million lire in the reclamation scheme because it hoped that malaria would be eradicated over a large part of the province of Apulia and Molise.

David Russell initially invested £1000 in the Gargano scheme. Tudor Pole told him: "With control of the *Banca di Pughlia*, we should be kings of a large section of a fruitful province, containing 500,000 people, and our potency for good could be immense." Tudor Pole was in Rome in June 1925. "I saw Mussolini speaking from a balcony. He looked like an ardent spirit, quite ruthless, a flame that was wearing out the body very rapidly." He also saw Padre Pio on this visit, who blessed the project, saying that the Lesina district had been "an abode of evil spirits for centuries."

A firm friendship developed between Daniele Pecorini and David Russell. The Count wrote to him in December 1925: "I distributed to all in the office and to my friends visiting me a piece of shortbread saying: 'This comes from a good man, and will give you a good disposition toward your people' and really I do believe it, and it is, more than I can say, touching to my heart in writing to you."

The Italian Minister of Finance signed the Lesina decree in the autumn of 1926, with the SACI having secured 2000 acres of land free. David Russell received a confidential memorandum: "It is very important that in financial circles in London it should be thoroughly understood that such attempts as the one recently made on the life of Il Duce do not represent any particular amount of political unrest worth speaking of, but are the isolated action of irresponsible individuals." In other words, it was safe for foreigners to invest in Italy.

The Gargano enterprise became a limited liability company in 1927, changing its name to Societa Anonima Industriele Meridionale (SAIM), with capital of 1 million lire. David Russell

Count Pecorini (second from left).

wanted to take his two sons to Gargano that spring, and asked Tudor Pole if he could arrange a hotel or suitable residence "where we might live on sweet lemons and fish from our own preserves." Tudor Pole dissuaded him, warning him that the sanitary conditions were bad, though there was little danger of malaria at that time of year.

However, the Russells did tour France and Italy, leaving London on 2nd March 1927. Alexis Aladin and Tudor Pole saw them off. They stayed in the Pont Royal Hotel, Paris. Alison Russell had tea with the painter Jean Despujols and his wife Donata, and after dinner she went to the Folies Bergeres with her husband. The next night they went to the Moulin Rouge. "Horrid vulgar and how both hated it," she recorded in her diary.

On 5th March they left by wagons-lit for St Margherita, where they had rooms overlooking the Gulf of Genoa in the Hotel Portofino Vetta for ten days. There were long walks and an excursion to Genoa. They arrived in Rome on 15th March and were met by Pecorini. The next day the Count and the Russian clairvoyant Pojidaiev quarrelled about guiding the Russells round the holy city, much to Alison Russell's amusement. Pecorini played Wei-chi with the boys, who threw coins into the fountains, and there was an excursion to the Coliseum by moonlight.

On 24th March the Russells moved to Naples. Sunday, 27th March was a busy day. They visited the Solfatara near Naples, the half extinct volcanic crater, 820 yards across at its widest. The ground at the bottom was hot and emitted a hollow sound when stamped on.

Virgil describes Aeneas's descent into the Underworld accompanied by the Sybil of Cumae, who showed him how to pluck the talismanic Golden Bough from the woods beside Lake Avernus, as a passport to Hades. The Russell family followed Aeneas into the Grotta della Sibilla, "an awful place," Alison Russell recorded in her diary. "The boys, David Russell and I were carried on the shoulders of our guides. We stuck and refused to go further. A filthy place, the walls black with smoke of the torches of centuries. My only dress was ruined!"

Pecorini wrote from London in late May 1927 where he was promoting Wei-chi: "I am glad to say that our Gargano business is entering into a new phase and a good one. I am pleased to tell you that we are little by little winning our battles with the bad spirits which kept our business back."

David Russell apologised to the Count in July: "The long light of our Scotch nights takes us out into the garden, often till between ten and eleven o'clock, and there is not much inclination then to settle down to play Wei-Chi."

In the summer of 1927 Pecorini made a trip to Milan, Turin and Genoa to sell Tullis Russell products, particularly sulphate paper for power cables. The Pirelli company wanted to test samples for deterioration. The exchange rate was "steady" and business prospects promising, the Count wrote confidently. In the same letter he acknowledged receipt of a cheque for 200 SAIM shares, and reported that definite approval had been given by the Ministry in Rome for the Gargano railway project. "After two years of struggle finally we got on firm ground for the railway work. A very good profit should accrue out of it, and a great benefit to that poor community."

Pecorini was always ready to defend Fascist rule, lecturing David Russell in his convoluted English:

never, under no Government, liberal or Papal, the streets of Rome, and I may say of the other towns as well, were so exempt from beggars, prostitutes, pickpockets, thieves, and their allies. I would say that Italy made more progress in this respect during these 5 years of Fascism than in the 50 years under Liberal Governments, or the centuries of Papal rule.

He sent "for the boys" a dramatic account of being caught in a thunderstorm in Venice in July 1927, describing hundreds of chimneys brought down, boats lifted from the water and many lives lost. "All of this in about 15 minutes. The sky was afterwards full of stars! Hundreds of poor pigeons were thrown dead on the pavements of the piazza."

There was a new Italian development scheme proposed. Tudor Pole claimed to have been approached indirectly both through Mussolini and the Mayor of Rome in connection with a redevelopment programme for the improvement of the city, and its restoration to a world capital, but with the classical antiquities fully protected.

The 60,000 square-metre plot of land proposed for redevelopment was situated about three kilometres from the centre of Rome, on the Via Aventino, between Porta San Paolo and Porta San Sebastiano. The land was directly south of the ancient walls of Rome called La Cinta Aureliana, which protected it from the winds of the north. The walls had been built by Marcus Aurelius, and the area had been papal property till the seventeenth century. It sloped gently southwards and had a magnificent vista of the old Appian Way, and the Alban hills. It was close to the terminus station for Ostia on the Tyrrhenian sea, and to the site of a new underground station that would link Porta San Paolo with the Piazza Venezia. It was proposed to form a development company, which would then divide the land up into lots, and arrange the construction of services in a five year plan.

The 1928 prospectus stated: "there is no risk whatsoever for the capital invested. The land itself is ample security for the capital, and now that the Italian lire has been put on a gold basis, even foreign investors have not to fear the danger of the falling off in the exchange."

Count Pecorini was chairman of the Societa Aureliana, and David Russell became a substantial investor. Signor Nardi, a high Fascist official was another shareholder. The lawyer Frederick Leveaux, the Quest member, had shares in SAIM and Aureliana. In April 1929 he offered David Russell his Aureliana shares for £2500 and his 150 SAIM shares for £440. David Russell bought his SAIM shares, but said he could not afford to take more than half of Leveaux's Aureliana shares. He had advanced Leveaux £1000 and would send a cheque for £250 for the balance, he promised in a letter of late May, also telling Leveaux that he had been in Edinburgh at the unveiling of the Wallace and Bruce statues by the Duke of York, "beautiful weather and a fine spectacle."

Meantime the land reclamation work at Lesina proceeded, with the dredger *Roma* deepening the lake. Mud and water were pumped half a mile across the surface of the lake and about 200 yards inland, to a region where the marshy land was on a lower level than the lake. In this ingenious recycling, mud built up on the reclaimed land and water drained back into the lake.

The scheme was growing more ambitious, with Tudor Pole reporting from Gargano that the syndicate was trying to buy the whole valley of Callinelli at Peschici, containing pine woods, a cove and beach and room for a model garden city by the sea for 20,000 people. "It's been my dream that this place should be developed as a Riviera on model lines, without casino but with tennis, golf, bathing, fishing and sailing . . . warm baths and so on. Italy has no real place of this kind, properly conceived and developed."

In early November 1928 Tudor Pole again visited Padre Pio. "He looked stronger and happier and promised his prayers for the work at Lesina and for us all. He said he felt the world was approaching a more spiritual phase but that the battle between the two selves in man was a struggle needing more faith and work than ever."

By April 1929, half the works had been completed at Lesina. There were 300 workmen and 24 horses on the job, with the dredger. Mussolini himself was now Minister of Public Works. It was a good year for business. In May Pirelli bought Tullis Russell paper and the Aureliana development was proceeding. Pecorini wrote in December to David Russell:

The town authorities are granting one million lire for the making of a great road at the south of our land, which will mean a great enhancement of the price of that land which lies along the road to be made. I really hope that this new year 1930 will begin to show a return in your investments in Italy, which should prove very advantageous. For instance the Aureliana land should bring at least 100% on the original capital.

The new Gargano railway was expected to open in October 1931, and there was more good news with the festive season's greetings from the Count:

The Laurentina land which we bought after the Aureliana has developed more quickly and we have already sold several lots at twice and three times the original value. I am quite confident that your good faith and confidence will be amply rewarded. I always think of you as the kindest and best man I ever met.

At the end of October the area around Ancona in northern Italy was struck by an earthquake, the shock of which was felt throughout Italy from Naples to Trieste. Forty people were killed, and David Russell sent a cheque to the disaster fund.

Tudor Pole was far from well, and in a letter of October 1930 David Russell wrote to George Leavey:

I feel that he has never spared himself, either in outlays or in thought, in watching over our interests. He has incurred expenses of which I had no knowledge, and appears now to be in a condition of health calling urgently for rest. It would be exceedingly difficult to replace him, and I feel that unless his friends take him in hand, his condition may become much more serious.

But Leavey was getting nervous about his foreign investments. He wanted SAIM to sell its Lake Varano concession at Gargano, and he wanted to realise his investment in Aureliana, the "Romeland" company, as Tudor Pole called it. But Tudor Pole warned him: "If you desire to withdraw your interests entirely from Italy and with as little delay as possible this end will be more surely gained by continuing as at present until the worst of the depression is over, when it will be possible to find a buyer for the whole undertaking."

Frederick Leveaux was also wanting to sell the rest of his "Romeland" investment. In May 1931 David Russell paid him £625 for half of his remaining Aureliana shareholding and also sent £600 to the Midland Bank, St James's Street, London, to be credited to Tudor Pole's Quest account. But the world was plunged into depression, and at Gargano delays and frictions with local landowners were causing problems. Tudor Pole reassured Leavey that Italy was "weathering the economic storm," but warned David Russell not to add to his Aureliana land investment because there could be a delay and more expense before the land could be realised at a satisfactory profit.

Leavey was not convinced by Tudor Pole's reassurances, but required the support of David Russell's shares to gain a majority for a decision to sell the Aureliana land. However, although the site was not yielding interest in money, it was yielding fragments of marble, pieces of porphyry and red granite, a section of column and a fragment of frieze. Walls and human bones were also being uncovered. Tudor Pole was fascinated by archaeology, but nonetheless pointed out the danger that if significant Roman remains were excavated on the Aureliana development site, the Italians would schedule the land as an "Antiquity Area" not to be built over.

Tudor Pole forecast a dividend of "not less than 20%" on SAIM shares for 1932. But negotiations to sell the Aureliana land dragged on through that year, with a convent, a friary, and a sisterhood showing interest, though economic conditions were depressed. Besides, the business relationship of Tudor Pole and George Leavey was deteriorating rapidly. Tudor Pole was on the SAIM board, supposedly looking after Leavey's interests, and he was also on the board of Combined Pulp & Paper Mills on Leavey's recommendation. But Leavey complained that he was paying Tudor Pole without getting a proper return on his Italian investments, and decided to dispense with his services. David Russell defended his closest friend: "To have the capital more than intact, as I understand it is, through these difficult times, is a position not to be lightly valued. I say this from my own standpoint as a shareholder."

But under Mussolini, matters in Italy were subject to sudden change. In September Tudor Pole reported a setback:

A new plan of Rome has appeared in such a form that the previous authority given to us for selling plots of land for any kind of building has been modified and under present arrangements only three or four villas with large gardens can be built on the upper portion of the land, but blocks of apartment houses could be erected in the lower portion.

Then the Superior Council for Antiquity and Fine Arts apparently annulled the development plan, and a community of Dutch nuns became interested in buying part of the Aureliana land for a convent and schools.

The financial crisis was affecting sterling, but Tudor Pole urged optimism. Count Pecorini wrote to David Russell:

I wish you were coming to Italy soon. You would see wonders in Rome, a 'novus ordo,' new broad roads all over Italy, and schools and hospitals everywhere. With a powerful grasp Mussolini has shaken Italy from the dead waters, and put it on firm ground to work and to hope for. For the land, we have really good hope to sell it to some Holland nuns who are now sending a party to inspect it and close the business.

By 1933 David Russell's investment in the Aureliana scheme exceeded £4000, and he had £1800 in SAIM. Leavey's SAIM shares were worth £11,250. He was taking £5174 in cash, and the balance payable in bills over three years. He rebuked Tudor Pole in a letter: "you are obviously powerless to prevent these Italians from doing more or less what they like."

David Russell told Tudor Pole that Leavey had made "a great mistake. I am certainly inclined to hold on to my shares." He wrote to Leavey about Tudor Pole: "What he considers his life's work is still unrealised, and that to him is infinitely more than any material considerations, hard as these may press upon him. I have done all I can to ease his mind of material cares."

Count Pecorini wrote to David Russell in June 1933:

> There is room for a tremendous lot of business. Your Artine and Artine boards and other specialities can go in very big quantities. It is a pity to lose time, when times are favourable! The first shipment is just arrived and it is all sold already. If we would sell in Milan, Venice, Turin, Genoa, Florence, Palermo, it would need a financial outlay superior to our strength and I wish you would give this matter your consideration.

Pecorini was at the mills in August 1933, to discuss business and reassure David Russell that his Italian investments were sound. Back in London, the Count wrote from the Savoy Hotel: "I received a letter from Rome today saying that the convention with the City of Rome for the building of 17 villas on our land has been approved by the Ministry of Public Works and now it remains only to have it signed by the City Authorities."

At the end of October Pecorini secured an order for 150 tons of paper for the Vatican, for delivery over six months. There was better news about the "Romeland" too: Mussolini was a personal friend of Bossiner, one of the Aureliana directors, and the company was granted permission to open a passage in the old city wall, leading directly on to the San Saba quarters. The Government ordered "immediate execution" of the scheme.

In March 1934 Pecorini wrote optimistically to David Russell about the Aureliana site: "Even at the moment of writing we have here in the office a gentleman on behalf of the Jesuit Fathers who is negotiating for the acquisition of the entire upper land." Meanwhile, David Russell had an idea: could Pecorini get Mussolini to write a lecture on leadership for the Walker Trust, though he knew it was out of the question for Il Duce to come to St Andrews? Someone else could deliver it. Count Pecorini promised to do what he could, and David Russell turned his attention to the mills.

15
Sunlight and Enlightenment

In a letter to Tudor Pole in July 1929 David Russell set out part of his philosophy: "Whatever our occupation in life may be, it is important that some definite purpose should run through it all, some purpose, it may be altogether apart from the mere 'occupation' that may appear to swamp our existence."

For some time David Russell had been considering the possibility of a publication "to record various happenings in connection with the firm and its employees." The first issue of the *Rothmill Quarterly Magazine* appeared in September 1929. It had a foreword by David Russell, a practice he was to keep up for the rest of his life, commenting on all kinds of events, historical and contemporary. He urged:

The firm wishes to encourage every activity that is likely to increase the general well-being and happiness of each one of you, and of the little community associated with the works: but I want you to take the initiative. I want you to think out what is required, to meet and to organise every activity that will add to the happiness of the community. You may rely upon the firm to help you.

The editorial reinforced the sentiments of the proprietor (or "Mr David" as he was called) by pledging: "This is a Works' Magazine—*for* the workers, and written almost entirely *by* the workers. Who of us are not 'workers?'"

David Barn featured in the first issue. Seventy-two years before, at the age of 11, he had begun work in the mills. He would be 83 in October 1929, and had retired about the age of 80. He had gone through all the branches of papermaking, from the time of the millwheel, later becoming a machineman, and he could remember the time when all machinemen used to wear paper hats. His comment was: "Folk nowadays couldn't make a paper hat!"

Contributions boxes for the magazine were placed in the mills. There was a series about the history of the firm, a warning about filling in sickness forms for National Health Insurance, news of flower growing in the gardens of employees, and amateur dramatics. The satisfaction of working and living at Rothes was expressed in Walter Rougvie's poem:

> O Rothes Mill, O Rothes Mill,
>   Where paper's made wi' mickle skill
>   And men work hard wi' richt gude will,
> At Rothes Mill, at Rothes Mill.

Housing for the mills formed a small town. In the 1920s 22 houses were modernised, with electric cookers, washers, boilers and irons provided gratis. Twenty-eight new three- and four-roomed houses were built, and 10 five-roomed, all-electric houses. Young trees and shrubs were planted. Once he had put his holiday snaps into the magazine box an employee could go down to the Markinch Institute which had been opened in 1924. It had a billiard room and games room. Nine daily newspapers were available there, and books could be borrowed from the library. Lectures and debates were organised, the subjects chosen by employees who sat on the management committee.

Employees practised with the Tullis Russell Silver Band or played golf, cricket, football, curling and bowling. One commentator in *The World Today* in 1925 had called the firm "not so much an impersonal employer of labour as a parent to the countryside." When David Russell went round the mills every morning any employee could speak to him. He knew their names, and the names of their wives, husbands and children. One Monday morning a young man arrived for his first day's work at the mills. He was told to wait until Mr Happer came. A man sat down beside him and chatted for nearly an hour. It was David Russell, showing an interest in a nervous new employee and putting him at his ease.

An Artificial Sunlight clinic had been installed in Rothes House and now an under-the-weather mill worker and his family could go there for treatment. In October 1926 David Russell had written to Nurse Nisbet, who lived in Edinburgh: "The more I read about the Artificial Sunlight treatment, the more I am satisfied that it has a very big future, and we are all anxious now to have you here in charge of the apparatus at Rothes."

Artificial Sunlight treatment claimed to be beneficial in nervous disorders, skin diseases, tubercular conditions, rickets, chest complaints and anaemia. It was considered necessary for city dwellers because smog interfered with the sun's ultra-violet rays. In 1900 an attempt at the London Hospital to use sunlight to cure lupus—

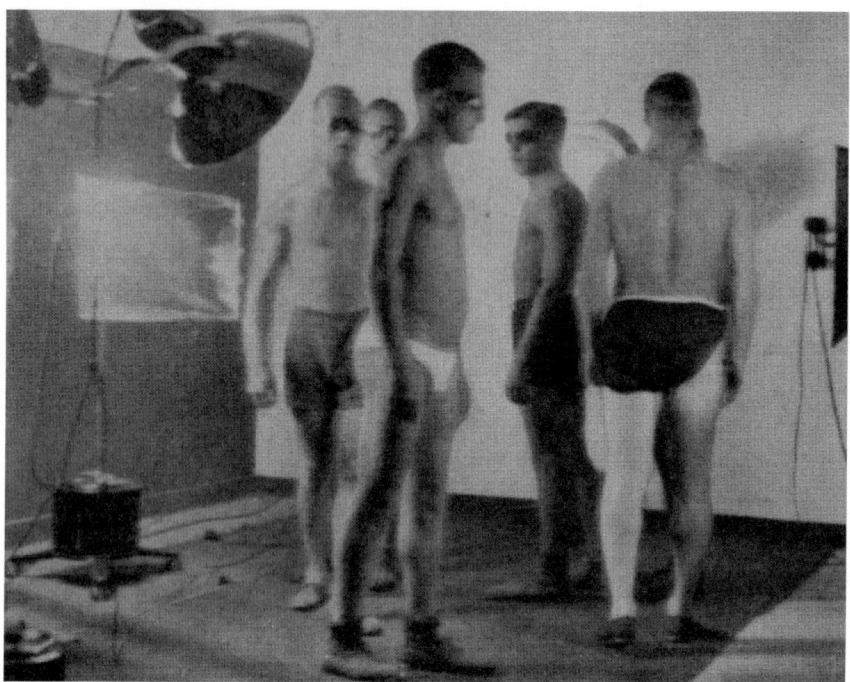
An Artificial Sunlight clinic of the type installed at Rothes House.

tuberculosis of the skin—was stopped by atmospheric pollution. But science decided to fight "the diseases of darkness," and ultra-violet lamps were developed. At the same time the dangers of too much light were recognised, and possible damage to eyes noted.

It was believed that the best lamps were those which produced plenty of ultra-violet light and little heat. Ordinary glass was not suitable for lenses or globes, because it arrested the ultra-violet rays. Quartz was excellent, but very expensive. Vita Glass was invented in the 1920s to transmit ultra-violet rays, and it was claimed that its use in windows created the same beneficial results indoors as in the open air. At the London Zoo animals relaxed under Artificial Sunlight lamps.

Nurse Nisbet went to London for a fortnight's training with Dr J. Howard Humphris, the pioneer of the treatment, at his clinic in Wigmore Street. For the sun-baths men wore bathing pants of celanese silks, and women silk vests which they slipped down once they were settled on the stools between the precisely spaced lamps. At another clinic the female patients wore white loin-cloths, the males blue ones, Nurse Nisbet reported to David Russell, who thought that Rothes should use the same arrangement.

The equipment that had been purchased for Rothes was state of the art: two multiple carbon arc lamps and a tungsten arc lamp. Nurse Nisbet stayed on in London, Dr Humphris having suggested that she should see how treatment was given at Drury Lane Theatre, where there were no absences through illness by those who were receiving regular Artificial Sunlight.

In the first few weeks the results of the treatment for workers and families at the mills were so successful that there were plans to enlarge the clinic.

In December David Russell reported to Tudor Pole:

The Sun Baths are making good progress. We now have over 30 patients, and no persuasion appears to be required to increase the number. We are still lacking some of our appliances, and have not put any notices up to the employees. It is quite obvious that, if we care to expand and to make the treatment available, a great many will respond. Nurse is settling down to the work in a most satisfactory way, and we are getting into touch with a number of cases of impaired health.

Pat Russell and his sisters also bathed in Artificial Sunlight.

The Russells were always willing to try out new methods in alternative medicine. In London in March 1929 Alison Russell had Sandor foam baths administered by Dr Hector Munro, who ran a clinic. The bath was designed to make the patient perspire profusely, without added heat and therefore added strain. Dr Swanberg was also in attendance, together with Sandor, the inventor.

The wildlife of Rothes evidently liked sun-baths. Nurse Nisbet reported to her employer in December 1929: "Such a funny little sparrow came into the Sun Room tonight and wouldn't go out. I put on one of the lamps but it just hopped round it and didn't seem to blink an eye."

In March 1930 David Russell's brilliance of mind was recognised by his election to the Royal Society of Edinburgh. But he could not afford to relax with his books in his Silverburn study because merger was still in the air. In September it was proposed that Tullis Russell should link up with all the esparto group of mills in a rationalisation of production, with redundant mills closed down. The Bank of England was to be the financial base. An alternative plan was for Tullis Russell to merge with Wiggins, Teape & Company, but to retain its identity in an arrangement outside the esparto grass mills proposed merger. This rationalisation was to extend to the control and marketing of grass in North Africa.

While his sons skated in January 1931, David Russell worked on a coat of arms for the mills, but he was worried about the future. The Revenue was demanding that supertax be paid on the profits of Tullis Russell, backdated for three years. David Russell knew this would make it impossible for the firm to remain as a private company. He wanted to go to Algiers, but had to stay to fight the taxation ruling.

But there were diverting amusements at Silverburn. He told Tudor Pole: "I am having one of Anne's hen's eggs every morning just now, and her two hens come to the dining-room window every morning at breakfast and call us, I suppose to know if the egg is satisfactory." Tudor Pole had sent a genoscope to test eggs for sex and fertility.

Tullis Russell won the supertax hearing, and there were intriguing developments to consider, with an invention to use paper towels in toilets. An order for 40 tons of paper milk bottles came in, and David Russell relaxed at Mentone on the Riviera. Home again at Silverburn, Sheila and Anne washed their faces in the May dew before coming into their parents' bedroom. David Russell was a loving father. Every morning he went to the day nursery before going to the mills. He whistled to the canary, and sometimes brought a triangular oatcake with butter and marmalade which he divided carefully between his two daughters. One morning Sheila missed saying goodbye to her father. She cried so much that he had to be phoned, and he came all the way home to say goodbye.

Every evening he went up to the night nursery to chat to his daughters and hear their prayers, regardless of dinner parties or other pressing engagements. He was full of fun: there was the time he drove a car round to the front of the house on a footpath under the day nursery window to amuse his daughters. Then one morning Aunt Dora, who was "difficult," came downstairs at Silverburn with a vivid description of the terrible night she had spent fighting off a mosquito. A few days later there was a showing of a new film by David Russell, featuring Felix the cat having a horrific fight with a wasp. The children loved it, but Aunt Dora was not amused.

The insect problem faced by the workers of the Dooria Tea Company out in Assam was very real, as David Russell explained to Tudor Pole.

Apparently only one mosquito, Moinimus, is responsible for malaria, and breeds only in clear, running water. We opened up our ditches on the Dooria Estate to avoid malaria, and apparently we have done the very worst thing possible. They are now planting a species of thorn all along

SUNLIGHT AND ENLIGHTENMENT

these open drains to cover them over with foliage, which is the best preventative against the breeding of the mosquito, as apparently it cannot develop in shade.

In June Tudor Pole wrote from the Royal Hotel, Rome: "The economic blizzard seems to be becoming a typhoon and I fear you must be in the midst of many perplexities." But the Russells had their summer holiday on Iona, and returned to give a garden party for friends at Silverburn. There were also tea parties at Silverburn in the summer term for St Andrews students. One hungry student, perhaps from the divinity school, seeing the table spread with home baking and strawberries and cream, delighted Alison Russell by telling her that "the food sure came straight from Heaven."

Since boyhood David Russell had had a passion for botany, and the gardens at Silverburn were full of the colours and scents of old favourites and new choices. When he moved into Silverburn he planted Virginia creepers, observing the growth of the shoots morning and night, and recording day and night temperatures. He noted that they grew mostly at night.

He also loved the bird life of the Silverburn policies, but sometimes the harmony went, as he told Nurse Nisbet. "The swallows and the sparrows had a great fight. Anne tells us that one of the nests has had the opening plastered up, and she is quite sure that the swallows have shut up a sparrow inside!"

In early September 1931 the Russells went to St Andrews for an air circus. Mollison was flying the little plane he had brought from Australia, and Captain Barnard had the plane he had flown from India.

The mills were in mourning in November. Taylor the cashier, who had been with the firm for 25 years, was killed by a motor car while cycling home, apparently dazzled by the headlights. He left two boys, both St Andrews students. However, as always, David Russell made sure that there was no hardship as a result of the tragedy.

That year Christmas in Fife was like spring. The clouds glowed with golden light at sunrise, and the birds were singing. The new year brought new business possibilities, but though the profits would be large, David Russell was not interested in making cellophane to compete against Courtaulds.

In June 1932 Sheila sat an examination confined to children born in 1921. Over 87,000 took part, of which 43,000 were girls. She ranked in the top 52. In August her parents went to a garden party at Freuchie in Fife. David Russell noted: "It was quite like a prewar party—an old-fashioned house, and old-fashioned hats and bonnets upon old-fashioned people." He met the Reverend Ian Simpson, the minister at Ceres, a nephew of Sir J. Y. Simpson. The minister kept "open house" for Oxford Movement people and had a thousand applications to join.

David Russell was fascinated by Queen Margaret of Scotland. It was a personal triumph for him when, after four years of negotiation, the Office of Works gave permission at the beginning of 1933 to refurbish Queen Margaret's Chapel at Edinburgh Castle, so that it could be brought into use again. Count Pecorini wrote to tell his friend that under the plaster of a thirteenth century church, Saint Giovanni and Paolo at Spoleto, a likeness of St Margaret with a necklace of pearls on her forehead, with her name underneath in Gothic letters, had been uncovered.

In early March 1933 David Russell lay out sunbathing at Silverburn. He heard Roosevelt's inauguration address on the wireless, and afterwards tuned in to Germany, listening to the students' songs, the cheering and the bells as the country prepared to hold its first and last free elections under the Nazis. On the last day of March the Prince of Wales visited Fife. It had been suggested that he should go to Tullis Russell, but his heavy programme made that impossible. However, he did go to Leven, near Silverburn, and inspected workshops and other premises occupied by the unemployed. The Russells, who had just arrived home from the South of France, listened to the Prince speaking on the wireless that night about his three day visit to Scotland.

While at the mills one day in early April, both the boys were weighed. David was the same height and weight as his father. "I wish I had them both working with me in the mills, but I shall still have some years to wait for that," he told Count Pecorini wistfully.

Pecorini had discovered another relic in an antique shop. It was an old panel painted on an oak table, with what was believed to be a depiction of St Margaret, with a "Scotch thistle" in the background. Many of the details were similar to the Spoleto frieze. The panel, which was supposed to be from the thirteenth or fourteenth century, had belonged to an old Spoleto family, no longer in existence, their palace converted into a bank. Pecorini offered the panel to David Russell for £100, which included the export charges. Stanley Cursiter, the director of the National Galleries, Edinburgh, who was shown photographs of the panel, had difficulty in reconciling the figure of Queen Margaret with the background. But Sir D. Y. Cameron was interested in the piece, and there was a suggestion that it would be placed in the National Portrait Gallery, Edinburgh. It ended up in Falkland Palace, Fife.

A London dealer alerted David Russell to the sale of the Monymusk Reliquary by Sir Arthur Lindsay Grant of Monymusk at Christie's on 22nd June 1933. The Brecbannoch of St Columba is a casket formed from a hollowed block of wood, the exterior overlaid with silver plaques and bronze. The casket is said to have been carried with relics of the saint before the Scottish armies whenever they went to battle, and was at Bannockburn with Bruce.

There was a vigorous newspaper campaign to keep the 1300 year old relic in Scotland. David and Robert Russell were prepared to pay £200, the estimated price, to secure it for the nation. But the relic was withdrawn from the sale because it was found to be entailed, with certain sanctions necessary before a sale could be completed.

The National Art Collections Fund put up £1360 for the purchase, the balance of the £2500 purchase price coming from donations raised through the National Museum of Antiquities, Edinburgh, which also had St Fillan's crozier and bell, and the Guthrie and Kilmichael-Glassary bells and bell shrines. David Russell contributed £50, but wrote to Sir George Macdonald of the Museum: "Is it at all possible that a place might be found for it at Iona, or at some other sacred centre in Scotland? It would seem out of place, somehow, that it should be in a museum."

On 2nd July 1933 the temperature at Silverburn reached 115 degrees in the sun and 84 in the shade. The Russell family took a break at Insh Manse, near Aviemore. In August David Russell wrote to Tudor Pole: "We are having to work late on Saturdays at both mills just now to overtake the rush of orders, and we can only hope that it is the beginning of a revival of trade." Lord David Hamilton was capped at St Andrews, and his mother was a guest at Silverburn. Alexis Aladin was also at Silverburn as a member of the family. David Russell was considering taking young David out of school the following April and bringing him into the mills for several months before he went to university.

September brought devastating news, which put the whole future of the Quest in jeopardy. Florence Tudor Pole wrote to David Russell that her husband had "cancer in an advanced form. There is little left except Christian Science that can help."

The diagnosis had been made initially by Dr H. W. Anderschou. A Dane, author of a book on *Cancer, Cause and Cure* (1922), Anderschou had opened the first Gallspach Institute in Britain at Markham, Guildford. Valentin Zeileis, the "Wizard" of Gallspach in Bavaria, a former coppersmith with no medical qualifications, claimed to have cured 250,000 patients in eight years to 1930. His method of treating any disease in less than a minute was to hold towards the patient's body a glass wand filled with helium gas and attached to a high frequency apparatus. The treatment lasted from one to three seconds three times a day, with 200 persons in the surgery at the one time. The "Wizard," who lived in a castle, had an income of about £500 a day, and a medical commission had criticised his methods.

Anderschou offered the Gallspach method ("Die Zeileis-Therapie") at his Guildford clinic using equipment developed from the "Wizard's" wand. The treatment involved the application of a high frequency current produced through a generator with a 350,000 volt capacity. The current was passed through radium built into an electrode and applied to the body of the patient in soft sparks—the so-called "Effluviens." It gave the patient a slight pricking sensation.

After this application the patient was exposed to 3 to 5 seconds of X-rays, followed by helium light exposure. The combination of applications was repeated two or three times daily with 4 to 6 hour intervals. "Gallspach treatment is thus the only treatment by which it is possible to reach and successfully regulate the invisible life forces proved by science to be of etheric-radio-active and electric-magnetic nature." Tuberculosis and epilepsy could be cured, and in the treatment of cancer "marvellous results are at hand," Anderschou promised.

He also operated the "Lakhowsky Oscillator," a machine developed from a suggestion in a book, *Le Secret de la Vie* published in 1929 by George Lakhowsky, a French professor, that cosmic rays were responsible for a great number of disturbances of health in human beings. Lakhowsky had designed a spiral copper belt for a patient to wear as protection against these rays, but Anderschou's version of the oscillator was a cage of spirals of pure silver, copper and iron wires in which the patient was placed. At the same time the patient was fed with mineral rich food, since Lakhowsky and Anderschou believed that deficiencies of minerals like sulphates of potash and magnesium allowed cancers to develop.

David Russell believed that the medical profession was "extraordinarily blind" with regard to cancer, and put money into the Anderschou clinic. Anderschou reported his successes to his sponsor in April 1932:

Young lady, paralysed for 2 years from the waist to the toes. Had entirely lost use of legs and control over the bladder. Had had electric massage and other treatment. After the first week the bladder was cured and she could stand. Before she left she could walk on crutches. Gone home where she is ordered 2 months' massage and she will then have to return for another 3 weeks' treatment and she will probably be cured.

David Russell visited the clinic in May 1933 and was "greatly interested" in everything he saw. A small Lakhowsky Oscillator was installed in the clinic at the mills. But Anderschou's diagnosis that Tudor Pole had a tumour between the bladder and rectum was wrong. In March 1934 a stone was removed from his bladder at Sherwood Park, Tunbridge Wells, a clinic run by Dr Douglas Cameron, an Aberdonian. David Russell went to visit his closest friend. "The stone was as large literally as an egg," Florence Tudor Pole told him. At Silverburn Anne and Sheila brought in bunches of flowers in the wonderful spring weather and some were sent to the convalescent TP, whom the children called "uncle".

David Russell's heart was always in the Highlands, and he told Tudor Pole:

We saw a little house at Pitlochry which we are very much tempted to buy. It is a small house right on the edge of an oak wood. It is said to be the highest house in Pitlochry, with a beautiful view, and gets the sunshine all day long. If we do buy it, it would be for the children, and small enough just to lock the door and leave empty, and near enough here to reach in about an hour and a half from Rothes.

He knew Pitlochry well. He had been sent to the Perthshire village as a boy with his brothers George and Robert because a change of air was considered good for their health. On one visit David and Robert had found an old pistol in the loft of a barn. When Robert pulled the trigger a bullet grazed David's shirt sleeve.

In April 1934 a pink-breasted parrot was caught with difficulty on the lawn at Silverburn. It was thought to have flown out of a porthole of a passing liner. The parrot attached itself to David Russell, and whenever he went away, it pined. It screamed loudly, particularly if someone was on the phone, and since David Russell could not bear noise, the bird was sent to Edinburgh Zoo.

It was a busy time for the business: in July the pollution of the River Leven by the mills, an old problem, was under consideration, while Rothes Mill was working till midnight on Saturday to supply speciality papers. But David Russell did not want Sunday work.

Sir David Russell (front row, far right) in an academic group after the installation of Jan Christian Smuts (front, middle) as Rector of St Andrews University in 1934.

The Russells attended the Holyrood Garden Party and were present when the King and Queen went to inspect the refurbished St Margaret's Chapel. Pat shot for Sedbergh School at Bisley and in October 1934 David went to St Andrews University to study chemistry, geology, natural philosophy, and natural science. He resided in St Salvator's Hall.

That autumn Jan Smuts was installed as Rector of St Andrews University. Students pulled his carriage through the town. David and Alison Russell attended the dinner given in his honour. Though he was not partial to oysters, David Russell ate them because they were on the table when the guests went in. But he sensed that they were not good, and advised his partner on his right to take alcohol with them, as he was doing. The woman on his left passed her oysters to the man next to her. There was a bad outbreak of food poisoning, and before he left on the train two nights later Smuts asked for whisky, though he had hardly touched alcohol during his visit. The supposition was that he was feeling ill.

The Rome paper business run through Count Pecorini was so unsatisfactory that David Russell considered closing it down,

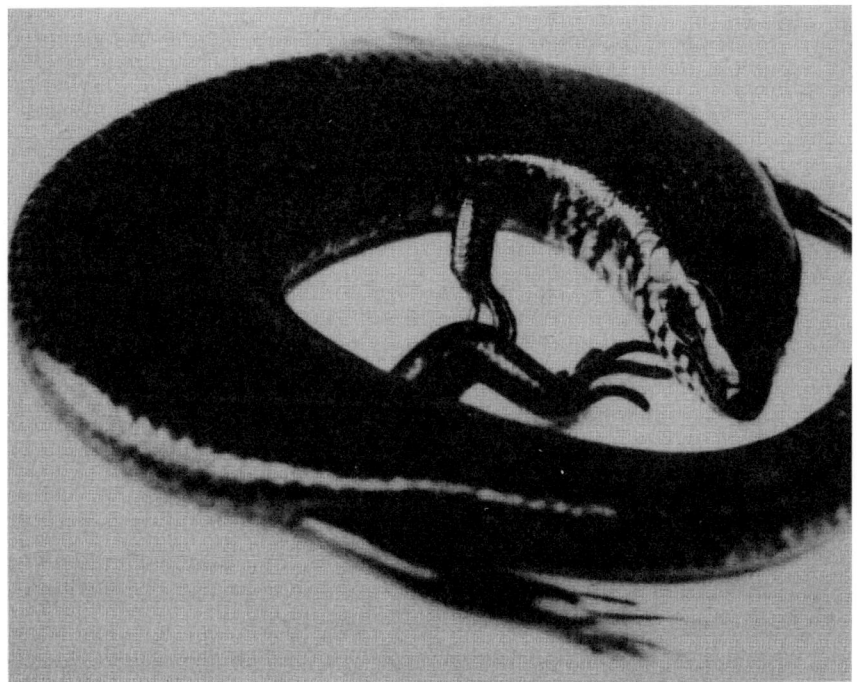

A dead lizard discovered in a bale of bagging from Egypt.

though the loss would be at least £1000. Ill in bed with flu at Silverburn and being treated by Farmer Hall, a distance healer, David Russell watched the sun rise over the sea. As 1934 approached its end he feared that he would be forced to convert Tullis Russell into a public company because the supertax issue had been raised again.

A small chameleon had been found in a bale of esparto grass at Kilbagie Paper Mill, Alloa, where Miss Bell's brother was chief chemist. Such creatures had been found in esparto bales at the Russell mills, but they had not always survived their long voyage. This one was brought to David Russell, and it spent the night at Silverburn so that the girls could see it. Their father thought that it should join the pink-breasted parrot in Edinburgh Zoo, so there was a foreign passenger on the 3.37 train from Markinch to Waverley on 14th December 1934. The zoo's director-secretary duly acknowledged the safe arrival of the long distance traveller.

It is a remarkable thing that a chameleon should make the journey from Africa in a bale of esparto grass. The slender bodied typical lizards seem to bear both the pressure in baling and the long fast quite well, but chameleons are not usually able to fast so long, nor, I should have thought, could bear so much pressure. I hope it will live for some time.

16

The Quest Continues

The Walker Trust's request to excavate in Constantinople had reached officials in August 1932, but the Turks were cautious, asking for a *croquis* or sketch of the area in which the St Andrews group wanted to make a historical or archaeological investigation. A plan of the sea walls at the House of Justinian was sent in reply.

Because of the delay it was decided that Professor Baxter would go out to discuss the extent of the excavations with the Turks, and to make a preliminary survey. Though he had his work at St Andrews as well as a worldwide correspondence with scholars to attend to, Baxter managed to spend five days in Constantinople in mid December 1932. To make sure that Baxter kept the Quest foremost in his plans, Tudor Pole told him: "You will feel the 'call' of this work more as each step is taken, because the spiritual issues involved are far greater than either the archaeological or the historical interests."

David Russell sent shortbread to Paris for the two Russian members of the Quest. As Christmas approached Baxter telegraphed from Constantinople: "Many introductions, useful advice, lantern bright, but delays inevitable." The Turks were still not issuing a permit to proceed, but the German Archaeological Institute promised to help Baxter with advice once excavations began.

In October Baxter was briefed by Tudor Pole on "inner guidance" with regard to the Quest. Tudor Pole wrote to David Russell on the last day of 1932: "Baxter's main and natural apprehension is that the 'taint' of psychism should not come to be associated with the Q in the minds of the St Andrews people and the Turks."

The Times of 2nd February 1933 carried a report of a talk on Constantinople which Baxter had given to the St Andrews Rotary Club, stressing the "vast potentialities" of that part of the world for British trade, and praising "the willingness of the Turk to learn." Tudor Pole was not pleased at this publicity. But Baxter himself was learning rapidly about the psychology of the Turk. He urged David Russell that it would be a move "of the first importance" in winning over the Turkish authorities to offer to repair the Golden Gate. One of Constantinople's most historic monuments, it had been built of large square blocks, glittering with gold, adorned with numerous statues and flanked by two great towers. Through this gateway each new sovereign had entered the city on his way to the Imperial Palace alongside the cathedral of St Sophia. Legend claimed that the victorious Christian army which some day would win back the city for Christendom would pass through the Golden Gate.

It was not the infidel that had caused so much damage to the Golden Gate, but the great earthquake of 1912, which had brought down the upper portions of the inner gate. Baxter inspected the large marble slabs lying in the grass, noting how frost was eroding the inner masonry. Through the Walker Trust David Russell offered £250 towards the cost of restoration work to the Golden Gate, estimated by the Turks at £1100.

Tudor Pole encouraged Baxter's efforts, telling him that it looked as if he would secure a concession both to survey and to excavate. "If so, what a splendid feather in your cap, indeed you will have succeeded where the Kaiser and the Austrian emperor and others failed. In 1906, 1908 and 1912 efforts were made to secure a concession covering this very area."

The lawyer and Quest group member Frederick Leveaux involved himself in the Constantinople negotiations. Through a Foreign Office contact he was informed in mid March that Baxter was now authorised to proceed with his archaeological investigations, with the proviso that if excavations on a large scale were necessary, the matter would be remitted to the Council of State for its permission. The news was telegraphed to David Russell on holiday at Mentone, but he was cautious. The Walker Trust required written authorisation.

Eager to witness over 20 years of Quest obsession reach its climax, Tudor Pole wrote to David Russell in April: "if it is intended that I shall be there during actual excavations or otherwise, then the way will open naturally and I shall be fit to go." David Russell had discussed the Quest freely with his wife and sons. In April Pojidaiev arrived in Fife, his gleaming platinum teeth objects of great curiosity. He was taken to St Andrews to see the cathedral. On his return to Paris he wrote to Alison Russell: "Meeting Baxter at your house has enabled me to fulfil the greatest test of linking up the Quest, which is my life."

The Russian clairvoyant was a kleptomaniac, and before his visit to Silverburn Alison Russell had hidden any tempting small objects which were lying about. Pojidaiev would pocket things, and a few days later they would arrive back in the post, with profuse apologies for having taken them by mistake. Count Pecorini's superb jade collection in Rome was constantly at risk.

The Times of 20th April 1933 carried an article on the Manichaean finds. In the autumn of 1930 eight or nine papyrus books had been discovered by native diggers in a remote village in Egypt. The books, which were in deplorable condition, had been divided up among several dealers. Chester Beatty had secured some for his famous manuscripts collection in London, but an enterprising German professor had located the remaining manuscripts and taken them to the Berlin Museum, and Beatty agreed to place his acquisition on loan to the same museum. The find gave Tudor Pole hope that the library of Justinian could have survived underneath Constantinople, though Turkey's climate was very different to Egypt's.

Anxious to get started in Constantinople, Professor Baxter was reading up Byzantine literature. The Foreign Office assured him that the note they held from Turkey authorising excavations was sufficient permission to proceed.

David Russell was consulted about a plan to establish a paper mill in Turkey. He was cautious about giving advice, recalling that a paper mill set up out there 40 years before had failed because of lack of supplies of raw material. Meantime Baxter was up till the small hours marking scholarship examination scripts in June 1933, and writing an oration for a graduation ceremony. He was now under intense pressure: the divinity schools in Scotland were being reorganised. David Russell told Tudor Pole: "Baxter is the man the Principal [Sir James Irvine] is relying upon to help him in the opening and organising of what may almost be called a new faculty in St Andrews. He is really the only theological professor who can undertake this work, the principal of St Mary's College having died recently." Baxter therefore would not get extended leave to go out to Constantinople.

There were problems over getting maps for Constantinople. Though the Town Prefecture maps were not for sale to the general public, David Russell had obtained a set. However, the Insurance maps, on a scale four times larger, were required for the Walker Trust dig. Tudor Pole fretted at the delay, warning that the Germans would "bring money and pressure to bear on the President Mustafa Kemal himself." According to Tudor Pole, the

Germans had dug close to the Quest site, and had narrowly missed piercing a secret tunnel in 1917.

David Russell thought of going to Constantinople on the Orient Express with his two sons, but changed his mind. But Baxter went back out in August 1933 to finalise arrangements for the dig. Aziz Bey, director of the Istanbul Museum of Antiquities wanted the Walker Trust to proceed with the excavation south of the Ahmediye Gardens, on the Great Palace site, according to the application. Though it was a bigger project than David Russell had anticipated, it suited Quest aims because it was believed that a tunnel ran from the Ahmediye Gardens area towards the sea to the outlying House of Justinian site, which Aziz Bey promised to keep open for a future excavation.

Tudor Pole wrote to David Russell in August 1933: "I am bowed down under a sense of wonder and an emotion far beyond gratitude, when I think of all you have done and are doing for the Q., for me, for all else." But there was tension between Tudor Pole and the two Russian clairvoyants. Pojidaiev complained to David Russell in September: "TP is a member of our work and we must bear his meanness and narrowness of mind."

It was the harrowing time when Tudor Pole thought he had cancer. He wondered if he would live long enough to see the completion of the Quest as he read Baxter's optimistic report: "My guess is that there are passages running in from the tower towards the palace, away from the sea, and that possibly one of those is what we are seeking. Things are in excellent train for our start."

But Tudor Pole warned David Russell in early January 1934: "We must not look for Quest fulfilment this year." When David Russell did his calculations, he found that to date £5000 had been spent on the Quest. He was still considering the proposal about a paper mill in Turkey, and he told Tudor Pole: "The guarantees promised are so complete . . . that it would be bound to be a success. I am unwilling to turn this down altogether, as it is another link in building up interests in that part of the world."

Tudor Pole had been obsessed with the Quest treasure in Constantinople for a quarter of a century, whereas Baxter was a recent initiate to the great secret. Perhaps inevitably, tension was growing between the two. Tudor Pole had apparently received a psychic warning, for he wrote to David Russell in February 1934: "Its effect was that Baxter should not be allowed to dictate Quest policy, because there was some factor in his mind (egotism or not quite single mindedness?) which enabled influences not favourable to us to percolate in and affect his judgements." But Baxter's problems were practical, not psychic. Principal Irvine of St Andrews wanted him to concentrate on his university work instead of taking on the Constantinople commitment. "Did Jim indicate to Baxter his reasons for desiring B. to come out of the Quest work, or rather the general archaeological research?" Tudor Pole wanted to know. Following the removal of the stone from his bladder, he received a message from BB that it would require "a second season's work" to complete the Quest.

Two days late, the Russells' Hellenic cruise ship *Letitia* approached Constantinople on Wednesday 16th April 1934 through the narrows that join the Sea of Marmara to the Bosphorus. David Russell was on deck, his eyes following the sea walls to the House of Justinian, the Quest site that had brought him to this mysterious place but whose secrets he was no nearer uncovering. His interest in Constantinople dated back to his boyhood, when the Russell family at Silverburn had frequent visits from Waldegrave Leslie, who had been in the British Embassy at Constantinople. In 1904 David Russell had met some Russians at the Sanna sanatorium in Sweden and bought some large illustrations of St Sophia. Since then he had spent years reading about the history of the city of minarets built on seven low-lying hills.

The Greek colonial city of Byzantium had a turbulent and bloody history under Persian, Spartan and Roman domination, having never achieved the promise of its foundation on the advice of the Delphic oracle. But when Constantine I, head of the entire Roman empire east and west, embraced Christianity, he decided to make Byzantium his capital. In May 330, six frenetic years after the laying of the foundation stone, Christian ecclesiastics performed the capital's inauguration ceremony. To indicate its political status the city was named New Rome: to perpetuate the name of its founder it was styled Constantinople.

But the buildings David Russell could see on the hills as his cruise ship turned towards the superb anchorage of the Golden Horn were Turkish. The city was besieged by the Ottoman Sultan Mehmed II in April 1453. The Golden Horn had been protected by a chain across its entrance, but the Sultan succeeded in hauling his fleet overland from the Bosphorus. The city fell at the end of May. With the last Byzantine emperor, Constantine XI Palaeologus, killed in battle, the line that had began with such hope and ceremony came to an end.

David Russell was driven through the streets, past the noisy *hamals* or porters staggering under heavy loads and surrounded by the barking pariah dogs that followed the traffic. The Russell family did not take to Constantinople, as he told Tudor Pole, who replied: "I agree that Constantinople is sinister and cruel and historically unpleasant, nevertheless it has become one of the comparatively few vital centres over a long period and may become so again."

During the two day visit David Russell took the opportunity to talk to Turkish officials about the Walker Trust's repairs to the Golden Gate. He suggested that such funds as the Trust could provide should be used to preserve the structure, and that the refacing of the walls with marble should be held over till further funds were available. Aziz Bey appeared to consider it a good suggestion. The excavation at the Great Palace was also discussed.

Tudor Pole was worried about the publicity of the Constantinople excavations and wanted to do it through J. J. Astor, the chairman of *The Times*. But Baxter claimed that he had journalistic experience, having worked for the *Glasgow Herald*, and he insisted on handling publicity himself. As always Pojidaiev and Bergengreen in Paris needed more money and David Russell responded, irritated: "Surely it would be possible for the Russians to live within the amount they have been getting? Is it necessary that Pojidaiev should continue to stay in a hotel?" Tudor Pole cautioned: "they hold peculiar views about the Quest and their proprietary interest therein and exaggerate the value of the BB indications. Nevertheless their position is very difficult and we cannot abandon them or even appear to be shutting them off from consultation in regard to Quest policies."

Bergengreen wrote to Tudor Pole in July, urging speed with the Quest. "To wait one year more could be dangerous." But Tudor Pole was beginning to have some doubts, as he confessed to David Russell. "One can say definitely now that Quest fulfilment via BB guidance alone would seem very dubious. Can it be made a useful adjunct?" He was anxious to bring Israel Sieff of Marks & Spencer into the Quest team. "He seems to have some vision, a broad outlook and of course ample means. If the inventory we possess can be relied upon there are a number of very early Jewish scripts which may throw a flood of light on pre-Christian Jewish history and thought."

Sir Ernest Budge, who had urged Tudor Pole to get on with the Constantinople dig, died in November 1934. Baxter was planning to go out to Constantinople in the spring of 1935. David Russell

THE QUEST CONTINUES

had been very ill with whooping cough, which he had caught from his small daughters. The family went out to Palma, Majorca, in February to convalesce, but the weather was frigid, 37 degrees Fahrenheit and snow. It was summer weather at home, his secretary Miss Bell reported. The Russells visted the convent of Valdemosa, where Chopin had stayed. Blind to the notice on the instrument, Sheila played two notes on the composer's piano, to the attendant's consternation.

As a young woman Alison Russell had been told that the best way to a man's heart was through his stomach, but David Russell was not particularly interested in food. However, on that visit to Majorca he spoke longingly in his sleep about "apricot ice cream."

Meantime Tudor Pole was discussing with the Marquis of Lothian an offer to liaise with the Prime Minister should difficulties occur over the Quest permit. Baxter was also busy. He spent four days in Constantinople in March 1935, touring the sites in a taxi. At a seance in Paris BB was not available, but "Jack" the communicator warned: "If work on the House of Justinian is undertaken this season, there must be 3 months available in which to finish it."

Baxter saw German archaeologists busy next to St Sophia, unearthing the foundations of the first church built on that site. He wrote to David Russell from Vienna on his way home in early April:

I have secured the permit. When I first went over the site where our map shows vacant spaces, I was amazed and disappointed to see how quickly new houses are springing up there. But on the whole it is a gain to us, for it limits the space over which our excavation is to extend. And when I found Aziz ready with a proposal that we should help him to restore the House of Justinian, with his plans and estimates prepared, I thought that providential.

The work on the House would give the team an opportunity to examine the vaults and foundations.

Tudor Pole warned David Russell: "The Quest work is so important that everything that has happened in your life so far has had its part in preparing you for the very vital arrangements now being made." On Easter Sunday 1935 Tudor Pole was in Constantinople, from where he wrote to David Russell: "I have no indication yet that full fulfilment is due but events may move quickly later on after work begins, and these are only my first impressions." But as he explored the House of Justinian remains Tudor Pole noted that they were deteriorating fast through "vibration," presumably from the adjacent railway. German work was proceeding on the land walls, and some of the archaeological sites were being built on.

The *Scotsman* of 3rd May 1935 carried an agency report from Constantinople that Baxter was about to conduct excavations on the site of the Great Palace. "According to M. Aziz, Director of the Istanbul Museum, discoveries of great archaeological interest are anticipated from the excavations." Tudor Pole was worried about the advance publicity; there was even more need for a press liaison person, he told Baxter. He was also worried about the excavators getting "fleeced," since a rumour had spread that "very wealthy people are behind this British archaeological research."

David Russell wrote candidly to Tudor Pole in mid May: "Our reason for deciding to ask permission to work on the site of the Palace was in a sense camouflage, and we appear to have gained rather than lost by having got permission to work upon the site in which we are most interested. So, can we really say that we have lost much through the building operations?" Tudor Pole cautioned: "Remember we are at work in an Eastern country full of intrigue and conflicting interests."

David Russell warned that it was "quite beyond the funds of the Walker Trust to develop a big exploration on the Palace site." For his part Tudor Pole was "bewildered by a turn of events which seems to be freezing me out of any real participation or collaboration in Quest matters and all that flows therefrom."

David Russell told Tudor Pole in June: "I never lay much stress on putting my point of view forward, provided I know that when the time comes I will be able to express it definitely, and I expect to be on the spot when the work comes to take a decisive character."

David Russell planned to go to Venice, and from there by sea to Constantinople for the commencement of the dig. But two of the Quest group seemed to be deserting: Pojidaiev wanted to go to Serbia, and urged Bergengreen to accompany him, though the latter, despite being 64, had his heart set on a new life in Paraguay. The two clairvoyants were apparently getting the wrong psychic message, for Baxter was about to strike treasure.

17
Excavating the Great Palace

For its time, the Great Palace begun by Constantine was one of the wonders of the world, sprawled over acres, full of fabulous artefacts. When the Bishop of Cremona went as an envoy to the Byzantine Court in 948 he was enchanted by golden mechanical birds singing in a golden tree in the audience chamber, where golden lions guarded the golden throne. A century and a half later Joseph, a monk from Canterbury, learned while at Jerusalem on pilgrimage that at Constantinople there was an incomparable richness of relics. He made his way there, and was overcome with awe at the holy treasures of the imperial chapel.

At the beginning of July 1935 the party which had been assembled in Constantinople for the excavation of part of the Great Palace under Baxter's direction was a small one, because he anticipated that it would be a season of "little more than experiment and experience." But they were fortunate to have new publications to supplement their own information about the Great Palace area. Following the fire on the site in 1912, Mamboury and Wiegand had made extensive archaeological investigations and in 1934 they were able to publish a compendious study, *Die Kaiserpalaste von Konstantinopel zwischen dem Hippodrom und dem Marmara-Meer*. It described and illustrated with plans and photographs the ruins in this area which could be examined without excavation, and demonstrated that modern archaeologists could distinguish clearly, in accordance with the ancient texts, between the upper and lower terraces of the Palace. A 1935–40 publication, *Constantin Porphryrogénète, Le Livre des Cérémonies*, by Albert Vogt, proved invaluable to Baxter and his team as it included a plan of the Palace.

Assisting Baxter was Professor James Corbett of the University of Notre Dame, Indiana; Henry Ricketts, a brilliant theology student from St Andrews; and, also from the university, Iain Gordon Campbell, who had made significant finds at Tentsmuir and in other parts of Fife, and had worked for three years on the

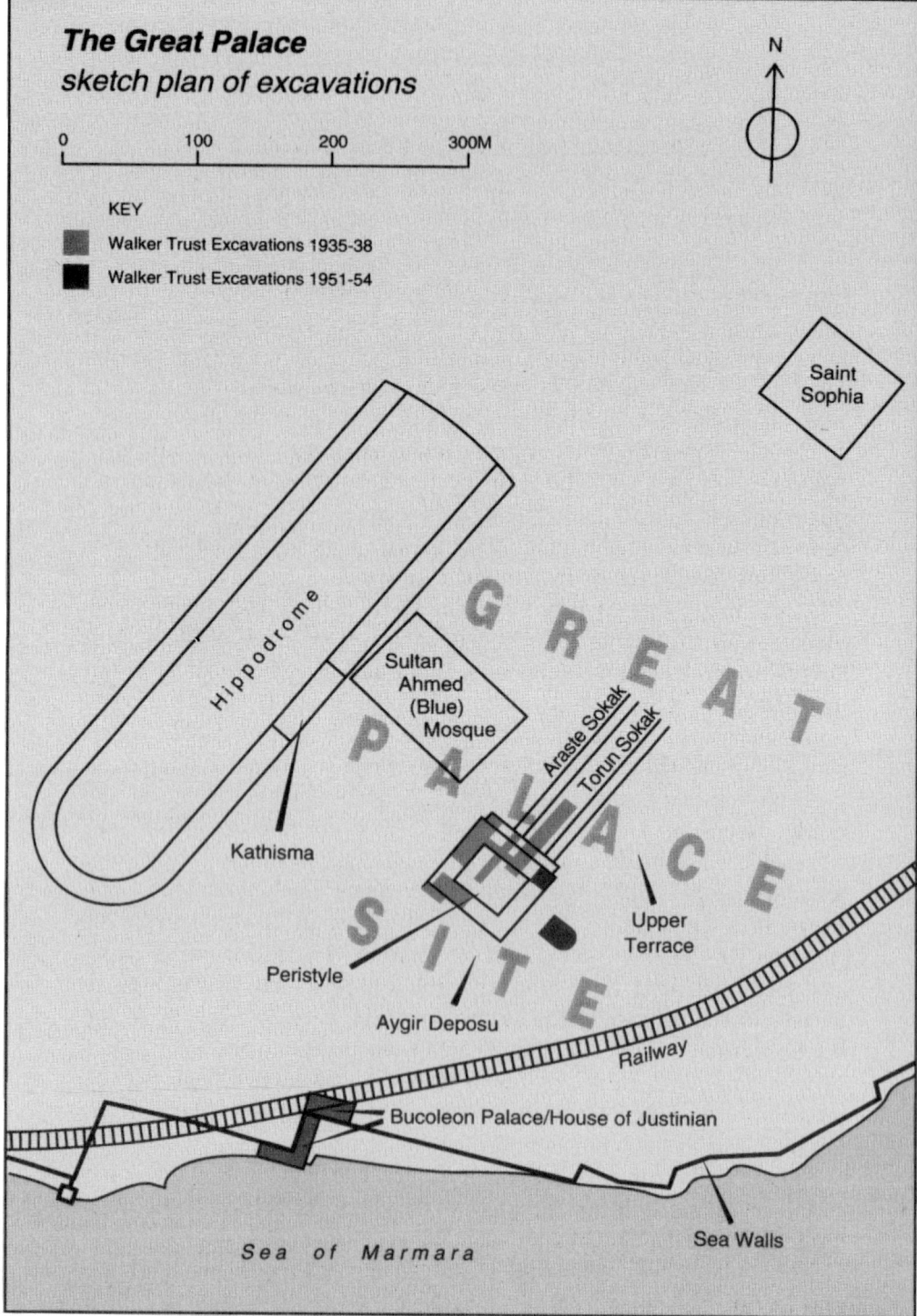

Roman excavations at St Albans. Bey Necdet Cumbaracilar was Government Commissar for the excavation.

Baxter began digging in one of the areas requested in the original 1932 petition, near the magnificent mosque of Sultan Ahmed. Also known as the Blue Mosque, it is flanked by six minarets and stands where the buildings that formed the first part of the Great Palace are believed to have once been. A gateway into the Hippodrome, presumed to be the imperial doorway, had been found recently. Baxter reasoned that from that point there would be a straight path along which the Emperor would come from his own apartment. One effect of the 1912 conflagration had been to reveal to the south-east of the Mosque a subterranean street (Araste Sokak) lined by the arcades of a seventeenth century bazaar. It was here that the Walker Trust excavations began.

The sun had set behind the Golden Horn on Wednesday 3rd July 1935 as James Baxter sat down to write to David Russell, telling him: "the great work started today." At 7.30 a.m. that morning five workmen had started digging the sunken road just south of the Blue Mosque. It suited Quest purposes because Tudor Pole believed through BB that there was at least one tunnel in this area, leading towards the sea and the House of Justinian. The plan was to advance north towards the Mosque, and in a week or so, having satisfied the Turkish authorities that the dig was under way, to carry out some restoration work on the House of Justinian, preparatory to digging the Quest site.

Baxter was blunt. "I have felt it without any doubt wiser to take on Mamboury to draw the official plans for me; if he hadn't been for us, he was sure to do us a lot of harm, and even already he has given me one or two useful bits of advice."

Baxter was itchy as well as tired after his long day, because of the mosquitoes and fleas: "Oh for Keating's!" He also needed drawing paper ("unprocurable here") for Mamboury. He could see the sliver of the new moon, "the colour of a ripe apricot," doubled in the darkening water of the Bosphorus as he thought about his wife and son in St Andrews. But he had a last piece of tantalising news for David Russell before he turned in: "Just half an hour before finishing, we struck a marble floor . . ."

They began to dig up the marble they had struck. The Turks worked for 2s per day, where the usual daily rate was from 1s to 1s 6d. After toiling from seven in the morning till noon each of the Turkish squad ate half a red melon and some bread. On the second day's digging a break in the marble allowed soundings to be taken, and an eight inch layer of cement was painstakingly removed. But Baxter would not complete the operation until the workmen had gone on Saturday afternoon, presumably because he feared careless talk over the weekend.

Inch by inch we then removed the covering cement as far as we could penetrate, and the excitement carried the crowd of us on till 6pm. We had had a very light breakfast, coffee and rolls at 6.45am, but hunger disappeared before the thrill of discovery. The mosaic is almost entirely intact. So far it covers between 2 and 3 square metres and represents a portion of what must be of large dimensions. The design is more than life-size: so far we have uncovered a monkey climbing a tree with foliage, but this must be only one corner. It may belong to the 6th–7th century, perhaps even 4th–5th—not enough data yet to show.

Baxter knew that he had a find of major importance, much more significant than what the British Academy had uncovered in the previous decade. But he reassured David Russell: "I have not lost sight of the Quest, but we had to begin somewhere . . ." Baxter was shrewd: the professor whose scholastic speciality was medieval Latin realised the fame and new status that his discovery would bring, and warned David Russell: "News of this find must not leak out, until my press announcement." He covered the exposed part of the mosaic with straw and earth, then tested his own security by taking a tram down to the Blue Mosque area and prowling around. The watchman's lamp approached and he was warned off with a shout.

Baxter's letter was handed to David Russell as he was leaving his office in Rothes. He was thrilled to read about the discovery as he was driven home to Silverburn in the summer evening. In his letter of congratulation he got the priorities right, telling Baxter that he had arranged for a supply of Keating's Powder to be sent out from Edinburgh c/o the Ottoman Bank, Galata.

A Greek with experience in uncovering mosaics was hired, since care as well as strength was now required for the excavation. "In some ways it is an embarrassment," Baxter told David Russell, "for it pins us down under constant supervision and public interest." Rather than stop work they had food sent from nearby restaurants and ate it in the archways round the mosaic. Appreciating that Baxter had his hands full, David Russell suggested that the work on the House of Justinian site could be postponed until the following year. He also felt that permits should be obtained for the other sites to prevent other teams working on them.

EXCAVATING THE GREAT PALACE

In Paris Pojidaiev spent his precious francs on a telegram to Tudor Pole: "Congratulations. Victory." Seemingly unaware of the discovery of the mosaic, and with the Quest foremost in his mind, Tudor Pole wrote to David Russell on 17th July:

Apart from topographical details, there is no reason to anticipate really interesting discoveries during the present season's work on the Palace site unless such work could include the sinking of shafts from the Byzantine ground level in an effort to discover some section of the underground network of tunnels and catacombs which were probably sealed up when the Palace fell into ruins and was abandoned.

The Turkish authorities were co-operative. Three weeks after the excavations had begun a deputation from the Museum, the Municipality and the Government came to view the part of the mosaic that had been uncovered and to assess the obstacles involved in following the extent of the discovery. The deep and massive walls of the arcades below which the mosaic was known to continue could not be removed without permission, and some of the ground belonged to private owners. The Vali or mayor of Constantinople gave much help. The question of removing the mosaic to a museum was raised.

On 23rd July a conciliatory Tudor Pole wrote to David Russell: "Unless it comes about naturally I won't press for any House of Justinian work this season. One cannot say exactly what is Q work and what is not, because they are working within the 'arc' on ground beneath which there is tunnel connection with H of J's subterranean systems."

A jubilant Baxter returned to London at the end of July to arrange publicity and to consult with David Russell, who had been doing some calculations. He had good news for Baxter. "I think we can count upon sufficient funds to see us through another season of, say, five months, upon a somewhat larger staff than you now have."

On the morning of Sunday 25th August 1935 David Russell and his son David arrived in Constantinople after a three day journey on the Simplon Orient Express. They hurried to the dig to see the extent of the mosaic that had been uncovered. The background of the sizeable area of flooring was composed of finely imbricated white tesserae, framed in a richly coloured, multiple border. The designs on the mosaic were arranged in three registers, each with its own ground or base. The first register showed a hunting scene in which four dogs wearing collars pursued a hare. Then two children were depicted, one stretching out his hands towards the hare, the other holding a dog. A small tree divided these from the figure of a griffin holding a lizard in its mouth. There was a monkey with a bird-cage on its back, and a child driving turkeys or guinea fowl.

The second register showed a combat between a lion and an ox, a bear in a tree, another griffin, two panthers devouring a gazelle, a mother nursing her child, a baying dog, and a stag in the coils of a serpent. The most striking representation on the third register was of a fisherman lifting a fish out of the water. Baxter considered this the finest of all the pieces. "The effect of transparency produced when his foot rested in the water reveals the most skilful and delicate artistry." As David Russell looked at the animals on the mosaic he imagined a succession of emperors passing to the Hippodrome, the burden of affairs of state lightened by the spectacle of the sports. The mosaic-floored passage (later identified as the north-east side of the Peristyle) was 30 feet wide and on its south side appeared to have been lined by an open colonnade, through which the sun would have streamed to illuminate the mosaic designs in a fabulous kaleidoscope of humans and creatures. Marble seats on the other side of the passage were found, resting on a wall 12 feet thick, founded upon rock 27 feet below.

During David Russell's stay he and Professor Baxter had lunch with the Vali, who told them that under Kemal Ataturk, the founder and first President of the Turkish Republic, the country was anxious to take her place among the nations of the West. To show what it had contributed to civilization, Turkey wanted to "learn to read the records of the past." The Vali spoke of archaeological investigations being carried out by the Turkish authorities in Constantinople, and of the new boulevard that was being constructed along the land walls. David Russell offered £50 as a donation to the work, and suggested an exchange of students with St Andrews University. The delighted Vali proposed the health of his Scottish guests in champagne.

Young David Russell took the place of Iain Gordon Campbell on the dig while David Russell senior returned to his desk at Rothes and the problems of running paper mills in the depressed 1930s. Baxter left Constantinople in mid September, telling David Russell: "I think the mosaic should be safe enough, but naturally one cannot but wish to have seen the last blanket happed over it for the winter." About 40 people saw the St Andrews party off at the station. At David Russell's request Baxter had asked to be allowed

EXCAVATING THE GREAT PALACE

After centuries part of the mosaic pavement in the Great Palace yields its grand design.

Enjoying the fruits of their success: (left to right) David Russell and Professor James Baxter with Turkish officials in Istanbul.

to take back several small pieces of the mosaic for chemical and colour analysis. "When I showed the permit to the customs officer at the station, he said that for our honesty he would not examine any of our luggage at all."

But Baxter did not receive a warm reception at St Andrews. Principal Irvine was not only worried about the time that he was spending away from the university; he was also anxious that the Walker Trust funds, intended for the benefit of the university, were being swallowed up in the large-scale excavations in Constantinople. This forced David Russell into making a remarkable admission: not one penny from the Walker Trust was going into the Turkish dig. The money was coming from his Iona Trust and other sources, presumably his own pocket. As plans were made for another season's dig he realised that this put him in a vulnerable position, but he agreed with Baxter: the mosaic should be followed to wherever it led. But there were risks in this decision. Buildings in the path of the mosaic would have to be demolished, with possible compensation problems. Also, the Turkish authorities were indicating that they expected the Walker Trust to erect a permanent building to cover the mosaic.

EXCAVATING THE GREAT PALACE

Tudor Pole was unhappy with developments. He felt that the Quest, centred round the House of Justinian, was being neglected if not abandoned through Baxter's obsession with excavating the Great Palace, and that Baxter was excluding him. He reminded David Russell: "Baxter said from the first that he welcomed collaboration, and yet from the first every suggestion I have made has been turned down, rarely any reason given."

Baxter's two articles on "The Secrets of Byzantium" appeared in *The Times* in late October 1935. Tudor Pole complained about the "very real embarrassment" of the omission of his name, and that a reference to the Great Palace site being "scrutinized and studied" over the years was not only misleading but untrue, since it was he who had studied the House of Justinian site over many years in his Quest investigations.

David Russell replied: "I cannot myself see how anyone could ever regard the omission of your name in 'The Times' articles as deliberate, or how that omission in any way relieves you of your status." He thought it "inadvisable" to refer to the earlier origin of the work. Frederick Leveaux was also angry that his name had not appeared in the articles.

Baxter had the type of personality that could not take criticism. He dispatched angry letters, pointing out to David Russell, with regard to Tudor Pole's and Leveaux's contributions: "The present success, indeed all the plans on which we are now working, owe absolutely nothing to any information supplied by them, and even should the Quest form part of our own future programme, this utterly deplorable and childish attitude of both men completely corrupts that atmosphere which is necessary for any success." He complained bitterly: "They wish now to come upon the scene after their own failures and futilities to bask in the sunshine of our success." He warned David Russell that any suspicion of a psychic connection with the dig would bring to an end the co-operation of the Turks.

Baxter then wrote to Tudor Pole: "you muddled my relations with Halil, you messed the Foreign Office contact, you left a sheaf of difficulties in Istanbul." He said that Tudor Pole's complaints to Ralph Deakin, the imperial and foreign news editor of *The Times*, had cast aspersions on "my sincerity and truthfulness." He warned Tudor Pole:

If this excavation which has begun so well is to continue at all under my guidance, it must be completely dissociated from your quest. I am glad that hitherto your data have not entered into it, for from now on I wash my hands completely and finally of it and you. How can anyone hold to the accuracy and reliability of spiritual information supplied by colleagues whose discretion, fairness and straightness are submerged by jealousy and the ambition to see their name in linotype?

He also wrote: "If your connection, control or consultation be still insisted upon, I must altogether abandon the task of pursuing the mosaic to its natural end in the Golden Hall."

As always, David Russell was the peacemaker. It was not as bad as Baxter had portrayed, since Deakin was anxious to cover the next season's dig in *The Times*. But Baxter refused to read a conciliatory letter from Tudor Pole, and he was not impressed by Leveaux "stringing out legal and hair-splitting arguments" in his letters. Tudor Pole wrote pointedly to David Russell in early December: "Whilst I propose making no reply to JHB's really venomous attack, I expect that you will hardly feel able to allow this to pass undefended, for it lays very serious imputations upon the character and actions of one of your oldest and most loyal friends."

As Christmas approached, Bergengreen sent David Russell his greetings from Paraguay. He had apparently obtained a concession to hunt crocodiles, and offered to supply skins to David Russell, who declined his offer politely. Family festivities and not business were taking up his time, as he told Tudor Pole on 27th December. "We gave a dance at Silverburn last night for young people, the first we have given for many, many years. It was, I think, a complete success."

Baxter lectured on Constantinople at St Andrews at the end of January 1936. He was eager to get back out in April, to identify the layout of the Great Palace. In mid February Anne Russell heard on the late news on the wireless that 20 minarets had had their tops blown off in Constantinople in a storm.

David Russell was at a dinner party for 10 given at St Andrews by Ramsay MacDonald on 26th February. He was placed next to the former Prime Minister, who had just been elected to the Scottish universities' parliamentary seat. They found a mutual fascination in the subject of St Sophia, the Constantinople cathedral that was the emperor Justinian's most magnificent achievement. "I feel that a useful contact has been made," David Russell told Tudor Pole.

Baxter arrived in Constantinople for the second season in April 1936. He was treated as a great friend of Turkey and ushered through customs. Having left his card with the Vali, he went down to look at the dig, which was "intact and flourishing with weeds." David Russell had a supply of Aquaflint Stone Preservative sent out to Constantinople so that Baxter and the Museum authorities could experiment with its use for the mosaic. David Russell also investigated the possibility of sending out a boring machine to save opening trenches, and to bring up specimens of flooring.

The programme of the second season's dig was to follow the mosaic-floored passage westwards towards the Hippodrome and eastwards towards the sea, probing at the same time to north and south in the hope of establishing from architectural remains the mosaic's relation to the Great Palace. The terrain was the difficulty: the first find of the previous July had been made in the sunken road about 20 feet below the terrace of the Blue Mosque. On each side of this road the ground had been built over since the Turkish conquest, and Baxter thought that excavation there would be comparatively unprofitable and slow.

On 24th April he began digging west of the uncovered mosaic, towards the terrace of the Blue Mosque. In the first few days several heavy walls were found behind the arcades, evidently designed as supports for the terrace. When one wall was laboriously removed,

A Turkish labour force excavates the Great Palace on Baxter's protracted dig.

marble paving was found, with the mosaic underneath it. William Macaulay, an artist from the Edinburgh College of Art, began to make superb coloured tracings of the mosaic.

In early May 1936 David and Alison Russell went out to Constantinople with Pat, with young David following later. David Russell senior was enchanted with the illustrations on the newly uncovered part of the mosaic. An old man, perhaps a shepherd, sat in contemplation, a staff in his hand. Beside him were a cow and calf, three goats, and a small bush or tree composed from exquisite green glass tesserae.

But excavation at that depth was dangerous, especially in such sultry and oppressive weather of sudden thunderstorms. An unstable section of ground had been marked off for removal, but was left. When it gave way it buried two men. The 60 workers engaged in the dig threw down their picks and spades, shouting as they rushed to the scene of the accident. David Russell also ran over but within minutes the heads of the two men had been uncovered, and they were helped out, unharmed.

It was a frightening lesson on the problems of digging in Constantinople. A fire brigade arrived, followed by an ambulance to take the two men away. The police lined up the workers and counted them to make sure nobody else was under the earth. It showed David Russell the very serious liabilities of employers of labour in Turkey, with compulsory insurance and compensation among the provisions of recent legislation.

Apart from some repairs to the buildings, no work had been carried out on the Quest site at the House of Justinian. Despite the brilliant success of the Great Palace excavation so far, David Russell had not forgotten that it was the Quest that had brought them to Constantinople, and that Tudor Pole had devoted so much of his life and psychic talents to its fulfilment. On the train home from Turkey he wrote to Baxter, suggesting that they should buy two of the dwellings at the House of Justinian to make work on the site easier, though that would add to the already spiralling costs in Constantinople.

But problems were beginning to build up on the excavation. In October opinions ascribed to Ernest Mamboury appeared in the French newspaper *La République*. Mamboury was alleged to have said that Baxter was not an archaeologist, and that he was carrying out the excavation "as a delegate from a religious mission." Since Baxter did not have the special knowledge to bring the enterprise to a successful conclusion, Mamboury advised the Turkish

Government to take over the dig, working within the Great Palace limits as set out in his published work.

David Russell read a translation of the article with alarm, realising the danger it could do to the Walker Trust's relationship with Government officials, and to the fulfilment of the Quest. But Mamboury claimed that the article had resulted from a casual conversation with a journalist, and that he had been misrepresented. As for Baxter, he was determined to proceed with the dig under his control, but David Russell's mind was on Italy.

18

The Romeland Investment

On 2nd October 1935 Mussolini had addressed a huge cheering crowd from his Roman balcony, telling them: "A solemn hour is about to strike in the history of the Fatherland . . . with Ethiopia we have been patient for forty years. Now enough!" Early next morning Italian troops crossed the frontier, beginning the invasion of Ethiopia.

David Russell was becoming increasingly anxious about his Italian business interests. In July Count Pecorini had written a frantic letter about an Italian company that had used Tullis Russell's Artine brand to print 60,000 illustrated pamphlets. The company claimed that the paper was of poor quality, and that the illustrations had turned from black to grey. The manager not only refused to pay, but demanded damages. A discount was agreed, and 21 promissory notes accepted, but the company collapsed. The Count was left with a loss of 23,000 lire (about £700). "See, please, if you can do something of meeting me on my loss," he pleaded. David Russell must have met it, for Pecorini sent a telegram: "Deeply Moved your Liberality receive profoundest thanks."

There was also trouble with the "Romeland" investment. Signor Osio, president of the Italian Bank of Labour and one of the leading figures of the Fascismo, wanted to buy 17,000 square metres of the Aureliana holding. He planned to "beautify" the land by creating gardens, tennis courts and bathing pools. Pecorini's enthusiasm for the sale was obviously based on self-interest. "One of the reasons which made us very anxious to sell was that the Italian Government, in order to keep the iron existing in Italy for the needs of war, does not give for the present any licences to build, this measure will cause a falling in the price of land, and a rising in the prices of apartments."

The best land with frontage to a main road was sold to Osio, thereby reducing the value of the rest. David Russell wrote to Tudor Pole: "We shall be very fortunate if we get out of the Rome

Land investment without losses." Tudor Pole was disillusioned: "Freedom as we understand it is no longer possible in Italy." He protested:

It almost looks as if there was an element of *force majeure* in the sale of the land to a Fascist banker. The financial position in Italy is likely to become so serious in the next year or two that it is evidently wiser to withdraw from financial commitments in that country. The position is disappointing, but probably the sale at Lire 39 is better than holding on, in view of the critical situation. Also it must be remembered that when the land was bought at Lire 20 per square metre the Lire stood at over 115 to £1.

Tudor Pole went to Rome to see what could be salvaged and produced a convoluted plan to get round the Italian Government's legislation to prevent money being taken out of the country. The Aureliana funds were to be invested in Italian government bonds. A loan from the bank would be secured on these, and the money used to buy Dutch and American cheques, mainly for small sums, the property of various religious institutions in Rome. These cheques would be sent through the Vatican mail bag to London for collection and exchange into sterling.

David Russell began to be paid out in instalments for his investment, with Tudor Pole going to Italy to collect sums of money. There were also investments in cargoes of Red Sea salt to get more money out of Italy. These were dangerous transactions, since the Italian Government was determined to stop leakage of money from the country. According to Tudor Pole, if the authorities discovered that Italians were utilising money from the sale of land in Rome for settling foreign debts, they could be imprisoned for two years and fined 10 times the sum involved.

In a letter in October 1935 Count Pecorini lamented to David Russell: "How unfortunate all this trouble with your country. If it will bring to war the destruction will be appalling!" The situation was embarrassing, since Marconi had been elected Rector of St Andrews University in November 1934, but could not attend to deliver his address. David Russell hoped he would come in 1936 or 1937, but Marconi died, leaving his rectorial address unfinished, and an unanswered question: "Have I done the world good, or have I added another mistake?"

Meanwhile, Sheila Russell was happy at St Leonards School, St Andrews. Anne was at home and had a new governess. "She wants to study history and Greek and to be an Archaeologist!" her father told Pecorini proudly. The Count had published his autobiography, called *Japanese Maple*, and warned his Scottish friend: "You will read in its short pages a compendium of that wild life, which I passed through in my juvenile days." But David Russell was charmed. "It all reads with such a reality of life, so true and so beautiful."

In late November there was promising news about the Aureliana land shares. Tudor Pole wrote to David Russell to tell him that an offer had been received from a French businessman for the Aureliana shares belonging to David Russell and George Leavey. David Russell's 42 shares were worth around £3,600. "Pecorini hesitates to advise, but he says that if the buyer realised all the recent laws against freedom in building, taxes, etc., he does not think he would offer so much for these shares."

In February 1936 there were cases of cerebrospinal meningitis at Sedbergh School, and parents were taking their sons away, but Pat was already at home with measles. Young David was at St Andrews University. In March Tudor Pole told David Russell in a letter that students at Oxford and Cambridge were disillusioned at the inability of their elders to "preserve world conditions without the constant danger of war." David Russell replied: "St Andrews, I believe, was the only university in Britain that refused to approve of the suggestion that they should refuse to fight in defence of their King and Country."

He reminisced:

As far back as 1903, when I had the privilege, or misfortune, to travel with the Thyssens [the German steelmaking dynasty] I was told by a friend who lived with the family that in all gatherings of German officers the one subject of conversation was war with Britain; and when Professor Kay [of St Andrews] was at one of the universities only two or three years before the war, the professors expressed their sympathy for the misfortunes that would befall the professors in Britain when the inevitable clash of arms came.

In April Pecorini wrote to David Russell:

There are very few people in this spinning world who act with such love and kindness towards his fellow boarders . . . therefore I cannot help thinking of you and of a "cara avis." And this much more so in this time of war, when hate and not love seem to be the strong ruler, and I am sure you also, like myself, cannot help suffering infinite sorrow.

His country house was at Bassano del Grappa, only an hour from Venice, and he wanted the Russells to go out in the autumn. "Your boys would love the climbing of Mount Grappa, where the Italians won their decisive victory in 1918. Your lady would like the garden."

Tudor Pole had a new business venture, called Hyganic. "I am investigating an ingenious system for reducing house and street waste products and sewage into a first class antiseptic organic fertiliser, through the action of natural ferment and air pressure alone. This may be the true solution of the sewage and waste product problem of the world's cities."

But Constantinople was constantly in his thoughts, and he warned David Russell: "Every year that passes us by seems to bring nearer another world cataclysm and we should not allow the slow and orderly progress of archaeological research to blind our vision to the need for speed in matters pertaining to the Quest itself." David Russell wrote to his friend: "I have always had the feeling, on my own part, of unpreparedness. Sometimes I have thought that it will be my sons who will play the part I am trying to play now."

However, the excavations continued in the summer of 1936. A maharajah was in residence at the Palace Hotel, where Baxter was staying, and there was hope that he would visit the mosaic and perhaps make a financial contribution to the work. In June 1936 Bernhard Gauer from Dusseldorf, the foremost mosaic expert in Europe, estimated the cost of lifting out, cleaning, relaying and restoring about 250 square metres of mosaic, bringing it up to Museum standard, at £3400. But it was too expensive for the Walker Trust. The possibility of covering in the mosaic under a building was again under discussion, and David Russell hoped that the authorities would help with the expense.

But these were decisions for the future. Baxter was preoccupied with following the mosaic passage, no matter how many maharajahs were in Constantinople. At the end of June he wrote to David Russell: "On Friday I uncovered about a square yard, without getting any definite pattern. But the interesting thing is that the direction of those shell-like shapes is changed: instead of lying at right angles to the Hippodrome, they now point towards it. Does this mean that the passage is turning?" He warned: "The rest of this summer's work will probably be prosaic, rather than exciting; but the mosaic at any rate will be a window-dressing piece."

Young David was out in Constantinople that summer. David and Alison Russell went out in July. The dig was beginning to look like an established presence in Constantinople. Huts for the workers had been completed, and there were the usual emergencies. Big

Ahmet, one of the "characters" in the squad went down with appendicitis, and another worker was put out of action with sunstroke. Increasingly worried about the expense, and by Baxter's careless bookkeeping, David Russell suggested that the marble overlaying the mosaic could be kept and sold as paperweights to bring in a small income.

The Turkish authorities had relaid the road between St Sophia and the Walker Trust excavations, in the hope that the new king, Edward VIII, would want to see the uncovered mosaics during his visit to Constantinople in early September, but he spent too long in St Sophia, and the diggers were disappointed.

Back in Fife, on 9th September 1936 30 Tullis Russell employees, heads of departments and those with long service to the company went by charabanc to Silverburn, where a congratulatory address was made to David F. O. Russell on his coming of age. He was presented with a silver salver and a 12 bore side-lock shotgun, and received a walnut desk from the staff. The spokesman for the workers told him:

We realise that the conduct of business interests for a number of years past has been beset with difficulties, and it seems probable that for some years to come the problems of industrial leadership will demand that courage and determination to succeed, which we are so well aware are characteristic of your much beloved father. We should therefore like to express to you, Sir, today, that whatever the future may bring, you yourself will have the whole-hearted support of us all in the conduct of the Firm's business.

Baxter returned to St Andrews for the new term, and that October Pat went to the university to study modern history, philosophy, chemistry, English literature, French and economics. Like his brother he was destined for the family firm, but their father believed that they should have a breadth of education so that, as he had done, they could develop interests beyond papermaking.

David Russell took an equally close interest in the development of his daughters. In her late teens, Sheila read *Desert Encounter*, "an adventurous journey through Italian Africa" by Knud Holmboe. She hurried to her father's study to tell him that she wanted to be a Mohammedan. As always when a member of his family came in he put down his pen immediately. "That's very interesting, my girlie," he said. "Come with me." He led her through to his book room, climbed the steps and took down a copy of the *Koran*. "Take it, and after you've read it we'll talk about it," he told her.

David and Alison Russell (centre, front) with the staff of Silverburn House in 1936.

Autumn 1936 was a royal season, with the Duke of Kent at St Andrews in November. The Russells listened with sadness to the abdication broadcast of Edward VIII at Silverburn on 11th December. David Russell wrote to Pecorini that month, thanking him for his kind remarks about David's coming of age. "You will understand how much I am looking forward to the time when he will have completed his studies at St Andrews and will be with me at the Mills. I hope that with the coming of spring you will have the blessing of new health and renewed vigour." But two days later a telegram announced Pecorini's death. Despite business problems David Russell had found the Count a warm and civilised human being, and Pecorini had admired the business and spiritual integrity of his Fife friend. He left David Russell a little wooden statuette that had apparently been unearthed in the Aureliana land development, a reminder that there was more to life than making a profit.

In January 1937 there was a serious flu epidemic. The Russells at Silverburn were afflicted, and the mills badly affected. But as always, David Russell found something to occupy his mind while he recovered. For some time he had been preparing an appeal for funds to recondition the farm of Burg on the west coast of the island of Mull. Burg had become the property of the National Trust for Scotland, of which David Russell was a founder member, and on the executive council. He wrote to Tudor Pole:

> It is distressing to see all these lands becoming derelict, and we are hopeful that the work we are planning to do on the Burg may help others in the district. A great deal of land in the west of Mull is going derelict, and I am most anxious, if possible, to show that it can be reconditioned upon an economic basis.

The problem was sheep disease caused by bracken and poor soil, and also the absence of cattle, which keep down bracken. David Russell prevailed on the West of Scotland College of Agriculture to start a pilot project to eradicate bracken and improve the land.

The Pilgrim Trust was asked to give financial help for Burg, where there is a fossil tree estimated to be 50 million years old. The Trust gave £500 for the repair of the buildings and the improvement of the roads, covering expenditure for the first few years and relieving David Russell's mind. He was also one of the prime movers in getting the battlefield of Culloden conveyed to the National Trust for Scotland.

His house on Iona, and the Highlands were a constant concern. He felt that the countryside was being depopulated, and that the natural leaders, the crofters, were going to the cities because of the economic penalties of living in the country. "As you go further north, where the conditions become less dependent upon all the artificialities of modern civilisation, you get to a greater extent what you call the qualities of independence or leadership." But there were also changes nearer home. "Children from the country places in Fife are being taken into St Andrews and other places by bus for their education, and there form the town habits—cinemas, etc—and they can rarely go back to the quiet of country life."

In March 1937 David Russell took a restorative Hellenic cruise with his family, sailing from Toulon. In January he had told Tudor Pole: "From an archaeological point of view, this year's work should be productive in determining our position in relation to the Great Palace as a whole." But Tudor Pole fretted. "Have they started work yet in the Near East?" he enquired in May. David Russell replied with a cutting from *The Times* on the 18th of that month. It stated that "The operations are again financed by Dr David Russell, of the Walker Trust, St Andrews." He told Tudor Pole:

I wrote to the Editor, taking strong exception to its wording. I have written to him before to impress upon him the importance of referring to these excavations as the Walker Trust (St Andrews) Excavations, and also the importance of omitting any reference to my name. I take particular exception to its being said that the expedition is being financed by us. As yet the [foreign] editor (Deakin) has not acknowledged my letter.

Nurse Nisbet of the Artificial Sunlight Clinic had first met David Russell in 1921. In June 1937 she wrote to him:

I feel I owe you almost everything that makes life worth living; the books you gave me to read and your own attitude to life; the happy atmosphere of your home and your own and Mrs Russell's friendship and all the care and consideration I have had at your hands; the very work I loved to do, and all your lovely gifts and kind thoughts that are too many to write about.

Young David began work in the mills in October 1937, in the costing department, much to his father's satisfaction. Though David Russell senior was now 65 he was not contemplating retirement, but he was pleased to have one of his sons with him. The healthy life of the mills went on, with free mid-morning milk given out.

On holiday at Taormina, Italy, in 1938, David Russell wrote to Tudor Pole: "Hitler's bluff must be called before long or Germany will overrun Europe and make France's position untenable. We must make a very real and serious effort in 1938 to fulfil the Q work at the House of Justinian. I don't think 1939 will be possible and after that, still less possible."

In late March David Russell was planting shrubs at his house on Iona. Tudor Pole had advised him to keep up his grass stocks at Markinch in view of the international situation. But Tudor Pole was getting increasingly annoyed by the way in which Baxter had taken over the Constantinople excavations to the exclusion of the Quest. David Russell wrote candidly: "I must confess that I have felt all along that the trouble really has been that you have never trusted me sufficiently. There is no doubt whatever in my mind that, although you held your work to be of world importance, it has been blocked by the intrusion of personalities . . ."

Friends in influential places briefed Tudor Pole on the international situation in May 1938. He passed on their comments to David Russell: "Italy is becoming Hitler's pawn. Hitler will welcome 'friendly talks' with Britain, to gain breathing time and to try to prevent alarm. But nothing is to be allowed to obstruct

Germany's outward march, penetrating by her influence Czechoslovakia, Hungary, Romania, the Balkans."

David Russell had always been interested in Gaelic culture. In 1938 he donated the Queen Elizabeth Coronation Trophy, to be presented annually at the Mod, "for the purpose of encouraging the cultivation of the language and music of the Scottish Celts." It was first awarded at the 41st Mod, held in Dundee in September. The hand-beaten silver shield was designed by Alec and Euphemia Ritchie of Iona, and made by a Glasgow craftsman.

Trees were another of David Russell's great loves. He planted them at Silverburn, and took hundreds of photographs of conifers to observe their growth patterns. At the expanding mills new buildings were designed so that trees did not have to be cut down. He was also a member of the Men of the Trees organisation. Its founder, Richard St Barbe Baker, came from a family of tree lovers, tree growers and explorers, and had worked as a forest officer in Africa. He found the Kikuyu people burning the forests to grow food, moving on every few years as the soil perished in the sun, literally making deserts. But by means of a new dance ceremony he was able to interest the tribe in tree planting. This prompted him to found the organisation.

The Men of the Trees grew into a worldwide concern, and in the summer of 1938 petitioned the Prime Minister to revise the forestry policy in Great Britain with "a clear definition as to what land should be used for agriculture, for national parks and for forestry," urging that "the forest land be naturally regenerated where possible, or planted in mixed forests with the object of providing a sustained yield for all time."

Tudor Pole wrote to David Russell on 24th December: "It will be the test of a long and loyal friendship, and sincerity, if you and I are able to recognise that the views held by each other are honestly held, even if the paths we each believe should be followed are not the same path."

In January 1939 David Russell wrote despairingly to Tudor Pole: "Why can't we put the fear of death on our enemies? Perhaps you will hardly call this a pacific attitude, but we have to do something to change the attitude of the people, or is it the *press?*" But a tragedy at home took all his attention. His brother Robert died on 4th February 1939 at nine o'clock in the evening from septic pneumonia. It was a peaceful passing. David Russell had always been so patient and understanding with him, and Tudor Pole provided a moving epitaph: "He was so abnormally sensitive, like a raw wound that could not heal. His whole life was really a clearing up through sorrow and pain of past mistakes."

Tudor Pole asked that in the event of war he be sent back to Palestine and Egypt for intelligence work. But the threat of hostilities was not affecting Tullis Russell business. In July 1939 the mills were as busy as they had ever been, running almost continuously over the weekend, including Sunday, though trade returns showed other mills running considerably below normal output. As a precaution, at the end of August Tudor Pole covered an esparto cargo for Grangemouth for War Risks.

19

The Expropriation Question

Baxter had begun his third season's work on the Great Palace site on 4th May 1937 with over 100 workmen under him. On his 1936 visit David Russell's discussions with the Vali about expropriation had been relaxed, since he understood that the area had been set aside for a national museum. As a gesture of goodwill the Walker Trust lodged a deposit of £200, but it was returned. When David Russell went out again in July 1937 Baxter told him that Bey Aziz Ogan, the director of the Museum of Antiquities, wanted to see him about expropriation, but it was not raised at their meeting. However, in a letter of 9th August J. P. Perkins, the Constantinople lawyer who was handling Walker Trust affairs, warned: "I am afraid that there can be no doubt whatever as to the liability of the person excavating to pay for the value of the land where the excavations are taking place, whenever expropriation becomes necessary."

James Watt, David Russell's shrewd lawyer, suggested offering £2000 to clear up the entire expropriation obligation. Perkins wired on 28th October:

One hand failure fulfil your definite obligation under Turkish Antiquities Law must result cessation work and possibly also diplomatic representations and action damages here or Scotland. Other hand while £2000 certainly insufficient, consider price will be well below 36,000 liras. Please cable final instructions, Museum waiting decision.

David Russell wrote to Anthony Eden, the Foreign Secretary, but the reply was not encouraging. "Although Mr Eden is not familiar with all the facts, the matter seems to him to turn entirely on Turkish law, and if Turkish law requires that archaeologists should bear the cost of the expropriation of the land on which they excavate, he cannot suggest any grounds on which the Walker Trust could claim exemption." He did, however, offer the ambassador's help in Ankara if Perkins considered that there were extenuating circumstances which would justify a claim for the mitigation of the law. Following discussions between Perkins and the Embassy, the Prime Minister Neville Chamberlain urged the Walker Trust to set in motion a definite claim for the mitigation of the law.

In January 1938 Tudor Pole wrote: "I feel more strongly than I can say that a Q. move forward is now inevitable and that there is no longer any obstacle that cannot be removed, or which need hold us up any longer." He suggested that the Walker Trust should be released from its obligations at the House of Justinian, and that the Quest team would arrange its own excavation. As he reminded David Russell in April: "The concession was secured as a 'cloak' for Q. work and was inspired by it; there would have been no concession had there been no Quest."

In February 1938 Professor David Talbot Rice of Edinburgh University urged David Russell to publish a comprehensive record of the dig to date for the benefit of Byzantine scholars. It was now evident to David Russell that outside finance would be necessary to continue the Great Palace excavations over several years. An archaeological institute was needed, he told Baxter.

I told him [Talbot Rice] of the talks we had with the Ambassador, and expressed the opinion that, unless we could secure adequate support for the establishment and endowment of an Institute or School in Istanbul, which would mean the guarantee of continuance of work over an extended period, we should have to endeavour to get sufficient funds to carry on the work over a minimum of three or four years. This summer and next winter will have to be devoted to these problems, and to the determination of our future policy.

In May David Russell drew up three clear objectives for the 1938 season in Constantinople for Baxter's guidance. First, the Walker Trust needed to reach agreement with the Museum, the Vali and the Government that the responsibility for expropriation, present and future, would be taken over by them. Second, Baxter was to plan, with these three authorities, a programme for the opening up of the area between the Blue Mosque and the terrace walls, so that it could become an "archaeological quarter" or a "national monument." Third, during these negotiations Baxter would undertake only the work necessary to fulfil the terms of the permit, to meet the convenience of visitors and to complete for publication a report on the three year dig. David Russell wanted individual members of the dig to write chapters on their speciality subjects such as the mosaic and pottery. It was to be one of the most comprehensive works of scholarship on the Great Palace ever published, and it was hoped that it could be brought out by Oxford University Press in October.

Baxter arrived in Constantinople in May for the season. The huts were blistered with the sun, and he had them repainted dark green. He replanted the annuals in the garden, and had the place weeded. A local proprietor, Abdulkadir, was in conflict with the excavators, demanding large compensation for a wall made unstable by digging. Baxter had the workers fill up the hole with earth and stones, and Abdulkadir was apparently satisfied.

The Vali advised Baxter that the best way of dealing with the expropriation question was to ask for a Government Commission instead of trying to negotiate with individual owners. But there was a new town planning scheme which could threaten the site of the mosaic.

Baxter never found it easy to work with others, and there were clashes with members of the dig. In March Dr Günter Martiny, an archaeologist and architect on the dig, had sent David Russell a damning report on Baxter, headed: "Professor Baxter is incapable of directing the excavation in the Arasta-Sokak." Martiny claimed that Baxter knew nothing about excavation, and had no interest in the day-to-day running of the dig, though he took visitors round and gave them "wholly false" information. He accused Baxter of being unfair to the workmen and delaying the payment of both tradesmen and taxes. "He reserves the best treatment for those of whom he is afraid."

Baxter countered: "He (Martiny) is too much of an intriguer and mischief-maker to be of any advantage, and if he is to be continued beyond the month, I am going to resign now. Also I want that matter of my fee fixed soon. Please do what you can for this." David Russell wired back that it was "absolutely essential" for Martiny to work on the dig to complete his report for future publication.

Baxter went to Ankara to consult with the authorities about expropriation, and there was hope that the Walker Trust's obligations would be relaxed. Meantime he was advised not to enter areas belonging to new proprietors, and to clear up and secure the ground, especially towards the Blue Mosque.

There were distinguished visitors to the dig, including the uncle of the King of Iraq, accompanied by a Foreign Office official from Ankara whom Baxter had met the previous week. The official was responsible for the preparation of the Turkish pavilion in the New York exhibition the following year, and wanted to display finds

THE EXPROPRIATION QUESTION

from the dig, painted life-size on glass with soft lighting behind. Baxter reported the uncovering of "A bit more of that most easterly part of the mosaic—another foot. Evidently a house or large building, but the comforting thing is that the mosaic goes right on, under the street." He concluded by saying that there was no urgent reason for David Russell to come out to Constantinople.

Baxter was about to have another distinguished visitor. Through Tudor Pole David Russell had met Prince Frederick Ernst of Saxe-Altenburg. The Prince, who was in his thirties, had been working in Mexico, principally with US archaeologists, on Mayan sites. He had spent much time following up the connections between the Celtic church and the missions from Iona and Ireland to Germany and elsewhere on the continent. He had toured Scotland and stayed a night at Silverburn. Tudor Pole told David Russell that the Quest group had been awaiting the arrival of one from a "long way over the sea" and that he had "little doubt intuitively that Prince F. fills the role and has been preparing and being prepared for cooperation with us all, ever since his 17th year." He had another qualification: the spirit BB, now unveiled by Tudor Pole as Prince Oleg, had been a great friend of the family at Altenburg.

The Prince went out to Constantinople in July 1938, with complete access to the dig granted by David Russell. Baxter judged him "well-read and intelligent." But he was suspicious of him and apparently warned Martiny that their visitor was a spiritualist. The Prince told Tudor Pole that Baxter was no longer persona grata with the Turkish authorities or the local people.

For three years David Russell had defended Baxter against criticism. But his patience was wearing thin, and he wrote to him: "You refer to Martiny as an intriguer and a mischief maker. You will remember that in the autumn of 1936 you accused me of intriguing with the Turkish authorities, without the least shred of evidence. Such accusations should not be made lightly, and without hearing the other man's point of view."

Once again there were emergencies to be dealt with on the dig. A workman from the previous year turned up with a leg complaint, claiming damages. But despite such problems, the dig had become a popular place to work, and every morning up to 40 workmen lingered at the gate, hoping for a day's labour, even though higher daily rates were being paid elsewhere in the city.

Baxter wanted the mosaic site to become a tourist attraction for visitors arriving on the English cruise ships, who would pay a small fee and buy the postcards that David Russell had had printed. The professor was feeling the heat, day and night, and he was fretting about money. In early July he wrote to David Russell: "The essentials seem to me to be that my work and responsibilities be not unworthily recompensed, that the amount and times of payment for my services be stated, the extent of my powers in the choice and direction of the staff be defined, and my part in the publication of the report."

Baxter went on: "I cannot continue, as I have done in the past two years, to give my time and my name only to be out of pocket, and that seriously." He claimed that as he and his wife were being driven home from Silverburn one evening, David Russell had agreed to join him in the editing of the Great Palace volume, "you taking charge of the photographs and drawings, I of the letterpress. Up till now I have been acting in the good faith that this arrangement still stands."

Then he came to the crux. "[The book] is my only means of justifying to the learned world my absorption in this work during the last five or six years, and it is also the only means of continuing among the people here that authority and prestige which is necessary for the future of the dig." He asked David Russell to send a wire: "either Accept or Refuse."

Baxter did not appear to see that his relationship with David Russell was being damaged by such demands. David Russell was becoming increasingly worried about the mounting expense of the dig, with the expropriation question not yet settled. The excavations appeared to necessitate the diversion of a road, but David Russell was worried about the security of adjoining buildings, and told Baxter that the work would have to be postponed till the following year.

There was criticism of the excavations in the local press. The *Son Posta* protested that the dig was approaching too near to the foundations of the Blue Mosque, and many official and private visitors came to see for themselves. At the end of July at a meeting with the Vali Baxter pointed out that he was about to close down the dig. The Vali made a phone call to try to speed up the expropriation decision. Iron objects, including arrowheads, a lance head, and what were probably iron masks were found on the dig, with some coins and a quantity of pottery, "of considerable value and interest," Baxter reported. He was obtaining beams to support weak walls.

He inspected the House of Justinian and noted that it had deteriorated even further in a year. Martiny recommended that

THE EXPROPRIATION QUESTION

The depth of the excavations of the Great Palace, Istanbul.

bushes should be cleared from the walls and roof, and that holes in the foundation wall be filled with cement for safety. It was 86 degrees in the shade, and the Prince was spending a lot of time at the main dig, getting on Baxter's nerves. The excavation had closed officially on 31st July, but there were still about 10 to 15 days of work, mostly earth moving, to be done.

David Russell wrote to Baxter on 4th October 1938:

> The future, as you know, is full of uncertainties. We have hoped for financial help from many quarters. It is impossible as yet to say what the position may be next year. If no financial support should become available, it will be very difficult to carry on; and, even if we should be prepared now to risk further outlays in the hope that support might become available next year, the ultimate decision must depend upon the settlement of the question of expropriation.

He rebuked Baxter. "What has distressed me perhaps more than anything else has been your failure to get on with those who have worked with you." He warned: "now the question may well be asked whether it will ever be possible to find an archaeological staff with whom you could work in harmonious co-operation." He ended: "It is not I who can give you peace, but yourself. You have had a great opportunity, and you have failed to rise to the demands it has made upon you."

Baxter replied: "If our relations have grown tangled and unhappy, it has been by no deliberate choice of mine; I should be only too happy to repair what is possible and to recover our original trust and happiness." He wrote on Boxing Day 1938: "The whole of this Turkish experience has been a broadening of life with great new interests, friendships and ties; it has been, taking it all in all, a great enrichment." He blamed Tudor Pole for causing trouble. "You will remember that in a talk I had with the Principal [Sir James Irvine], he had expressed his distrust of TP and rather warned me against him, saying that he had never felt much confidence in TP."

Kemal Ataturk, the first President of Turkey, died on 10th November 1938. He had modernised the legal and educational systems of his country, and encouraged the citizens to adopt a European way of life. David and Alison Russell had met him, and he had talked enthusiastically about the Great Palace dig. The President's wife had the Russells to lunch and sent round to their hotel a gift of several thousand cigarettes with KH (Kemal Hanim) embossed on them in gold. On the way home, David Russell offered them to the customs officials. They almost fell down to worship him before wrapping the cigarettes in their handkerchiefs as precious souvenirs.

As well as losing confidence in Baxter, David Russell was also beginning to doubt Tudor Pole. Along with Frederick Leveaux, he had got together with two new Quest members, Prince Frederick, and the Earl of Ossery, to put pressure on David Russell to begin work next season on the House of Justinian site, or else the new group would have to "send representatives to Turkey early in the New Year with a view to securing the grant of a new permit in respect of the H of J site." David Russell's Christmas message to Tudor Pole was: "Have none of you any trust, any faith?"

In January 1939 Baxter proposed Bey Fethi Okyar, the Turkish ambassador in London from 1934 to 1938, for an honorary degree from St Andrews University. The ambassador was involved in negotiations over the Great Palace site, and wanted to give the St Andrews team a more permanent right to excavate in the whole area in which it was interested, instead of having to go through the formality of renewing the permit every second year. Baxter wrote to David Russell: "I feel very strongly that our requests to Fethi Bey should be in [his] hands a day or two before the Senate's letter [telling him of the honour], otherwise he may think that we are using the proposed degree as a lever."

Baxter planned to go out to Turkey in March to ask the authorities to slow up the negotiations for completing expropriation so that the Walker Trust could get a better exchange rate. "As for the Dig itself, we ought simply to confirm our undisputed possession of the whole area for a long period of years, until all work is terminated on the site, no matter by what agency. Even if others contribute, it should be through the Walker Trust and not outside it."

At the end of April Baxter was staying at the National Liberal Club, London, having heard that the House of Commons was pessimistic about Hitler leaving any doors open for negotiation. "I have been repeatedly advised to remain at home," he told David Russell. But he had arranged an interview with a member of the Cabinet to get guidance.

It must have reassured him, because he went out to Constantinople in May 1939 and met the new Vali. He asked for a permit for the Great Palace site for five to seven years. There was heartening news about expropriation. Only three proprietors had produced allowable claims, with several others in process, and there was no immediate need to make payments. "There is general satisfaction at Fethi Bey's honour [his St Andrews doctorate] and Mr Perkins is sure it will be of the utmost value to have his support," he wrote to David Russell.

The dig was untidy. There were a lot of weeds, and the mosaic was very dirty. Also the visitors book was full. Baxter reported that he would cash cheques at the most favourable rate he could obtain. On 8th June he telegraphed to David Russell on Iona: "Have now seen all relevant authorities, progress very satisfactory. All rights conceded our area." Fethi Bey had smoothed the way. The Walker Trust was to receive the usual permit for two years, but with it a personal letter from the new Minister of Public Instruction assuring the St Andrews team of solid and continued rights in the area with which the Trust was concerned.

The damp weather had made the mosaic "greenish." Baxter had planted a dozen packets of seeds of climbing nasturtium to cover some of the "uglier" walls of the dig. He found the young plants well up. He reported to David Russell: "There is a renewed goodwill and friendliness towards our country as a whole, and this has profited us much." He added: "I have had three enquiries about cheque-paper and newsprint . . . there is so great a desire now to buy British . . ." But David Russell was not aware that the St Andrews professor was involved in a London-based trading company interested in doing business in all kinds of commodities with Turkey, import and export, including the settlement of refugee workers from Nazi Germany.

Baxter was preparing to leave Constantinople, and he told David Russell that a small amount of work would have to be put in that year to meet the conditions of the permit. "I think you will be satisfied, for we have secured our rights in the area, for a period of five or seven years, and the collaboration we hope for, though one of tactful negotiation, seems not too far off."

David Russell did not want further work undertaken that year till the expropriation negotiations were concluded satisfactorily. But Baxter went back out in July. Frederick Leveaux the Quest member was in Ankara, and Baxter wired David Russell from Constantinople on 13th July: ". . . received from Ankara notification of his [Leveaux's] application on behalf of British Byzantine Archaeological Committee for permit at 'House' under the supervision of G. Spurrell Mileham, alleging our recent inactivity there and sufficient preoccupation with mosaic for the desirability early opening whole Palace site."

THE EXPROPRIATION QUESTION

Leveaux visited the Great Palace site and explained in a letter to Baxter that the Archaeological Committee was only a month old, and had been constituted "for the purpose of (inter alia) the furtherance of Byzantine research in all its branches, and in particular, for the undertaking, within the area of ancient Byzantium, of excavations, with the concurrence of the Turkish authorities."

The president of the Committee was the Marquis of Lothian, ambassador designate to the USA. The chairman was the Earl of Ossery. Among the Committee members were Professor David Talbot Rice; Professor Thomas Whittemore, who was engaged upon the restoration of mosaics in St Sophia; and the mining engineer E. W. Janson, a cousin of Lord Lloyd. Janson had become a Quest member. G. Spurrell Mileham was an archaeological architect, who would act as field director for the first season, with Talbot Rice probably acting in the same capacity at a later date.

Tudor Pole was joint treasurer. It was the most severe test to date of the friendship between him and David Russell. David Russell warned him that if anything went wrong in Constantinople as a result of the new group's intervention, he, Tudor Pole, would be solely responsible.

Leveaux made it clear that the first season's plan was to undertake an archaeological investigation of the part of the site of the House of Justinian between the railway and the sea, making soundings and then excavating. He told Baxter in a letter that he had received "the assurance of the Turkish Government that they are fully satisfied with regard to the Committee."

Baxter saw his position threatened. But he had his hands full dealing with potentially serious falls of stones and earth from the arcades on to the mosaic, which was poorly protected by a covering of straw and sand. He asked David Russell for a "contractual relation with the Walker Trust in writing" so that his position could be secured. "For the past few years I have simply trusted to your word, but what can I show if my health be impaired here or I meet with an accident or am detained from home by war?"

He pointed out that his word was David Russell's only guarantee of the permit. "On receipt of your undertaking, I shall at once smash their [the Archaeological Committee's] chances." It was a critical moment in Baxter's career; he claimed to have two tempting opportunities to leave St Andrews for academic posts elsewhere, and if he accepted one he would have to surrender or transfer his permit.

Baxter entered a series of exhausting meetings with the Turkish authorities. Lord Lothian was trying to exert diplomatic pressure. On 21st July Baxter sent David Russell a wire: "Final decision as predicted permit concession. Inalienably ours Baxter." The St Andrews professor had defeated the opposition. David Russell was prepared to let the British Byzantine Archaeological Committee excavate the House of Justinian site, but under the name of the Walker Trust, with the Committee bearing all the financial and legal responsibilities, and with a Trust-approved archaeologist in charge. "I must confess I am not enamoured of collaboration with FL or TP," Baxter told David Russell in a letter from Somerset in August. He added: "If war does come, we must take steps to secure our Turkish rights with a necessary moratorium."

As David Russell holidayed on peaceful Iona that August, war seemed a distant prospect. He had written to the magazine *The Lady* in response to a travel article, rebuking the writer: "It is misleading to say that the people of Iona are extremely poor. They are comparatively speaking comfortably off, and are well-educated and progressive." Now he was about to witness the beginning of a remarkable experiment on Iona, one in which he would play a major part.

20

The Iona Dream

The romantic dream had began in the heady 1920s in a haze of cigar smoke as Angus Robertson, president of An Comunn Gàidhealach and a distinguished Gaelic authority addressed the New York Chamber of Commerce. Civilisation had a debt to repay to the island of Iona for its contribution, he told his audience, some of them well-heeled descendants of cleared Highlanders.

The American Iona Society was formed on a show of dollars, but the 1929 Wall Street crash stopped fund-raising. However, the scheme was revived in the austere 1930s. The plan was to establish a Celtic university or college on the mainland, with the Iona monastic ruins restored to form a place of retreat.

The question as to who first had the idea of rebuilding the Iona ruins has not been answered satisfactorily until now. David Russell would have been the first to insist that it is the realisation of the scheme, and not the identity of the instigator that is important. However, for the sake of historical accuracy it can be stated categorically that it was David Russell's idea. At the end of last century, even before the Cathedral itself was restored, he was photographing the ruins and dreaming about their restoration. When he started the Iona Retreat from 1920, for students from the Scottish divinity halls, he was attracted to the monastic site as a permanent home for the Retreat. The Reverend George MacLeod, who also wanted to restore the ruins as a home for a Community, but at a much later date, was one of the tutors on the 1930 Retreat.

In 1931 David Russell had commissioned Reginald Fairlie to prepare plans for the restoration of the ruins. In March 1933 the Very Reverend Charles Warr, minister of St Giles' Cathedral, Edinburgh, and a trustee of the Iona Cathedral Trust, had written to David Russell: "Some day I hope your dreams will be realised, but these are difficult times in which to make such an appeal. Nevertheless, the success of your persistence regarding St Margaret's Chapel is a good augury for your ambitions regarding the Isle of the West!"

The Fairlie plans were requested by the Iona Cathedral Trust in late 1935 because there was apparently a race on to rebuild the monastic ruins, as Warr explained to David Russell in a letter of 21st October.

> The Trust have had a communication from the American Iona Society in New York, asking if they are prepared to consider that Society rebuilding the ruins and restoring them as near as possible to their original form, and adapting them as may be suitable as a retreat of worship, meditation, study, and instruction. We are going to give careful consideration to this offer, which contains one or two stipulations which will require negotiation. Should anything come of it, I am in great hopes that it might be worked in with the Rev. George MacLeod's scheme for a Community settlement, and I am asking the Trustees to allow him to attend the Meeting when the American offer is considered.

In mid November MacLeod prepared a confidential memorandum on the rebuilding of the Iona monastic buildings.

> Since the public press notices regarding the Celtic College on the mainland with its "spiritual centre" still in Iona, I have had a talk with Mr Angus Robertson, the Inspirer of the whole project. While of course I cannot speak for him, nor could he speak for the American Iona Society, it is worth saying, unofficially, that he appeared to look on such a scheme as outlined above as in no way antithetical to his conceived purposes but complementary to them.

David Russell had an agency collect the many press reports on the American Iona Society's plan. The four preferred sites for the mainland academic institution were: Dunstaffnage Castle, reputed resting place of the Stone of Destiny; Benderloch, associated with the Ossianic saga; Ardchattan Priory, founded by monks from the island of Lismore; and Dunkeld Cathedral, site of a monastery associated with Columba. Dr John Finley of the *New York Times*, vice-president of the American Iona Society, had briefed David Russell about the scheme, which was reputed to be backed by several million dollars.

David Russell wrote to Tudor Pole in early December 1935:

> The idea of building a university on Iona had naturally been ridiculed by the other universities in Scotland, and obviously it would be a hopeless proposition. The suggestion now is that a college should be built somewhere near Oban, or elsewhere in the west or north, and that the monastic buildings at Iona should be restored. Upon being told this

confidentially, I immediately set about having reproductions made of drawings made some years ago, so that they might be available at a meeting of trustees which was held a few days ago, and I learnt only on Friday night that there is some prospect of such a scheme developing.

What is much more interesting than the idea of restoring the building itself is that those who are really most interested in its fulfilment have as their main object the establishment of a retreat and training centre for the clergy of Scotland. It is becoming more and more fully realised that some other training than the university training now being given is necessary for the spiritual welfare of the clergy.

One point that was emphasised in the conversation I had last Friday night was that the idea of this being an American scheme should drop out, and that it should take the wider aspect of making an appeal to the Scottish people, wherever situated throughout the world, i.e., there would be an endeavour to bring in Colonial interests.

The following year Fairlie's plans were exhibited at the Royal Scottish Academy's annual show of painting, sculpture and architecture in Edinburgh. Among those who viewed them is a man whose name has never featured in the history of the restoration of the Iona ruins, but who must now be given credit for his contribution. Clare Vyner of the Northampton family who had Torloisk estate on Mull, was owner of the famed Fountains Abbey near Ripon in Yorkshire, said to be the largest and finest monastic ruin in Britain.

Vyner went to see Reginald Fairlie, to propose a scheme. He had connections with social service affairs south of the border, and he suggested that the Iona ruins could be restored and used as a centre for social work in the Western Isles. Vyner promised to give financial support and to bring his influence to bear on the realisation of the scheme which, he believed, could be linked to the Church of Scotland. The year (1937) in which the Moderator (the Reverend Dugald Macfarlane) was a native of the Western Isles would be an opportune one in which to launch the scheme.

An intrigued David Russell received a copy of the Vyner scheme. He had written:

The training I visualise would be definitely undenominational and no suggestion that they were being trained in any way for the Ministry, but there would naturally be a certain amount of theological study, as it is essential that the two should be linked together. The major portion of their training should be to enable them when they leave Iona to be useful servants to the people amongst whom they are going to work, and just to name a few of the points which could be included, these would be health and hygiene, agriculture, fishing and gardening, weaving, etc. The period of training limited, say, to two years, that pay should not be expected, but all reasonable expenses met.

On completing their time on Iona, these students or "missionaries" would be appointed to different parishes or districts and there they would carry on the work which at the present time is very largely left undone, as being no one's job, and is best visualised by that which is done by such people as the English Society of Friends and the Brotherhood Movement.

George MacLeod wrote to David Russell from his parish of Govan, Glasgow, in November 1936.

Thank you for sending me the Vyner papers. I am frankly not impressed with the picture. Undenominational Social Service has had its days. Stormier clouds are on the horizon and what alone will stand up to the next two decades is The Faith.

I intend this early spring to make up my mind finally whether I am "in on" an experiment beginning at Iona. If I am, I shall claim that it will be of firmer stuff than this spreading of arts and crafts to the (largely denuded) Western Isles. I shall go for Fifty Thousand Pounds right away, if not from one man (there are latent Nuffields north of the Border) then from no more than five. Even then more will be required, and would come, as the work evolved.

If I am not on: then it is no concern of mine what happens to the buildings; but I would privately prognosticate dereliction for a vaguely Christian Social Scheme in those stern walls. I rather think the very stones would cry out.

David Russell arranged a meeting between Clare Vyner, Charles Warr and Principal Harry Miller of St Mary's College, St Andrews University, at the Northern Club, Edinburgh, on 12th January 1937. MacLeod must have been attracted to at least part of Vyner's plan, for the following month they met in Govan, with the object of drawing up a scheme for submission to the Iona Cathedral Trustees. Following the meeting Vyner reported to David Russell:

The major issue "Iona" seems to be very much in MacLeod's hands. His idea of making it a setting off place for a pilgrimage of national scope may be excellent. If he goes ahead with his idea, it will be a very alive business and obviously is a concrete scheme and as such is probably the one to hope for.

David Russell wanted to incorporate Burg Farm on Mull within the Iona scheme, but Vyner thought that impractical. "One would do better with ground on the Ross of Mull which is so much nearer," he advised. Though Vyner's scheme was not taken up, it must be pointed out that his idea of trained people going out from Iona was close to MacLeod's scheme of ministers going out to work in the deprived cities. Also, MacLeod later acquired the fishing station of Camas on the Ross of Mull, as the type of training place that Vyner had proposed, the Social Work departments of Glasgow and other areas sending young people there to work out their frustrations in labour and prayer.

But there were forces conspiring to frustrate MacLeod and his supporters. In 1937 the Duke of Argyll's permission was evidently sought for the building of a big hotel at Martyrs Bay, where the first Danish slaughter of monks had occurred on Iona. David Russell wrote to Robert Hurd the architect: "It is rumoured that the Duke is opposed to the idea, but his heir has been approached, and will give permission as soon as he is able to do so." This would certainly have destroyed the peace and seclusion that was essential for MacLeod's scheme.

But in March 1938 Hurd informed David Russell of a much bigger development.

I have now heard from the Marquess of Bute privately, that he has seen the Duke of Argyll and asked if he might purchase the island of Iona. He was met by a definite refusal. In view of this, Lord Bute suggests that there is nothing to be lost by putting down our fears and objections in a Memorandum, and quite bluntly sending it to the Duke of Argyll and if necessary, should we not obtain a satisfactory reply, publishing it later. Any such move, I am certain, would receive the most overwhelming support from the general public, which would soon show the Argyll family that they cannot play fast and loose without hearing about it. I return herewith the copy of the Valuation Roll which we lent to Lord Bute.

David Russell knew about the Bute family. John, 3rd Marquess, a man who combined awareness of his aristocratic status with a formidable intellect, had been Rector of St Andrews University from 1892 to 1897. A convert to Catholicism, Bute, who had an interest in the Middle Ages, wanted to restore the Catholic element to St Andrews University by having the teaching seminary of Blairs transferred from Aberdeenshire to St Andrews, a scheme which was opposed by the Catholic authorities. But under the deed of trust, the Iona monastic ruins could not be included in the sale of the island to be turned into a Catholic seminary. Presumably David

Russell thought that Lord Bute would have been a more caring owner of Iona than the Duke of Argyll.

The first meeting of the sponsors of George MacLeod's "Iona Experiment" took place in Edinburgh on 7th April 1938. Sir D. Y. Cameron the artist and David Russell attended, along with divinity professors and ministers. The parish minister on Iona was a sponsor ex officio. David Russell wrote to Tudor Pole on 3rd June 1938: "I think all will go well with George MacLeod's Iona scheme. I scarcely think that difficulties will ever crop up of such seriousness as to hinder the developments he has in view."

In a memorandum which he left among his papers David Russell recalled: "In 1938 Dr George MacLeod asked me if the plans could be used by the Iona Community. I said they were Dr Fairlie's and I could only give that permission provided he agreed. In his reply Dr Fairlie said: 'If Ian Lindsay can be persuaded to take charge, all will be well.'"

Though he had the Trustees' permission and David Russell's plans for the restoration of the Iona buildings, George MacLeod did not have the money. He wrote to the richest man he knew, Sir

Family and friends at Cnocmor, Iona. Left to right: the Very Reverend Andrew Nevile Davidson, minister of Glasgow Cathedral for 27 years; Peggy Martin; Alison Russell; Sheila Russell; Anne Russell; Ian Lindsay, the architect who drew up the original plans for Sir David Russell for the restoration of the monastic buildings on Iona, and who was also architect for the actual rebuilding for a time.

James Lithgow the Clyde shipbuilder, whose yacht came into Iona in the summer. MacLeod asked him for £5000. The battleship builder invited MacLeod to spend the night, and put a proposition which MacLeod often recalled in interviews: "If I give you £5000, will you give up your pacifism?" MacLeod replied: "Not on your life!" He got his £5000.

MacLeod had enough money for one summer's work on Iona. He recruited students from the Scottish theological colleges and ordered the wooden huts in which his Community would live during the restoration. A special service was held in the Cathedral in May 1938. Advance parties arrived on Iona in June, to erect the huts close to the ruins. But the Duke of Argyll did not like MacLeod's restoration scheme, and he withdrew permission to pipe in water from a source outside the area of the sacred buildings.

Holidaying at Cnocmor in the summer of 1938, David Russell could hear the hammers as work went on to put up the huts. But there was a setback: angered that it had not been consulted about the restoration scheme, the Ministry of Works announced that the Iona monastic ruins would be scheduled, and the apprehensive Cathedral Trustees withdrew permission for the summer programme. MacLeod managed to persuade the Ministry of Works to let the huts remain, and agreed not to begin work on the ruins till the following year.

Despite the threat of war, MacLeod's squad returned to Iona for the summer of 1939, to angry complaints that the huts were spoiling the sights of the ruins, and that a motor lorry on the sacred isle was a sacrilege. But young people on Iona wrote to the *Bulletin* newspaper, saying that they were "glad to see this sign of life and adventure in [their] Church, and welcome[d] it as a relief from a great deal of drabness elsewhere."

David Russell's own young people were not on Iona. His son David had joined the Black Watch Territorials in 1938. In July of that year Pat had gone out with a party of eight, mostly from St Andrews University, to the Grenfell Medical Mission in Labrador. It had been founded by Wilfred Grenfell, the selfless medical man and missionary who had built hospitals, schools, co-operative stores and a lumber mill to help the inhabitants on the 1000 mile harsh coastline. Hundreds of young people spent a summer or longer working in the Mission. The St Andrews connection was a strong one, since Sir Wilfred had been Rector of the university from 1928 to 1931.

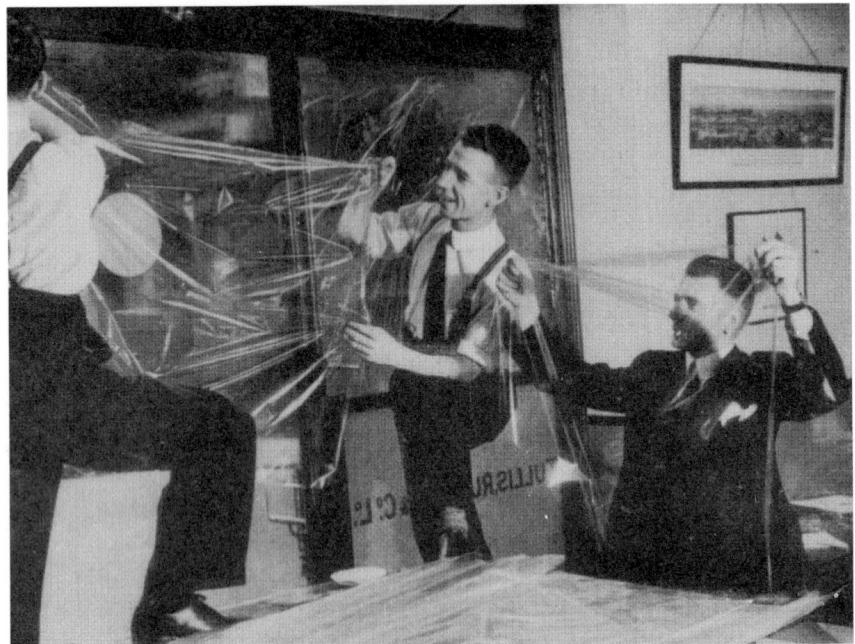

Protecting the windows of Tullis Russell's London office against expected bomb damage, 1939.

Pat came home from Labrador in a cattleship in late August 1939. Tubby Clayton, the founder of the Christian Fellowship Toc H, was with David Russell at Silverburn on 3rd September, the day the Second World War broke out. Clayton went straight to Kirkwall and on to Scapa Flow, taking Pat with him, and discovered that there was no provision of comfort for the thousands of men from all the forces gathered in the chilly north. Friends and the Pilgrim Trust helped; Sheila organised hundreds of boxes of books, games and comforts, particularly for the men in drifters and mine-sweepers on the Northern Patrol. She wanted to be a nurse, but was persuaded to meet an urgent need in the Naval Control office at Methil by joining the WRNS. It was a seven day week.

Young David was the only Black Watch officer at Leuchars Aerodrome, with 48 men under him. Later he was made a signals officer. Tudor Pole's son Christopher was with an anti-aircraft unit; his brother David had motored across France from Grenoble and caught the last civilian steamer from Dieppe on 3rd September. Pat asked Principal Irvine of St Andrews about taking a commission, but was advised that his place was with his father in the mills in the absence of his elder brother.

David, Alison and Sheila Russell watched searchlights from Silverburn in the clear sky, a beautiful but frightening illumination. Three planes from Leuchars took part in the raid on the Kiel Canal and returned, riddled with bullets. While petrol was still available David Russell took a day in the Highlands with his daughters on 14th September. Anne was not going back to Overstone School in Northamptonshire, but instead would be near home at St Leonards School, St Andrews.

Wood pulp cargoes were being sunk. "Have you any news concerning the whereabouts of the *Aberhill*?" Tudor Pole asked anxiously at the end of September. The war was getting closer to home, as David Russell described graphically in a letter to his friend on 18th October.

You have probably read of the raid on the Firth of Forth on Monday. I happened to be writing at Silverburn at the time and heard some heavy firing on the Forth, which is not unusual, but, as the firing was in salvos and irregular, it was obviously not practice firing. Then there was firing to the north and north-east, that is inland, which obviously could not be practice firing. I looked out and saw planes racing away to the east at a high speed, and heard a very loud explosion, which I thought must be a plane come down with all its bombs.

Alison was walking into Leven, and Sheila was on the golf links, but no one seemed to treat these happenings, except as incidents of interest, and everything went on as usual. No warning was given and there was no alarm.

The *Royal Oak* was sunk at Scapa Flow, and David Russell was getting anxious about the esparto boat: "We are daily expecting the arrival of the *Aberhill*. It is to be hoped that she will soon get through." Though his father needed him in the mills, Pat was called up in November. A Government rationing scheme for paper came into operation on 1st March 1940, an "ill-considered measure," David Russell believed.

At the outbreak of war the mills had had practically a year's supply of pulp stock, but the Government took 400 tons, and diverted 900 tons. Spanish grass was plentiful, if ships could be found. But the *Maindy Hill* that had run so many esparto cargoes from North Africa had been sunk, and timber and wood pulp supplies from Scandinavia were cut off. At the beginning of May Auchmuty Mill had to be shut down for several days, and looked as if it would have to go on a three day week, but Rothes Mill was running full-time on orders of national importance. David Russell told Tudor Pole: "Under the present restrictive orders, it is quite impossible to make paper from home materials, except at a dead loss, and apart from that, permits are difficult to obtain."

Despite the destruction of war, MacLeod's squad was busy rebuilding the monastic ruins. In his memorandum David Russell recalled: "In 1939 Mr Ian Lindsay was asked by Dr George MacLeod to prepare detailed plans dealing with interior arrangements within Dr Fairlie's plans drawn in 1931. These plans are dated October 1939, and are in the name of Orphoot, Whiting & Lindsay."

David Russell had been enchanted by a silver cross by Omar Ramsden in the Empire Exhibition in Glasgow in 1938. When he took George MacLeod to an exhibition of silverwork by Ramsden in London, MacLeod was dazzled by the cross. But it was not for sale. Ramsden's widow said that her husband considered it his finest work, and he had intended that it would stand in Iona Cathedral one day. David Russell persuaded her to let him buy the cross so that it could go where its creator had intended. MacLeod wrote to him: "what enthralls me about it is that it conveys both the Celtic idea and the modern design—and if that is not the sermon of all we are trying to do, I do not know what is." There was a day of peace and hope when the Ramsden cross was dedicated in Iona Cathedral on 13th June 1940.

Tudor Pole was doing ARP (Air Raid Precautions) work in London, and David Russell was getting more distressed as he listened to the wireless at Silverburn. "I wish the BBC would give up giving the impression that it is a glorious thing to be outnumbered," he told Tudor Pole in August. Tudor Pole was having a bad time in the Blitz. But there was a funny side, as he told his friend.

In one of the houses down near us, a lady landed safely in the basement, coming down slowly from the 2nd floor amidst all the debris. Immediately afterwards, a gentleman from the 3rd floor flat arrived beside her, in his bath, bath, water and nude gentleman all intact. His descent had been delayed by a beam, but this did not upset the bath, but he was most apologetic because the towel had not come down too. This true story was told to me by one of the wardens who helped in the rescue.

At Silverburn the Russell family's sleep was also disturbed by the drone of planes, because of the convoys gathering and sailing constantly from the Forth. At the end of September the house was shaken violently by an explosion. A Dutch ship with a crew of eight had struck a mine near the shore in shallow water which had been missed by the minesweepers. The boat was practically blown to pieces, and five of the crew were killed instantly. In London Tudor Pole was on a bus in a traffic jam when he noticed the unexploded bomb on the back of a lorry which drew up alongside. The hope was that it could be taken out of the city safely. But he was preoccupied with one of his greatest schemes.

21
Another War

During the fighting in the mountains around Jerusalem early in December 1917, two British officers were discussing the war and its probable aftermath. The conversation took place in a billet on the hillside at the mouth of a cave on the eve of a battle. One of the two, a man of unusual character and vision, realising intuitively that his days on earth were to be shortened, summed up his outlook thus:

"I shall not come through this struggle and, like millions of other men in this war, it will be my destiny to go on now. You will survive and live to see a greater and more vital conflict fought out in every continent and ocean and in the air. When that time comes, remember us. We shall long to play our part wherever we may be. Give us the opportunity to do so, for that war for us will be a righteous war. We shall not fight with material weapons then, but we can help you if you will let us. We shall be an unseen but almighty army. Give us the chance to pull our weight. You will still have 'time' available as your servant. Lend us a moment of it each day and through your Silence give us our opportunity. The power of Silence is greater than you know. When those tragic days arrive do not forget us."

Tudor Pole was the survivor from this conversation, which he wrote up, and in the spring of 1940, during the evacuation of Dunkirk, he saw that he could give his dead comrade the opportunity to help by instigating the Big Ben Silent Minute. At nine each night men and women in Britain, the Commonwealth and elsewhere were asked to devote one minute of their time to pray for peace and to create a channel "between the visible and invisible worlds through which divine help and inspiration could be received." King George gave his support, and, using his contacts, Tudor Pole succeeded in converting Prime Minister Churchill to his cause. David Russell gave Tudor Pole generous financial support, and during the shortage supplied paper for printing 50,000 Big Ben booklets.

The Dedicated Minute was being kept in Britain, Australia, New

Zealand, South Africa, Canada, and the USA. Members of the navy were even observing it. Tubby Clayton thought that the Minute should contain a reading from the Bible; George MacLeod thought that such a formalised reading might prove irritating to many listeners. As David Russell told the Reverend Melville Dinwiddie, the Scottish director of the BBC, in July 1940, MacLeod wanted to hear a wide variety of different religious voices on the Silent Minute, including the Archbishop of Canterbury, a rabbi, a Christian Scientist, and a spiritualist.

Edinburgh Education Committee took "no action" on the matter of schools participating in the Silent Minute, but the managing director of Richmond Park Laundry, Cambuslang, proudly told David Russell in October: "at the stroke of 12 o'clock while we do not stop plant and machinery the workers suddenly stand, bow their heads and pray, if they so desire and in their own way." The laundry workers also sang a war hymn before their meal, with community singing afterwards.

The Russells went to Iona for their annual holiday, and David Russell reported to Tudor Pole: "we had German planes over Iona on Thursday night. The planes are said to have flown three times round Mull, but whether that was the case or not, I am unable to say. We heard the raiders overhead for some time, but only in our half-waking sleep as they passed over."

Back home, they climbed the Lomond Hills where the blaeberries were bright-red, and the hills beyond the Tay glowed with autumnal colours. In late October Tubby Clayton preached in the chapel at St Andrews University. The previous night glass had been broken in St Mary's College in an air raid on Edinburgh. Polish troops gave a concert in St Andrews. The Polish officers' choir sang. The pianist had been a pupil of Paderewski's, and the wife of one of the officers danced.

Young David was stationed at Lerwick. The indifference of the men at drills depressed Pat with the 947th Defence Battery at Cucklington Camp, Somerset. Alison Russell went by bus three times a week to St Andrews to work in a Hospital Supply Depot. Canteen and ARP work took up the rest of her time. She was trying to do too much, and in January 1941 had to be treated in Edinburgh by Dr Swanberg for a blood effusion on the left retina after bronchitis. Her general health declined and she was taken into hospital in Edinburgh. On Wednesday 12th March, the last day of Pat's leave, she had to have a blood transfusion. Her diary for the following day records: "We had a real 'blitz,' tho' only passing over on way to Clydeside where much damage was done. The noise was awful. Practically no sleep." She shouted for the night nurse, but could not make herself heard because of the enemy aircraft. Her life had been saved by the brilliant gynaecologist Ernest Fahmy.

David Russell also had to be careful about his health. In the absence of his sons he was putting in a long day at the mills at an age at which most men were retired. Photographs of workers on active service appeared in the *Rothmill Quarterly Magazine*, including 2nd Lieutenant David Russell, Black Watch; Lieutenant-Bombardier Pat Russell; and Sheila Russell in the uniform of the WRNS. There was also instruction on allotment management.

Alexander Ritchie died at Shuna Cottage, Iona, in January, two days after his wife Euphemia. He bequeathed his books on Iona and Celtic art and literature to the library of Iona Cathedral. The Russell family grieved the loss of two steadfast friends who had been honorary grandparents to the children. But there was something to celebrate the following month, when young David Russell was made a captain and adjutant of his battalion, the 7th Black Watch.

These were difficult times in which to run paper mills. In 1941 95 per cent of the production of Rothes was for Government consumption, with pulp coming from Canada and the USA. At Auchmuty, in the absence of esparto, straw, waste paper and cotton wastes were being used, and there were even boots and shoes in the collection. "We are using reeds, mustard straw, wood chips and shavings, and we have been working upon the possibility of using sawdust," a weary David Russell told Tudor Pole.

He could hardly wait to get to his beloved Iona, where in June the early morning heat and sunshine reminded him of Constantinople. Regulations insisted that Iona eggs were to be sent south. "If they had to send their eggs to Glasgow and get them back, they might quite well be four months old—such a ridiculous position as to be obviously absurd!" he told Tudor Pole.

At first David Russell felt that it would be a short war, but he had changed his mind by 1941. "The ideal of rest in activity is not easily attained in these times: but they are great times to live in, for anyone who knows how to direct his thoughts and activities," he wrote to Neville Gorton ("Gorty" to the Russells and his pupils) who had been young David's housemaster at Sedbergh, and then headmaster of Blundell's School. In February Gorton had become Bishop of Coventry.

Anatole Bergengreen, the Quest member, was still in South America. In May he wrote to Tudor Pole from Asuncion.

> Here in Paraguay all is well and quiet—we are living like in a paradise, divided from the other world with endless space and oceans. I and my daughter are living in our country house on Rio Verde, surrounded by dogs, cats, horses, donkeys, pigs and chickens. I have a workshop, and make all the necessary work for the house and boat.

Someone in Fife was not so settled. In July Robert Hurd asked for David Russell's support in a delicate matter concerning St Andrews University.

> You will probably know of the critic, writer and broadcaster Edwin Muir, who lives in St Andrews. He is a very modest but brilliant man who has risen from nothing—having left school in the Shetland Isles [he was an Orcadian] at the age of 12. He frequently reviews books in the *Listener* and the *Scotsman*, and with his wife, has translated a number of well known German novels, the most famous being *Jew Suss*.
>
> Naturally the war has hit him pretty hard. Reviewing and broadcasting about literature has been cut down to a minimum, and so on. Although he is about 50, he had to set about finding some means of livelihood when the full effect of the war began to reduce his income to nothing. His wife, who is a graduate of St Andrews, took up teaching at St Leonards Girls School. He, not having a university degree, had to search in humble spheres, so he took a job at the Dundee Food Office, stamping food cards. This he carried on with, working very long hours; and in the intervals lecturing on literature to the WEA [Workers' Educational Association] in Dundee, until his health and heart collapsed some months ago, so that he has had to take things much more quietly since, although he is now much better.
>
> I am not writing to ask you personally to help him, except in this way. Do you think it would be possible for the University of St Andrews to provide some kind of suitable employment for such a distinguished man?
>
> It is pretty dreadful, really, when such a good writer and critic who does live in Scotland has to half kill himself stamping ration cards in order to keep his son at school and his home intact; especially when he happens to live in the immediate neighbourhood of a university.
>
> The trouble is that he is so retiring that he is not at all good at pushing himself forward. He has no idea at all that I have written to you and would probably be very cross if he knew.

David Russell did what he could, but Muir was not given any teaching at St Andrews, where David Russell was sitting for his portrait, which was to hang in St Salvator's Hall at the university. He confessed to Hurd:

> I cannot say that I like having my portrait painted—I don't see any purpose in it—but I did enjoy the talks with Keith Henderson during the painting of it. I feel quite unable to say whether it is successful or otherwise, but in the opinion of Keith Henderson and of others of my family, it appears to be considered a great success, and so, I suppose, I should be satisfied.

Alexis Aladin's son was staying with the Russells on Iona in August 1941. Permits and green identity cards were necessary for going to the sacred isle, since it was within No 1 Protected Area, Scotland, principally because of the movement of convoys in the surrounding waters. Young Aladin was a pupil at Dr William's School, Dolgelley, North Wales, where Miss Nightingale, who was bringing him up, was on the staff. He was interested in studying civil engineering at Edinburgh University.

In late October the Russells returned from London to find a British major and two Polish officers waiting for them at Silverburn, with the proposition that a training centre could be established there, with accommodation for two or three hundred provided—"not in the house, fortunately," as David Russell told Tudor Pole, but in the old buildings around it.

Tudor Pole wrote to David Russell on 22nd October:

> I have been in London ever since the war broke out and have only missed one of the blitzs. If I were not engaged upon work which I believe to be of real spiritual value, the tremendous tension here and the inside information which comes my way from time to time, would have broken me down long ago. I am only telling you this because I want you to know how grateful I am to you for having made it possible for me to devote my whole time and strength during this tragic war period to work of this kind.

Sheila Russell started work at the Royal Infirmary, Edinburgh, as a nurse in November 1941. Pat was getting leave, and David was trying for some so that the family could be together for Christmas. "They have hardly met for four or five years," their father told Tudor Pole. He bought a flat in Eglinton Crescent, Edinburgh, to make it more convenient for the various members of the family to see each other.

In February 1942 Rothes Mill was running full-time on war work, but Auchmuty Mill was short of materials, though there were plenty of orders. Straw was being used, but the farmers were hoarding it, and when they were willing to sell it was at a price, and transport proved difficult. An order for 20 tons of red and black photographic paper was received from New York. Tullis Russell had experience of producing such papers as the company supplied Ilford. Hyganic, Tudor Pole's waste recovery business, was flourishing; the RAF was buying the fertilizer product because it helped to make good turf on aerodromes.

David Russell's elder brother George had a malignant mole on his back, and a tumour on the brain had been diagnosed. He died on 8th April 1942, aged 73. It was a loss, because both families had been close, and it was an untimely reminder that David Russell himself was growing old. But there was to be no respite from anxieties. Sheila had exhausted herself with her dedication to nursing, and required treatment from the Swanbergs in London.

David Russell was helping the Iona Community with paper supplies for its publications. The St Columba Hotel and farm on the sacred island was to let, with entry at Whitsunday. The Reverend George MacLeod wanted to take it for his Community, "To experiment at that central place with right approaches to farming for crofting country. For if, with intensive culture, we succeed I am serious in my hope that we will have a small boat, a fishing smack, going to Oban once or twice a week selling vegetables and jumping freight charges."

In August 1942 Captain David Russell of the 7th Battalion the Black Watch disembarked with the 51st Highland Division at Suez, after 60 days at sea. On 27th October his father sent a telegram to Tudor Pole: "Report from German sources of annihilation 51st Division is cause of much distress. Can you get reliable information? David." Tudor Pole replied: "Rumour officially stigmatised. Gross exaggerations stop losses below expectation hitherto stop Consider these statements accurate writing. Wellesley." The "annihilation" headline was supposed to have appeared in a Scottish newspaper on 27th October. Tudor Pole complained to the Ministry of Information's military adviser, who apologised for the distress caused, but advised him to take the matter up with the newspaper concerned.

Captain David Russell sent a telegram to say that he had been "slightly wounded." The truth was much more alarming. On the first day of the battle of El Alamein he had been hit in the head and shoulders by shrapnel, but had his wounds dressed and continued fighting for three days. His Military Cross citation stated that he continued to carry out his duties as adjutant with "great courage and determination." Later in the advance, though weakened through loss of blood, he helped the battalion transport to get through despite the heavy enemy shelling and mortar fire. He insisted on remaining with the battalion and carrying out his duties until a relief could be provided two days later, after which he spent three weeks in hospital.

There was more distinction in the family. Billy Blyth, David Russell's nephew, had led the assault by the Seaforths at Wadi Akarit, where the Black Watch had come to their support. Meantime Pat was with the 334/101st Light AA Regiment, Royal Artillery, on shooting practice in the south.

David Russell confided to Bishop Gorton in November 1942: "Much as I value the idea of the Silent Minute, I have never felt that I could pass on Tudor Pole's Big Ben 'literature' to my friends. It has never seemed to express what I would wish to say." He also gave a character assessment of Tudor Pole, whom he had known and supported for 30 years. "If he could cut out all desire to be a man of the world, his true gift would shine much more brightly."

David Russell never stopped learning. A tutor from an Edinburgh agency came along to the Eglinton Crescent flat to teach him mathematics, since he felt that his school mathematics, learned in another century, needed updating so that he could keep up with new developments in the mills and elsewhere.

Pat was sent overseas in January 1943, to his parents' great anxiety, since both sons would now be in the heat of the war. Willie Braid the coachman died in February, in his 92nd year, having spent over 70 years with the family at Silverburn. It was a changed world. At the end of April David Russell complained to Tudor Pole about a distraction to his workforce. "We are finding great difficulty in keeping the machines running whenever there is dog racing on. It means other men taking longer shifts, and there seems a complete indifference to what this means to others."

There was that other, constant worry. On the first day of May Tudor Pole used his psychic gifts to reassure David Russell: "I don't 'see' either of your boys going over during this war." In fact Captain David Russell was in Tullis Russell territory in North Africa. Carl Basiaux the esparto dealer had been imprisoned by the Germans at Sfax, but had been released and was at Sousse, where he gave Captain Russell and the soldiers a dozen bottles of wine and a sheep from the farm he was living on in return for David Russell's and Tudor Pole's kindness to him in the esparto dealings.

ANOTHER WAR

But Tudor Pole warned David Russell against Carl, whom he believed had been in Vichy pay.

No grass concessions were being worked in Algeria, since all available labour was being used by the military authorities. There was no point in Tudor Pole going out, though David Russell was anxious to know what the position was as he holidayed on Iona in the summer of 1943. He had lost his "right hand," because Miss Bell had both arms in plaster after an accident. As regarded the future, Tudor Pole warned him that "the word had gone out" in London that the war could not be won before 1945.

David Russell had been a council member of the Royal Society of Edinburgh for years, and in 1943 he was elected a vice-president. He somehow found time to sit on committees while running the mills, with equal commitment. He was also a vice-president of the National Trust for Scotland, and was a member of the Royal Institute of International Affairs, the unofficial and non-political body founded in 1920 "to encourage and facilitate the scientific study of international questions."

Captain David Russell's battalion had returned to Britain in November 1943. He came home on leave for Christmas, "almost completely unchanged," his father noted proudly. But Tudor Pole was having a rough time. On 23rd February 1944 his Duke Street office was bombed. It was an eerie scene: the walls and windows were partly gone, but the pictures, ornaments and Chinese screens were intact, and his papers were in order on his desk. The war was also reaching Silverburn. In mid May there was a German plane near Leven. The Russells heard firing, then thankfully, the all clear before midnight.

Pat, who was with his AA regiment in Egypt, spent a weekend in Jerusalem, and wrote to his parents about joining the London Scottish. At the beginning of the summer the Russell family had a short holiday in Somerset, then went up to Iona with Alexis Aladin, who had been in Canada, training for the Fleet Air Arm. As he heard the buzz-bombs over London Tudor Pole wrote to his old friend at Silverburn: "All that lies in my power is being done to help in the safeguarding of your boys."

David Russell drew spiritual strength as he walked about Iona in the summer of 1944, where the rebuilding of the monastic ruins was a visible example of an act of faith. But the war had reached these shores too. Men from torpedoed convoys were washed up and buried, "known only to God," beside Scottish kings. But the sea had been good to George MacLeod. In September 1940 it looked as if the rebuilding would have to cease because of a shortage of timber. Then the deck cargo of a Swedish ship carrying wood from Canada had to be jettisoned. It floated to Mull, opposite Iona, and proved to be the right length for the MacLeod squad's purpose.

While MacLeod had harnessed the power of prayer for his project, David Russell was considering harnessing the wind power on Iona for his house. The Lucas-Freelite set was designed to commence charging in a breeze of about 10 mph. The pledge was: "Provides light from the wind," for an outlay of £35. That summer oatcakes were sent from Edinburgh, and Mrs MacPhail at the Iona shop was asked to supply "emergency rations."

Young David Russell had landed in Normandy on 10th June 1944, four days after "D" Day. He had recently been promoted to major, second in command of his battalion. Captain Pat Russell, who was now attached to the London Scottish, was in Italy, at San Egidio, a small village near the ancient towns of Perugia and Assisi on the road to Florence. He wrote to his parents on 18th August. There had been torrential rain, and he had dined with the man who owned the land they were camping on. He had had a large meal of spaghetti, roast geese and chicken.

On a morning in late September a telegram was delivered to the Russells' flat in Eglinton Crescent, Edinburgh. David Russell received many business telegrams, but this one was from the War Office. Captain John Patrick Russell, Royal Artillery, attached to the London Scottish, had died of wounds in Italy on 7th September. A second telegram was delivered that day. Major David Russell, MC, of the Black Watch, had been wounded on 12th September and was dangerously ill.

22
A Grievous Loss

It was Pat Russell who had once told his father that he would stand beside him all night, or sleep on the floor, in order to be with him on his business travels, and it was Pat who had always wanted his brother David to have the same things as he had.

Miss Bell called it "a nightmare." As David Russell drew heavily on his massive reserves of inner strength and continued to run the mills he waited for news of his elder son. Major David Russell had been wounded in the left foot, shoulder and lung by a shell at Le Havre. He was seriously ill and in an oxygen tent, but there was comfort nearby. Dr Loudon, who attended him at No 6 British General Hospital, BLA, had worked in the Royal Infirmary, Edinburgh, and the nurse who was attending him was a friend of Sheila's from the Royal Infirmary.

Major Russell was brought back to Salford Royal Hospital, Manchester, in October 1944. By the end of the month he was visiting his family at the Edinburgh flat from Edenhall Hospital, Musselburgh. Christopher Tudor Pole had escaped from a burning plane at Asmara in north east Africa. His father, who had reassured David Russell that his sons would be safe, wrote: "Somehow if we are to live sanely at all we *must* realise more fully that death is an incident in life and *not* a tragic and irretrievable calamity."

David Russell had long since been convinced that there was an afterlife, but he was sceptical about mediumship. "The truth cannot be got that way," had been his opinion in 1920 about communicating with the dead at a seance. But Tudor Pole wrote to him in November 1944: "When Pat awakes and when the way opens naturally it should be right and possible for you to hear from him in one way or another." A fortnight later he promised: "I will let you hear immediately Pat makes himself felt and heard."

Tudor Pole had already dealt with the experiences of a dead soldier in *Private Dowding*. He explained:

For the consolation of those who have lost their loved ones in war or as the result of an accident, the following fact should be recorded.

There exists in the Borderland region a number of groups and organisations similar in function to our Red Cross Societies on earth. Their members are drawn from those who have been specially trained in what might be termed rescue work.

These important activities are undertaken by volunteers, many of whom were alive on earth not so long ago. They are equipped with hospitals, rest houses and educational centres on a scale adequate to meet all urgent needs.

Pat had died defending his battalion's headquarters at Croce. Eric Linklater wrote about that hill in San Marino:

There is—or there was—a village called Croce upon it. And in the ruined houses on the ridge and among the tattered trees that grow there, are the ghosts of dauntless men.

In every prolonged and stubborn battle there is varying fortune, and where some triumph, others suffer. It may happen, however, that those who gain no ground are remembered with as deep a respect as those who go victoriously forward over many miles.

Captain John (Pat) Russell, R.A.

Wartime wedding: Sheila Russell and Edward Erdal, January 1945.

A GRIEVOUS LOSS

They may have set an example of fortitude that captures the imagination as surely as their happier comrades who took towns and villages—and this is the battle honour that the London Scottish won, who fought at Croce. (Quoted in the *Rothmill Quarterly Magazine*, 1944.)

The cessation of esparto grass supplies after the fall of France in 1940 and the shrinkage of rag stocks hit British paper mills hard. Tullis Russell was one of the few firms which still used manila ropes as a raw material, but there was a reduction in their quantity and quality, especially after the Philippines fell into Japanese hands, and manila had to be replaced by sisal from Kenya. However, like other companies using esparto, the Fife mills were fortunate to possess digesters and boilers that could be adapted to straw cooking.

Auchmuty Mill had suffered in the straw shortage at the end of 1940, but the assistant secretary James Rae, who was one of four on the Scottish committee set up to examine all aspects of supply, helped to get The Papermakers Straw Trading Co. into operation. This was a non-profit-making company which eventually came under the jurisdiction of the Paper Control and the Ministry of Supply. The company purchased baled straw from farmers and hay and straw Merchants and delivered it to the mills, charging the cost to the Paper Control. As the mills used the straw they paid for it at a uniform price fixed by the Paper Control. In this way the price of straw at farm was controlled and the price paid by the mills, no matter where situated (the majority of the mills able to process straw were in Scotland), was kept at a uniform level. The company was successful in obtaining reasonably adequate supplies for essential needs at Auchmuty Mill. Two threshing mills were bought by Tullis Russell to clean the straw, and the surplus grain was fed to the chickens of Fife, to the benefit of the food supply.

Early in the war Tullis Russell had been put on the Vital List of firms making products essential to the war, under contracts or subcontracts with the Ministry of Aircraft Production, the Admiralty and the Ministry of Supply. With its quotas assured and its labour force protected by an Essential Works Order, Rothes Mill was able to work to capacity all through the war, turning out products for munitions and military construction of all kinds—insulating papers for electric cables and fine wires for aircraft, magnetic bombs and ship-degaussing apparatus, for aerodromes, naval and military installations, laminated plastic base papers for a wide range of uses from bomb detectors to instrument panels, cartridge papers for mines and for use in starting up aircraft, papers for candle flares ("window" to the RAF), and for converting to gas detection purposes. Many of its products were on the Secret List.

There might well have been Rothes papers in the plane that 21 year old Sub-Lieutenant Alexis Aladin RNVR was in, which failed to return from a practice flight from Crail, Fife, on 3rd January 1945. It was a grievous blow to the Russell family, since he had been brought up as one of them. The following month the esparto agent Ivan Basiaux died at Marseilles, having ruined his health through long dusty drives, bad water and poor food, as well as anxieties over his business affairs.

The flat in Edinburgh was convenient for Alison Russell because she was involved in clubs for girls in the city, but David Russell had to endure crowded and often blacked-out trains as he commuted to the mills four days a week. His son David fretted as he convalesced, knowing how much his father needed him in the mills, where an experiment—not scientific, but spiritual—had failed.

In 1940 the Reverend George MacLeod, founder of the Iona Community, had had the idea of a "factory-community," with a minister having a room in a factory and sharing the experiences of the workforce. It was not a novel concept, since there were factory chaplains in the south. It was agreed that the Scottish experiment would begin at Tullis Russell, with the Reverend Ian Fraser taking up appointment in the mills as a minister in industry under the aegis of the Iona Community from September 1942 for two years.

The difficulties over Fraser's appointment began with the employees maintaining that the minister had first to work "as a man with the men" before making a religious approach. Fraser produced a memorandum about seating arrangements in the mills canteen. He complained about "class distinction in factories" through separate tables for different staff, and warned: "Though not serious at the moment this may be the beginning of a policy which will have serious consequences in the division of the mill into separated groups who squabble because they have never met on a separate footing."

The canteen dispute was compounded by an advertisement in the *Scotsman* for a lecture in Edinburgh on "Common Wealth: Piety and Politics" given by the Reverend Alex Miller of the Iona Community. David Russell complained to MacLeod:

This has brought a shower of questions and criticisms about my head. Is the Iona Community a Communistic organisation? etc., etc.; and all this has been accentuated by one of the staff bringing in a copy of *World Digest* with an article, "A Parson in a Factory," in which this is said: "Unless she (the Church) is prepared to stand for some form of communal control and ownership in business etc."

I am in a sense single-handed here. I depend upon my staff, I trust my staff, and I count upon the trust being mutual; and I cannot support what my staff, with some reason, resents, and I am afraid these developments are going to rule out the possibility of extending Ian Fraser's activities here beyond the two years, i.e., after October, and much—not all—of what I had hoped for will have failed in realisation. You speak of disciplines in the community. We have our disciplines too in business, as in our lives.

MacLeod replied robustly:

Providence got us together on this first chaplaincy experiment and now honours us with difficulties, which is a proof that something is really happening. If we can't get a factory chaplain a success in *your* place, and in the person of Ian Fraser, I am pretty well satisfied that factory chaplains are a flash in the pan which will either degenerate into bluff: or—if they get down to it—will through a misunderstanding be turned out everywhere as a menace: which would ultimately end in the Church emerging over against the trend of modern industry to the very great improvement of both.

The other personal worry, on my side, I raise finally to dismiss. There was a time when this sort of issue (as a preview of the shape of things to come) would have worried me in what it implies for the whole future of the Community: that we will lose our larger backers and leave the Abbey half roofed, because we have gone broke. I am now quite satisfied—if it came to that—to have it so. The Church might get "safer men" to complete the roof but I am quite convinced that such a completion would merely house an unreality: so convinced am I of the coming expression of Christianity for the twentieth century. All that, to prevent any personal issue arising whatsoever in any action you feel personally you must take or that we must take.

Fraser wrote to David Russell in late June 1944:

If I am going out, let it be quite simply and clearly because, in the view of one or two powerful individuals, Christianity and business will not mix, the methods of business cannot stand Christian challenge and so have to get rid of the challenge. A hatred of the idea that Christianity should at any point challenge the status quo in the mill is absolutely basic to the present controversy.

David Russell rejected the argument and told George MacLeod that an industrial chaplain had to be "part of the management—in other words, one whose sphere of activity would be the spiritual, mental and physical welfare of the people." In October 1944 the Reverend Fraser's appointment was terminated, but the depression following the failure of the experiment persisted with David Russell until after the war.

Tudor Pole had suggested that David Russell should try to contact Pat through a clairvoyant and had recommended Mrs Mona Rolfe, director of the London School of Psychology, who was seemingly, in touch with her dead husband and son. But in March 1945 Pat apparently communicated through the automatic writing of Geraldine Cummins, whose "Cleophas" scripts David Russell had had published. Tudor Pole quoted Dostovyesky: "Our highest thoughts, our noblest feelings are not rooted in this world. From His many other worlds God took the seeds and sowed them in this earth, and tended His new Garden . . . And all growing here depends on its contact with other worlds, and this consciousness is alive in us." He told David Russell: "*Direct* communication is what I long to see established between you [and Pat] and I see no good reason why it should not come."

David Russell loved family life at Silverburn, but his children were now setting up their own homes. In January 1945 Sheila had married Edward Erdal, the former tutor to the Russell boys, who was now chief assistant engineer to the port of Beira, Portuguese East Africa, and in July Major David Russell married Catherine Robinson from Colchester, a captain in the Auxiliary Territorial Service. The couple settled at Kennoway in Fife.

On 1st November Tudor Pole advised his oldest friend: "Do keep a chair at your table free for Pat, his chair; but he would like it to be done unostentatiously—just to feel he can join you at meals, as at other times." That same month Field Marshal Viscount Montgomery of Alamein was at St Andrews, to give a lecture on "Military Leadership" in the Leadership series arranged and financed by the Walker Trust. Montgomery also received an honorary degree. Students swarmed all over the conqueror's car, and when he was eventually able to step out at University House, women wanted to shake his hand.

James Watt, the brilliant lawyer with an unrivalled understanding of the esparto trade and an insatiable appetite for work, who had looked after the Tullis Russell interests for many years, died in December 1945.

Sir David Russell in 1946.

In the New Year's Honours List for 1946 David Russell was knighted for his many public services. His first grandchild, a daughter to David and Catherine Russell, was born in April. The papermaking industry had always been directed by men, but Anne Russell was on the board of Tullis Russell, and in June 1946 she decided to combine business with pleasure by going out to South Africa on a cargo boat. "It is extraordinary to see with how little concern these young things set off for a long journey," a bemused Sir David told Tudor Pole. Sheila and Anne met in Southern Rhodesia, and Alison, the Erdals' first child, was born there in September 1946. But Edward Erdal was suffering from chronic malaria and anaemia, and Anne also caught malaria.

At the mills business was good for speciality papers in large quantities but in September 1947 the main steam turbine broke, causing a six week delay in production. "We tried to place the order for the new power plant as far back as 1940, but were not given permits till after the end of the war," Sir David complained to Tudor Pole.

He continued to go to Iona, and there was no ill feeling with George MacLeod over the industrial chaplaincy failure. MacLeod wrote in August 1948: "As you know, you first 'plotted' a rebuilding of the Abbey, but your considerable gifts so far have been lost in the contemporary goings on of Student Retreats and current expenditures." He thanked Sir David for the gift of £2000 from the Russell Trust, founded in March 1947 in memory of Captain J. P. O. Russell, towards the completion of the refectory as a memorial to Pat. Sir David also gave a facsimile copy of the *Book of Kells* to the Iona Community.

MacLeod made a confession:

I begin to look with wondering eyes at the Nunnery. I wonder whether *that* should be a ruin or a six month summer hostel for youth with a quiet resident Man of God. I think of approaching Thomson [of Scottish Motor Transport] who loves youth. But the Trustees will be the first hurdle! Unprepared, I am sure they will be tempted only to think of The Garden.

Sir David continued to pursue his interest in alternative medicine. Years before he had invested money in a company set up by Tudor Pole to develop the Emion process of ionisation. Now the clinic at the mills was treating a woman with a wound that had been open for a year and was thought to be tubercular. Sir David was interested in using Emion's immunised herbal antibiotic on it. Tudor Pole wondered if St Andrews University would run trials on

A GRIEVOUS LOSS

A royal occasion at Kirkcaldy in June 1948. Sir David and Lady Russell meet King George VI, Queen Elizabeth and HRH Princess Margaret.

Zytocin hygroscopic powder, a pure herbal product used as an inhalant for tuberculosis of the lungs, asthma or bronchitis.

Sir David was taking Emion Zytocin tablets, which were claimed to be a specific for catarrh, influenza, asthma, intestinal and bacterial infections. Annie, the one-time under-nanny had become cook/housekeeper and the mainstay of the Russell family. One of her many initiatives was to cut out items from the newspapers she thought Sir David would be interested in. When she developed conjunctivitis he gave her Emion tablets to take, and was able to report that she was much better. He also ordered some herbal preparation for his brother-in-law Ben Blyth, who had been operated on for cancer of the bowel.

Sir David wanted to use Emion products on other members of family. At Anne's wedding in 1948 to William Macaulay, the mosaic tracer who had been on the Constantinople dig, the bride's father gave out cold-cure tablets to the wedding party, though the bride would not take any. He ordered over 2000 Zytocin tablets and thought of testing them out on the herd at the mill farm. They were used in the Artificial Sunlight Clinic and appeared to cure colds, bronchitis, catarrh and asthma.

For 20 years David Russell had been writing a regular foreword to the *Rothmill Quarterly Magazine* on subjects which he thought would interest and instruct the employees. The range was astonishing, from "The Peace of Iona" to "The Lesson of Dunkirk." Many readers wanted to have the forewords in book form. Sir David had some time on his hands to do this, since his son David was now running the mills. The Russells continued to see the Irvines at St Andrews, but Mabel Irvine was now blind in one eye, and the other was threatened.

Ben Blyth died in mid October 1948. On New Year's Day 1949 Tudor Pole had a message for Sir David: "I am often aware of Pat, but he has never allowed me to act as intermediary and I respect his wishes." Tudor Pole was also thinking about Constantinople. A psychic message from Paris intimated that the hour of the Quest would be "brusque and unexpected." He elaborated: "I for one cannot lose the strong belief that those ancient trunks and their contents are still there, more or less intact and awaiting recovery when the hour strikes."

The discovery of the Dead Sea Scrolls in caves in what was the British Mandate of Palestine in the late 1940s showed both Sir David and Tudor Pole that the library of Justinian could have survived in an underground chamber in Constantinople, since the Old Testament scrolls were 2250 years old. The chief priest of St Mark's Monastery, Jerusalem, was apparently asking £250,000 for them, a reminder of how valuable the Quest library would be.

In early December 1949 Sir David was signing business letters when he found he could not see the electric lamp. A thrombosis of the left eye was diagnosed, alarming in someone whose life was books. He rested and thought about the disadvantages for Scotland of too much centralisation in London: "If we wish to work a few women in the Rag Picking House after 6 o'clock for even a few hours, we have to get permission from London," he told Tudor Pole.

Early in 1950 Sir David went into a nursing home in Edinburgh. An old acquaintance, the Russian clairvoyant Anatoly Bergengreen, died in his mid seventies on his Paraguay ranch. He had led an idyllic life there. He made his own furniture; his daughter planted fruit trees and grew vegetables. They had horses, pigs and domesticated parrots. But there had been a time of terror when they got caught up in the civil war of 1947. The house had been occupied by 11 men armed with guns and machetes. They had looted and burned, shooting at the door behind which the Bergengreens had barricaded themselves.

A GRIEVOUS LOSS

Michael Pojidaiev died in his sixties in a Paris hospital around the same time. "He has left behind him a large number of sculptures which it is very difficult to know how to collect and deal with," Tudor Pole wrote to Sir David, who was still convalescing. Alison Russell was also not well, and they took car runs into the country to restore their health. On 6th August 1950 a party of 14, including five grandchildren, helped Sir David to celebrate his seventy-eighth birthday. Sheila and her family had returned from Rhodesia and were going to stay at Corriemar, the house in the grounds of Silverburn.

Sir David and his wife went to London later that year to be treated by Dr Swanberg. The capital had had other Scottish visitors—the Stone of Destiny had been taken from Westminster Abbey. Sir David wrote to Tudor Pole: "I make no excuses for the removal of the Coronation Stone from Westminster Abbey, but in the first place it was a 'theft' by Edward I of England!"

The Russells' eldest daughter Catherine died of pneumonia in January 1951. She had spent most of her life in the institution at Larbert, but had been faithfully visited by her devoted family. Her mother had made her dresses.

Sir David had always been receptive to new developments, and he listened intently to Lovell of Jodrell Bank's broadcast on "The New Science of Radio Astronomy." But there were older methods to be relied on. Sir David was friendly with Joseph Cecil Maby the bio-physicist, founder of the En Rapport Group, "a select and intimate society of like-minded, instinctly harmonious people all sharing the same basic ideals, aims and civilised sentiments regarding life, nature, God, man and spirit." Maby was a gifted diviner who used technology to make his own instruments. The mills were short of drinking water, but Maby divined two well points. One was dug immediately and yielded water. Maby believed that people could be disturbed by water below a house, and at Corriemar he demonstrated the presence under a room of a disruptive stream which Sheila had sensed. David Russell had proposed that Maby should give a paper on his water divining instruments to the Royal Society of Edinburgh, but the subject was not considered scientific enough for the distinguished members.

But Tudor Pole believed that dew was beneficial, and urged Sir David, who was almost 80, to go barefoot through the grass in the early morning. Tudor Pole had moved to a house at Hurstpierpoint, Sussex, allegedly for his retirement, but he was still active on many fronts and the Quest was still foremost in his mind.

SIR DAVID RUSSELL

In 1951 the Iona Community was integrated into the Church of Scotland after many attacks on it and its founder at the General Assembly over the years. George MacLeod thanked Sir David for his "generosity, understanding and goodwill, and [his] advice from early days till now as a very active Sponsor of the Iona Community."

23
The Dig Resumed

On 20th January 1942 Professor James Baxter sat down in his St Andrews study to write to David Russell. But there was none of the euphoria of that letter written on a sultry night in Constantinople in 1935, as he was about to start the dig of the Great Palace that would bring him fame through the discovery of the exquisite mosaics. There was no fire on in his study in South Street, and correspondence had accumulated. But the letter from David Russell needed answering. Baxter wrote bitterly: "If you have any will to the peace and love you so often speak of, if you feel any sincerity in the 'kindest regards' you sent, why don't you clear things up, tell me what has instigated all your ill-feeling, and try to put right a situation which has puzzled me and pained me beyond telling?"

But it was too late for a reconciliation. David Russell's long patience was exhausted. He had had so many reports from Constantinople about how difficult Baxter was to work with, but he had always given him the benefit of the doubt. Baxter defended himself plaintively: "I did my best, and gave my best, for the sake of the dig, and I don't think you have realized how much I gave, and at what cost."

But the cost was mostly on David Russell's side. Apart from the huge outlay in Constantinople, where Baxter had not kept a tight enough grip on expenditure, the report on the excavations was now well behind schedule because of Baxter's resistance to the plan for individual experts on the dig to write sections on architecture, pottery and other aspects. He wanted the report to be largely his work. It was a question of pride, not professionalism.

It was wartime. "I'm short of paper and have no envelopes," Baxter added as a footnote to his letter. Several days later David Russell sent his car to the professor's house to collect books and papers relating to the dig. David Russell edited the report with great difficulty. One author refused to have even his grammatical errors corrected, and other authors were unavailable for consultation because of the war. When the report was published by Oxford

University Press in 1947, under the title *The Great Palace of the Byzantine Emperors,* it did not carry Baxter's name. In congratulating David Russell on the "superb" publication, David Talbot Rice, Professor of Fine Art at Edinburgh University, and a member of the British Academy team that had carried out excavations on the Great Palace site in 1927–8, wrote: "I only hope that one day it may be possible to carry on the excavations."

Without realising it, Baxter had already nominated his successor on the dig. In November 1932 David Russell had written to Tudor Pole: "Baxter appears to think very highly of Talbot Rice. In his opinion, if we can get his services, the soundness of the archaeological work will be assured." But Tudor Pole did not feel that the time was ripe to extend the group who had Quest knowledge.

In November 1950 Major David Russell wrote to Talbot Rice on behalf of his father, who was having a prostate operation in Edinburgh, asking him if he was interested in taking charge of the resumption of excavations on the Great Palace site. Talbot Rice replied that he had heard UNESCO was considering taking a role in archaeological work in Constantinople, since the excavation of the city was beyond the skill and resources of the Turks. But having discussed the proposition with Sir David, he decided to accept. The Foreign Office offered to help if there were any difficulties transferring funds to Turkey, and the British Institute of Archaeology in Ankara offered help in obtaining permits.

Talbot Rice went out to Constantinople in April 1951 with his wife Tamara, also an archaeologist. He reported to Sir David: "In the neighbourhood of the old dig, houses have sprung up like mushrooms and it is almost completely surrounded. The only place which has not been built over is the garden of the Government stables; elsewhere there is not a chance or hope of extending the old diggings at all."

However, there were two possible sites for excavation. One was a small garden lying east of the large subterranean building identified by Mamboury and Wiegand as the Nea, one of the most important buildings of the Great Palace, which might yield a fine mosaic floor. Talbot Rice estimated that it would take 20 men three months to clear the garden and the substructure.

The other possible site, a large vacant area on the opposite side of the Hippodrome to the Blue Mosque had been cleared to make way for a new Palace of Justice. It was adjacent to the Hippodrome and Kathisma, or Royal Box. Some archaeological work had already been done there, and Talbot Rice thought it was a good site for the

Walker Trust to attempt with a large number of workmen over several seasons, though it was not a part of the actual Palace. "A large area has been expropriated, so that no trouble with owners etc. would arise," he assured Sir David.

He had also looked over the House of Justinian site, but concluded that it would not be easy to work there, since the area on the landward side of the railway had been built over completely and was consequently inaccessible. He reported to Sir David:

> The rest comprises only a small triangle of ground between the railway and the outer wall on the sea side, and house to the north east. One might penetrate its sub-structure from elsewhere and carry on under ground, but my view is that it would be wiser to begin a main dig elsewhere and to do a subsidiary one there when the other work has begun.

He suggested that the whole area between the railway and the sea could be taken over and restored, but that it would be a "terribly expensive" business, though well worth doing. "I do not feel that small scale soundings would be very practicable."

Sir David wrote to Tudor Pole in early May: "Talbot Rice is coming on Friday. Am I at liberty to disclose everything to him with regard to the House of Justinian? I shall be glad to know if this coincides with your wishes, or if there is anything you would have me hold back?"

Tudor Pole replied:

> I hardly know what to say about Q. work in relation to Talbot Rice. It is natural that professional archaeologists should be very critical of what must appear to them as psychic hunches about "buried treasure" received by untrained amateurs. If nothing whatever can be done or attempted until next year (tragic if true) then to raise Q. matters in detail with T.R. at this juncture, would serve no useful purpose.

Sir David wanted to spend time and money renovating and preserving the House of Justinian. But with no definite reason for asking the Turks for a permit for urgent work, he could not see how progress was to be made, he told Tudor Pole, and complained that BB's drawings did not conform to the House of Justinian and its environs.

Tudor Pole had his answer ready. "To prove the value of all the indications given, or to disprove them, is not a very big task. If 6 feet below the marked spot there are no signs of a blocked-up marble staircase, then we are on the wrong track and need go no further at that particular spot."

In July 1951 application was made to work the original Great Palace site, the Nea site and the Palace of Justice site, with an additional request that the House of Justinian site should be reserved for the Walker Trust, though it was not envisaged that work would be undertaken there during the 1952 season. But the Palace of Justice site had apparently become a political issue, and Talbot Rice was warned by the British Institute of Archaeology in Ankara that permission was likely to be refused

He advised Sir David: "In many ways the [Palace of Justice] site was not inviting; there was a great deal of earth to be moved, and it was not part of the Great Palace ... I do not recommend fighting for it; in some ways I think we are perhaps lucky to be out of the obligation." In Talbot Rice's estimation, congested Constantinople was too difficult a place to excavate in, and he suggested: "we could get far more valuable results in return for our money if we were to tackle a site where habitation ceased roughly in the fifteenth century or thereabouts, but where one could expect Islamic, Byzantine, Classical, and perhaps Hittite levels, one below the other." He cited the excavations undertaken by Yale University at Dura on the Euphrates, which after several seasons had produced new material relating to early Byzantine and late classical art and history. "I have something like that in mind, and would be most interested to hear your reactions."

But Sir David had never been one to leave a task unfinished, however problematic. The Walker Trust group would continue in Constantinople until the work had been carried as far as it could. However, Tudor Pole persisted in his belief that the House of Justinian site should be detached from the main dig, with an accredited archaeologist in charge, financed by the Quest group and not by the Walker Trust. He elaborated: "One cannot saddle Talbot Rice with the past or with the possible 'taint' of psychism. There is a lot of detailed material, some of which may prove valuable, which was never disclosed to Baxter; and which nothing would induce what is left of the Q group (apart from myself) to divulge."

In March 1951 Sir David wrote to Principal James Irvine of St Andrews.

It is essential that the area of the Mosaic we discovered should be cleared up for the Great Exhibition to be held in Turkey in 1953, in celebration of the five hundredth anniversary of the capture of Constantinople in 1453. The problem is what to do with the Mosaic.

THE DIG RESUMED

The Turkish Government has proposed that the whole area should be laid out as a national monument, like the Forum in Rome, but is little inclined to spend the money necessary for it. We have carried on negotiations, partly through the late Professor Whittemore, during the period since the outbreak of war, but no decision has been arrived at.

After consultation with Professor Talbot Rice, who knows Istanbul and the Turks well, Professor Michael Grant of Edinburgh, whom we met in Istanbul, and who, as head of the British Council in Istanbul, acted for us for a time after the outbreak of war, and Professor Calder of Edinburgh; and also with Seton Lloyd, the Director of the British Institute of Archaeology in Ankara, who has been home on leave, we have arranged that Professor Talbot Rice should go out to Istanbul to inquire into the whole position and to advise what should be done.

The first edition of *The Great Palace* report had sold out, and a reprint was issued. In December 1951 a new application to excavate was made, with the Palace of Justice site deleted. Sir David warned the Turkish authorities that if no reply was received by January, "the Walker Trust might . . . have to consider itself free from any obligation for the original site, whether by way of further excavation, conservation, or maintenance of guardians on the spot."

Talbot Rice estimated that the erection of a building over the mosaic would cost £1500, with the season's excavation adding £2000. But the Turks prevaricated about the Nea site, answering Talbot Rice's queries about the ownership of land in that area by claiming that there were numerous owners whose addresses the authorities did not have. Talbot Rice warned Sir David: "it looks as though work is not going to be at all easy, and I feel that there are going to be many difficulties ahead." When the authorities later wrote to say that the owners had been traced, they wanted a large sum from the Walker Trust for permission to dig there.

Tudor Pole's wife Florence had died in December. He was devastated at the loss of her devotion and her understanding of his psychic interests over the years. Corresponding daily with Sir David and thinking about Quest fulfilment kept him going. In February 1952 he warned: "the whole situation in the Eastern Mediterranean is extremely complicated and a single spark might at any time create a very grave situation." That same month permission was granted for continuation of Walker Trust work. Talbot Rice was told about the sapphire blue Glastonbury Bowl and the subsequent Quest. Asked if he believed in the possibilities of such guidance he replied:

"yes and no." However, Sir David felt that he was sympathetic. But he was still worried about inconsistencies in BB's drawings. For instance, the distance of the railway from the House of Justinian was given by BB as much greater than it was in reality.

Sir David tried to be patient, but he became exasperated by Tudor Pole's hints that there was secret Quest material that had not yet been divulged. "You showed me papers when we first met. I have borne a good part of the burden of the Janson yacht expedition; I have spent much money in trying to open a way through a university group; all to little purpose, so far as the Q is concerned. Who are left of the original Q group, and who refuses to divulge what you refer to to me?" he demanded to know.

The problem with the House of Justinian site was that there were squatters living in the vicinity, and if excavations were going to be allowed, a path would have to be left free for the traffic. Talbot Rice told Sir David that if the squatter problem could be solved, there would be no difficulty in sinking a shaft down three to four metres at point X on the BB plan. That would be sufficient to prove or disprove the contention that the blocked-up remains of a marble staircase could be uncovered below that spot. "So far as can be judged at present, Q work must depend on that assumption being correct, or fall down," Sir David reminded Tudor Pole. However, Tudor Pole warned that the shaft would have to be slanted, with great care taken not to affect the foundations of the railway embankment or the House of Justinian ruins.

Even if the marble staircase leading to the treasure was found, Sir David recalled that when Baxter had asked to be allowed to take home a few square inches of the mosaic, it had to be measured, weighed and signed for. Every article found had had to be delivered to the Museum, which would not let a single Quest item leave Turkey. There was also the problem of the weather. Tudor Pole maintained that work could go on for eight months, but the Byzantine scholar Steven Runciman had told Sir David that the weather at Constantinople was the worst in the world.

Talbot Rice and his wife flew out to Constantinople in late April 1952. Spencer Corbett, who had been working with the British School at Athens at Smyrna, was the architect. Though no permit had been received, Talbot Rice was told by the Vali and Aziz Bey that work could recommence on the Great Palace site to conserve the mosaics that had been uncovered by Baxter. A roof was erected over the greater part of the mosaic floor, while outlying portions were lifted and installed in the arcades of a Turkish building close

THE DIG RESUMED

to the site. The border of the mosaic floor was unearthed; it was a fine piece of work, the most dramatic image that of the moustached head of a barbarian.

No permit had arrived for the House of Justinian site, where Tudor Pole wanted Talbot Rice to sink a shaft. He asked if there would be any objection to him flying out with Frederick Leveaux to see for himself. Talbot Rice wrote to Sir David:

Quite honestly, I do not think there is anything that Tudor Pole could do if he were to come out now. What I suggest is that we should begin next season in the Aygir Deposu [in the Peristyle area], and that when that has been started, work on the House of Justinian should begin. Tudor Pole could then come out in time to start it, and he could as it were, be the "assistant in charge" of that particular site. Whatever is or is not discovered there, there is room for a full architectural study and survey of the building and I think Corbett should do that in any case. The fact that we have found considerable ramifications of underground chambers and substructures at the Aygir Deposu will give a good reason, so far as the public is concerned, for seeking them also in the House of Justinian.

The modest museum housing parts of the mosaic was officially opened and handed over to the Turkish authorities on 30th May 1952, but with much less publicity than on the Baxter dig. The Vali was present, along with other officials, and tea was drunk. As Talbot Rice prepared to return to Edinburgh, he wrote to Sir David, apologising for going over the expenditure estimates, but predicting: "On the eve of closing this season's work, I would like to say that I have really very sanguine expectations of what may result from next year's work." In his absence conservation work would proceed on the mosaics.

While out in Constantinople Talbot Rice had obtained the permission of the owner of the waste area to the north of the Nea site to work there for a realistic payment. He hoped also to get permission to work on top of the Nea arcades for a similar payment. Though the House of Justinian site was very restricted, the area Tudor Pole wanted excavated was open ground.

If one came into vaults and substructure there, as is probable, it might be possible to work under ground, as we did this year, without doing so very much on the surface. Such work is very profitable, for one can go a long way without the expense of moving hundreds of cubic metres of earth, but it is also slow and difficult, and if Tudor Pole is right, we would have to work very slowly and carefully indeed.

Sir David hoped that the 1953 season in Constantinople would bring to an end the work on the Great Palace, since it was proving a big drain on Walker Trust funds. In late April Talbot Rice began work in Constantinople with 10 men. Spencer Corbett was the architect, David Oates and Anne Wilson from St Andrews joined the staff as archaeologists. Talbot Rice planned to move on to the House of Justinian about mid May, and Ward Perkins would take over the project early in June when Talbot Rice had to go back to Edinburgh for university examinations.

24

In the House of Justinian

After waiting over 40 years for fulfilment of his Quest dreams, Tudor Pole arrived in a downpour in Constantinople on 15th May 1953. He stayed in a Greek pension with no bathroom in Moda, so it took him about an hour to cross by ferry to reach the dig. There had always been friction between himself and Baxter, but he got on well with Talbot Rice, who went over the details of the dig with him.

The remains of the House of Justinian form an arched loggia, standing on top of the city's seaward walls and facing towards the south. About half of the facade of this loggia is preserved. Before the motor road altered the landscape the loggia looked

Tudor Pole's obsession: the House of Justinian (Bucoleon Palace) from the sea. Note the arched loggia.

directly over the Propontis: boats could come in, and emperors land to take the staircase up to the palace; the same route could also provide a means of escape. Professor Baxter's researches had showed that when the railway was being made in 1869, beside the House of Justinian, underground passages had apparently been discovered, examined, then closed. Tudor Pole had reconnoitred the railway cutting in 1908, when he met Sir William Whittall, a Constantinople-based merchant who had seen the railway being constructed and who claimed to have helped himself to a marble statue of an angel found in a passage grotto when the cutting was made. But Tudor Pole believed that these were superficial tunnels on the hillside, well above sea level and the underground areas of interest to the Quest.

Tudor Pole wrote to Sir David on Thursday 21st May 1953:

All being well, Talbot Rice is placing 3 workmen (with Michael Scott in charge) to begin tomorrow the sinking of a trench parallel with the railway wall [at the House of Justinian site] and I shall be there tomorrow at 8.30am to superintend. The next ten days should indicate whether we are on the right Q track or not.

After two hours of digging vertically, a passage with no ceiling was struck at a depth of about eight feet. It was faced on either side by walls dressed with a mixture of cement, broken tiles and stones. The passage was dug for four and a half feet in the direction of the arched loggia. At noon they reached the entry to a descending passage shaft, possibly a stairway, since there appeared to be fragments of stone paving slabs.

The entry to the shaft was blocked by several layers of rubble, soil and concrete. By 3.30 p.m. the entry had been cleared sufficiently to allow Tudor Pole to crawl in for about seven feet, but he was driven back by falls of stone. Tantalisingly, he saw what looked like a stairway at the end of the slope. But the dig was short of torches as well as small pickaxes, and it was not possible to go further that day.

The next day, Saturday, was spent clearing the rubble from the entry to the shaft. Tudor Pole got in far enough to take measurements, which conformed with early BB writings through the planchette. In the near darkness he thought he could make out cut steps going down. He reported to Sir David: "I cannot yet say quite definitely and finally that I am fully satisfied that we are on the correct Q track but it would need wild horses to drag me away from here at this juncture." In reply Sir David urged him to stay, assuring him that funds would be made available.

BB's drawings suggested that further on the shaft would be traversed by a wall. The kerosine lamps made it hot work for the diggers, but they reached the wall at the point expected. Tudor Pole was eager to break through it, but Talbot Rice wanted a record made of the site first. There was a pause while the dig was cleaned up so that Ward Perkins could take photographs, including some of a marble plinth or capital that seemed to be wedged into one of the side walls. Spencer Corbett did not want to breach the wall, and believed there was a possibility of penetrating below it, sound archaeological advice which Tudor Pole accepted.

Sir David was waiting anxiously to hear if the Quest chamber had been discovered, after so many years and so much expenditure. In Scotland the weather had been deplorable, with railway bridges washed away and villages flooded. In Constantinople tropical storms held up the celebrations, including a firework display, for the 500th anniversary of the Turkish conquest of the city. Tudor Pole was busy underground with a pick, though he had something to celebrate, with his son-in-law John Carroll, chief scientist with the Royal Navy, knighted in the Coronation Honours list.

The dig was within seven feet of the place where Tudor Pole expected to locate stone steps, but one of the side walls and part of the roof had collapsed, an obstacle predicted by BB. Another obstacle was unpredicted: Frederick Leveaux had cabled to say that he was arriving within days, and Sir David wired Tudor Pole to complain that he was "gravely disturbed" by this news because he feared that Leveaux would cause trouble.

A decision had to be taken about how to proceed without damaging the stability of the railway, because Tudor Pole believed that the staircase was very close to it. Sir David gave permission for the dig to continue, with buttresses used if necessary. The atmosphere of drama intensified with an earthquake on the evening of 3rd June. It caused only a slight tremor, but it was as if guardians of the Quest site were angry at it being disturbed. Meantime a new section of mosaic pavement was being uncovered at the main dig at the Great Palace. It showed a camel being led through a desert, with an oasis in the background, perhaps a sign to the House of Justinian squad that they were about to fulfil the Quest.

But it took two days to set up tackle to get the marble capital out of the trench. It was fifth century AD Corinthian, and apparently had the letters TP incised on it, which was taken as a good omen by Tudor Pole. But the stone staircase continued to elude the diggers, though the weather was kinder. Leveaux had arrived, but so far had visited neither dig. Then, on 15th June, Sir David received a telegram from Tudor Pole: "During Bairam holidays when dig closed have discovered first steps of stairway. All measurements conform." At Silverburn Sir David waited for news of the entry into Chamber V. But on 19th June another wire came from Constantinople. "Traces steps in vault apparently not of Quest interest."

On an aeroplane to Rome on 26th June, Ward Perkins wrote in a letter to Talbot Rice: "T.P.'s telegram to Sir David was inspired by the conviction that he had found his stairs, and I was able to dispel this by the process that I have adopted throughout, that of allowing him to disprove his own theory." Ward Perkins believed that the trench had been dug in Turkish times for the purpose of quarrying stone. It was the "ghost" of a wall, where one had once stood, with masses of concrete on either side.

His letter continued: "Three days ago I was able, with his [Tudor Pole's] full consent and goodwill, to start filling in—not unthankfully, since he had burrowed quite a distance under the railway property, and I was frankly terrified lest this should be seen by the same high Railway Official." But the dig was far from wasted, Ward Perkins stressed, as the great concrete platform—the backing of the present sea wall—was contemporary with the earlier, not the later of what appeared to be two successive periods of construction of the extant structures.

At the main dig the trench nearest the sea in the Aygir Deposu area at the Peristyle had disclosed a building of considerable size which looked as if it had been a church. An ICI product, Bedacryl, was proving effective for restoring the colours of the mosaics, but the building erected over them the previous year was leaking.

On 13th July Tudor Pole returned to London, without treasure, but with his confidence unshaken. He told Sir David:

I now have the key I need, and I know the exact spot beneath the platform where the stairway in its spiral form continues and the direction it follows. I hope therefore that you will feel able and willing to facilitate the next stage of the Quest, *soon*, and in such a way as will leave me free to devote all my time and attention to this specific Q undertaking.

Sir David was anxious to see the work on the House of Justinian completed that year. Corbett had an injured leg, but was willing to go back out to Turkey for October, when Tudor Pole wanted to return to follow the staircase down to Chamber V, taking with him Douglas Williams, the deputy area planning officer of Somerset County Council.

The hole dug in search of the Quest staircase had reached 16 feet in depth, and Talbot Rice warned that reopening it would give the Turkish authorities the suspicion that a treasure hunt and not an archaeological dig was under way. Not only could the House of Justinian dig damage the railway; it could damage relations with the Museum and Aziz Bey, with the expropriation question still not resolved.

With far more tact and patience than Baxter had used, Talbot Rice told Sir David: "My own feelings are that Mr Tudor Pole is convinced, and that it would be almost impossible to unconvince him, even if he dug through concrete for a year!" He concluded: "I should add, in all fairness, that it seems to me impossible that what he hopes to find—i.e. manuscripts—could possibly have been preserved in the damp atmosphere of Constantinople."

Tudor Pole arrived back in Constantinople with Douglas Williams on 25th October 1953. The central section of the trench was cleared to a depth of about 17 feet by five workmen. An examination of a bridge platform showed what seemed to be broken steps disappearing into concrete. A probe behind a large flat stone deeply embedded in concrete in the wall of the trench gave a hollow ring when Tudor Pole struck it, a "descending" space, he called it. He wrote excitedly to Sir David: "The vibrations emanating from ChV are so strong and so close that one almost feels as if one were in the Chamber itself."

But it was not a lucky dig. There had been a railway accident a few hundred yards away, with passengers killed and injured. Tudor Pole caught a bad cold, and had to stay in his hotel. Leveaux turned up, but all the treasure he saw was two Austrian coins dated 1816 which had been found in the bottom of the trench, an indication of an earlier attempt to break into the House of Justinian foundations. Corbett's mother died, and on 23rd November Tudor Pole sent Sir David a telegram: "Owing Corbett's departure dig closing without completion of work envisaged stop returning London end week." In a letter written the following day he told Sir David: "The small spiral staircase we still seek lies embedded in the concrete without any outward sign of its exact measurements." He believed that only about 20 feet of concrete separated the group from Chamber V at its north-west corner.

Back home Tudor Pole experienced a numb feeling which persisted into December, as if a "tremendous" electric shock had struck him. Life seemed to go on as in a dream: "Could I have 'touched' some very powerful force out there, unawares, and if so what can be its significance? For the time being I cannot even say whether I should wish to see further Q research carried out; and this in spite of the fact that we appear to be so close to our goal." He wondered if a curse had been put on the Quest chamber, as the Egyptians were alleged to have done when sealing up their tombs. He seemed reluctant to go back out to Constantinople, and in February 1954 warned Sir David that it would take much longer than a few days to investigate the House of Justinian site by reopening the trench. "I want to have received clear guidance as to the correct method of procedure; not to reopen until this has been received."

Sir David spent £5600 through the Iona Trust, mostly his own money, in Constantinople in 1953. Through the Russell Trust he financed archaeological excavations elsewhere, giving £1000 to the British Institute dig at Beycesultan, and also £500 to a dig at Harran in search of a Royal Library. For 1954, Talbot Rice included no estimate for the House of Justinian in what was expected to be the last season in Constantinople. He wrote to Sir David:

My view is that to do any more there would be an absolute waste of money, and I would not like to be associated with it. I have always been ready to believe that something could be 'disclosed' by a vision of the sort that Mr Tudor Pole had. But I felt that if this guidance failed, it would be necessary to admit defeat. It did fail, though the archaeological results were definitely important and interesting. But there is no more that can be done on the site from the archaeological point of view, and I think it would be wrong to dig there again; indeed, in view of the nature of the site, I do not think that it would be possible because it is all solid concrete."

In December Sir David had heard from J. P. Perkins, the lawyer in Constantinople, that there was a possibility that the Walker Trust's expropriation liabilities could be wiped out for between £600 and £700. Sir David's relief was short-lived: in the spring of 1954 the Director of Antiquities at Ankara demanded £7000 expropriation money, a sum that would have meant a large payment from Sir David's private funds. He warned Tudor Pole: "It has reached what we regard as a stage where it may reach a diplomatic level. We are

IN THE HOUSE OF JUSTINIAN

therefore putting the whole situation before the Ambassador. If no willingness to reconsider the whole position is shown, then our interest in the site of the Palace will be definitely closed."

With his long experience of Turkey Tudor Pole cautioned that if a compromise was not reached, it could be dangerous to send out workers to Constantinople that season. "As to the Quest, I feel like someone who is holding a very delicate thread, the other end of which is centred within chamber V. And that one impatient tug at this thread might snap it and so destroy the clue of which it is the potential agent."

Talbot Rice agreed with Tudor Pole about the danger in Constantinople. He warned Sir David: "They [the Turks] are quite capable of putting a stop to work when we get there, of impounding the dig and perhaps even putting members of the staff in prison." He urged: "I feel that we should fight this, and I think the only way of doing so will be to approach the Turks at the highest level."

Sir David had been practically blind in his left eye for four years. His right was now affected, and reading had become difficult. But he read with great interest about the huge collection of ancient scriptural manuscripts in Greek, Aramaic and Hebrew found in the remote monastery of St Paul, in the rugged mountain range bordering the western shore of the Gulf of Suez. The manuscripts had been discovered in a deep vault hewn out of the rock under the floor of the monastery chapel, the same kind of chamber that Tudor Pole believed held the Quest treasure under the House of Justinian.

Tudor Pole was 70 in mid April 1954. He had the satisfaction of being told that healers were using the Silent Minute as a daily link between each other, their patients and friends. But he was low in health with a kidney infection. In a letter to Sir David in June he wrote: "How happy and busy Pat must be! Not only in helping over those departing from our world, but in creating channels through Borderland darkness through which the growing light from above may reach us here." But he added despondently: "As Q work seems to have come to a dead end, I should like to go hence, where I may be of greater use than hanging about down here."

Tamara Talbot Rice arrived in Constantinople in a heatwave in June 1954. The Bairam holiday and a closed bridge contributed to the traffic congestion. There was no excavation permit, but she threatened that unless she got verbal permission to resume work, she would cancel the entire expedition and return to Britain. She was told that the permit was ready, and that she could start. But the Turks still wanted £7000 expropriation money. She advised Sir David: "There are various courses open, i.e., to protract, to compromise, to go to law. We all feel that it is advisable to protract, at any rate, till we have all finished here, closed our account and gone." She began to clean the mosaics uncovered the previous year and to repair an alcove to put them in. The mosaics were filthy, and she advised putting glass in the building over them.

Sir David wrote to Tudor Pole in late June: "Although it does not seem possible to do anything this season about reopening the trench at the H. of J., or investigating that problem further, I would on no account at your age give up the idea of following up the matter later on."

At the request of the Museum authorities the large excavation in the Aygir Deposu area had been left open so that delegates to the Congress of Byzantine Studies in the autumn of 1955 could see the massive walls and constructions.

But there was still a great deal of work to be done on the Great Palace in the form of writing the second report of the excavations. It was in progress, under the supervision of Talbot Rice, so David Russell could relax at Silverburn, with the new diversion of television. With the increasing pride the Turks were showing in the mosaics he was optimistic that there would be a realistic expropriation settlement, and that the Walker Trust could withdraw honourably, at least from the Great Palace site.

25
A Life Concluded

The enemy planes that had droned above Iona had not only menaced the convoys and threatened the security of the country. Bombs could destory historic buildings and do irreparable damage to beauty spots. But there was also the enemy within, the spread of industry threatening the countryside. In 1940 a project, Recording Britain, was initiated under the auspices of the Ministry of Labour and National Service to form a permanent pictorial record of places and buildings at risk.

The scheme, which gave employment to artists in wartime, was supported by the Pilgrim Trust. The artists chosen were, in the Trust's words, invited to record in water-colour, gouache, pen or pencil, "any landscape, coast line, village or city street, building, or ceremony characteristic of a period and of a district, and in danger of destruction or injury at the present time."

The Pilgrim Trust gave a separate grant in 1942 to set up a similar scheme, Recording Scotland. Principal Irvine of St Andrews University, a member of the Trust, chaired the new committee. Reginald Fairlie and Sir David Russell were on it, with Miss Bell acting as secretary.

Artists were asked to collaborate, either by submitting existing pictures, or by making new ones. The committee then made an offer for the work, which might not be commensurate with the artistic merit. But there were problems, since wartime restrictions applied to certain areas, including Iona. Cadell had stood on the white sands painting the seascape in the carefree 1920s, but that could be seen as a sinister activity in the early 1940s because of the convoys in the vicinity.

Miss Bell got into complicated correspondence with Headquarters, Scottish Command, Edinburgh. Apparently she had "misunderstood" the position with regard to sketching. "No permit is necessary to sketch in *public places* in this country provided that the subjects prohibited under the above Order are not involved." These prohibitions included fortifications, seaplane stations (such as Oban), arsenals, docks, vessels of war. The list even included water works.

Despite these severe restrictions 147 pictures by 47 artists were presented and bought, to become a permanent collection at a total cost of £1600 provided by the Pilgrim Trust. Eighty of the pictures were reproduced in a book, *Recording Scotland*, published in 1952, a happy conclusion to a decade of dedication on the part of Sir David and others. The editor of the fine volume, printed on Tullus Russell Mellotex paper, was Dr J. B. Salmond, the former editor of the *Scots Magazine*, and the editor of the *Rothmill Quarterly Magazine*.

The Recording Scotland collection was exhibited in galleries in Edinburgh and Kirkcaldy, and in schools throughout the country before being presented to St Andrews University, as a tribute to its Principle, Sir James Irvine, who had died in June 1952. He had been one of Sir David's closest friends, and they had shared many things, including the loss of a son each in the war.

As well as paintings, Sir David appreciated music, and another of his closest friends was the pianist Dame Myra Hess. At the start of the war, when all the London concert halls were closed, she had

Dame Myra Hess and Sir David Russell, old friends united in a love of life as well as music.

instituted a series of daily lunchtime recitals at the National Gallery, ranging from solo recitals through chamber works to orchestral and choral music. The music gave many Londoners hope and heart in the days of the Blitz. David Russell made it possible for Scotland to hear Dame Myra, by arranging concerts sponsored by the Walker Trust at St Andrews, Edinburgh and other places. Wherever she was in the world, Dame Myra always had a card to send to her "dear friends" at Silverburn, where she often stayed. In 1946 she received an honorary doctorate from St Andrews University for her services to music.

Many of Sir David's old friends were now dead, but he made new ones among the young, who found him easy to talk to and a sympathetic listener. He kept his mind active by putting together a large collection of sayings and poems which had interested him or been useful to him throughout his life. He and Lady Russell were devoted to their two corgis, Vicky and Bambi, and he was convinced that Vicky was a reincarnation of a little terrier he had had in his youth.

In 1951 Sir David set up the Fundamental Research Centre in London to investigate and evaluate unorthodox scientific processes and inventions. In the quest for new energy forms, radiesthesia was defined as "the study of radiations, different from those at present recognised by science, which are believed to be associated especially with living organisms." It was claimed that radiesthesia could be detected by certain instruments, notably the camera demonstrated by George de la Warr at the Delawarr Laboratories, Oxford. But his "Black Box" was no ordinary camera, since no light fell upon the photographic plate. The active medium was claimed to be cosmic energy. A doctor could send the Delawarr Laboratories a blood sample from a patient, with the request that a specific organ be tested for the presence or absence of a named disease. The blood sample was placed in the "camera" at a particular angle to the earth's magnetic field. The "camera" then "photographed" the state of the specified organ, with any disease showing up black on the negative. The patient did not need to be present.

Sir David's fascination with medicine went back to his student days at Edinburgh University before he bacame a papermaker. His fascination with alternative medicine went back to his time at the sanatorium at Sanna, Sweden. In the 1930s he had put money into Dr Anderschou's Guildford clinic, where the cage-like Lakhowsky Oscillator was used to cure cancer. There was a smaller one at the clinic at the mills and it was also used at Silverburn.

Sir David believed that an international commission should be appointed to investigate cancer research, with non-medical members in the majority. "One cannot help having a suspicion that any orthodox medical man is likely to be biased," he told Tudor Pole. The De la Warr "Black Box" appeared to be a new tool for combating cancer. It was similar to the "camera" developed by the American Ruth Brown, whom Sir David met. Through the Fundamental Research Centre he evaluated the De la Warr "camera." But although Tullis Russell put a little money into the Delawarr Laboratories, Sir David was not convinced enough to authorise a larger investment. However, the "Black Box' is still in use today, and some Fife riders who "apply" it to their horses swear by it.

To Sir David, old age was a time of remembrance as well as a time for investigating the "science" of the future. St Leonard's Chapel, St Andrews, had been derelict for 200 years. The university had reroofed it in 1910. The Pilgrim Trust gave money for repairs, and the Russell Trust, founded in memory of Pat, refurbished it to his memory, the service of dedication taking place in November 1952. In December Tudor Pole reported: "Yes I can confirm that Pat is happy, congenially occupied and very much in

The interior of St Leonard's Chapel, St Andrews, refurbished by Sir David and Lady Russell as a memorial to their son Pat, a former student of St Andrews University, killed with the London Scottish in Italy in 1944.

touch with you." Though past retirement age, Tudor Pole was still active. His latest scheme was to drop thousands of leaflets with a Silent Minute message into Russia from a balloon.

A Royal Commission had been set up to investigate the relationship between St Andrews University and University College, Dundee, and to make recommendations about the future. It produced the St Andrews University Act of 1953, which effectively disbanded all the colleges. In particular, University College was to be dissolved, to be replaced by Queen's College, while the two St Andrews colleges lost their status as independent corporations. College councils were set up in both places. There had been friction between St Andrews and Dundee since the 1890s, and in January 1953, as the St Andrews University Bill had its second reading in the Lords, Sir David, who had been on the St Andrews Court since 1938, told Tudor Pole: "The past week has taken up most of my time in trying to straighten out some of the drafting of the Bill." There were "Complications and jealousies," and long meetings.

When the principalship of St Mary's College became vacant, Sir David put George MacLeod's name forward, though he confessed to Tudor Pole: "I am just a little afraid that George MacLeod as Principal of St Mary's would be too much of a revolution for the ordinary orthodox clergy." But MacLeod seemed intrigued by the idea. He wrote to Sir David in January 1954:

I would not refuse to consider such an appointment. I cannot conceive that any typical senate would consider the name of so divisive a man as myself and I shall not be in the least surprised if I hear no more about it.

I would consider it because

A. It is manifest that new ways should be tried at ONE of our Halls: if we are serious about the alarming lack of men coming into any Hall.

B. Very few seem prepared really to try new ways.

C. It may be that Iona's next stage is to flood its ideas into the normal training.

D. Because if the Community is to last—it will next June number nearly 100 full members—it must find its corporate feet and carry on its Glasgow work under its own corporate steam and not as MacLeod's baby.

MacLeod was not offered the St Mary's post. However, Sir David was kept busy with his other academic interests. The Walker Trust provided the salary of a lecturer in science at St Andrews for three years. Sir David envisaged that the person appointed would investigate the relationship between electronics and physiology, a subject that had always deeply interested him. He saw it as the beginning of work on biophysics. The Trust also continued to make money available for scholarships, and took into account students returning from National Service.

Alice Buckton, the owner of Chalice Well, had died in 1944, having created financial problems for herself by buying up surrounding properties in order to protect the well in the future. But in 1949 her trustees, unable to continue her wishes because of lack of money, sold the property to a school which had been leasing the buildings. In April 1952 Tudor Pole wrote to David Russell, telling him that the Chalice Well site, which was about to come on the market, would provide an "ideal sanctuary" for the sapphire blue Glastonbury Bowl, which had been found near there 46 years before. But Tudor Pole had to wait to get his wish. In 1958 he and a group of friends founded the Chalice Well Trust to preserve the well and surrounding land so that it would continue as a sacred shrine for all to visit. Thousands of visitors a year drink its water.

Sir David was becoming increasingly interested in faith healing. He told Tudor Pole in April: "In my opinion . . . George MacLeod is on very shaky ground when he says he cannot find any authority in the New Testament for the idea that healers in this world can be helped by those who have passed on, or by others in the Unseen World." The following month 50,000 letters were sent out to every minister of religion in Britain in a campaign launched by the healer Harry Edwards to utilise the power of the Big Ben Silent Minute.

At the Harry Edwards Shere sanctuary there were reputed miracles, with misshapen backs straightened, and sight restored to an eye that had been blind for 17 years. Sir David's sister Christian, who had introduced him to a new world by taking him to the Kellgren sanatorium at Sanna, Sweden, at the beginning of the century, was receiving healing from Edwards, but she died in late August in a London clinic.

Sir David was becoming concerned by some of George MacLeod's pronouncements, and detected flaws in his arguments. MacLeod had preached that the atom was God's, and should not be meddled with by man. "We might as well say that man should not have invented gunpowder, or high explosives, or any other such things. It is too late to preach such a Gospel now," Sir David told Tudor Pole. He saw the Iona Community leader ploughing a lonely furrow: "I don't think he really knows quite where he is going."

The industrial boom of 1954 kept the mills busy. In September Tudor Pole was in Tripoli, disillusioned with the esparto business. He reported to Sir David:

The grass weighing posts are awful; flies, stench, brackish water and not even primitive amenities. When one knows that a few shillings a ton added to the selling price could make living conditions at such arid and isolated centres just tolerable one feels that it is almost wicked to "make profits" out of such needless suffering among one's fellow men. The competition which makes British buyers leave no fair profit to the producers of its raw material may be good business but it is questionable on ethical grounds.

In December Tudor Pole was in a clinic in Surrey with an infection probably picked up in Libya.

There was another gift for Iona. Sir David sent the Trustees a cheque for £500 as a first payment to account of the cost of restoring St Oran's Chapel and St Columba's shrine, the work to be carried out in both places by the Community's artisans, under the supervision of architect Ian Lindsay.

Edward Erdal, Sheila's husband, had taken over a builder's business in Oban, with the prospect of harbour contracts on some of the Hebridean islands. "It will be a great blank for us when they leave Corriemar. But in some ways it will be a better life, nearer the earth," Sir David told Tudor Pole. But there was a family reunion on New Year's Day 1955, with 12 grandchildren at Silverburn.

Tudor Pole went to a three day psychic conference in Holland in January 1955, taking the sapphire blue Glastonbury Bowl with him. Meantime, Sir David enjoyed memories of the time when his family were young. When on holiday, they used to go from Mentone along the shore and over the Italian frontier to a favourite bay. Their passports were checked by a little Italian customs officer with a face like a monkey. Anne had a monkey doll, almost the image of the man, and one day she made up a passport and gave it to the man. He stamped the passport solemnly, then laughed heartily.

In February 1955 Tudor Pole showed that he was far ahead of his time with regard to ozone layer damage when he wrote to David Russell warning:

These American and Russian atomic explosions do not affect our weather *directly*. But they damage the earth's etheric protective envelope which surrounds the planet from 50 to 100 thousand feet up, and so let in to our own atmosphere "currents" that disturb its conditions and so in this way climatic and other arrangements are upset, with consequences not yet fully apparent.

Tudor Pole's Big Ben Council had some 7000 members and friends, but the organisation needed money to keep going and as always,

Wellesley Tudor Pole in later life, after years of psychic and business involvement on many continents.

A LIFE CONCLUDED

Sir David helped. He spent Easter at Dunkeld in splendid weather. Lady Russell went on a National Trust Gardens Cruise, and then the Russells sailed from Crinan to Iona for their summer holiday on their son David's new boat.

Scottish papermakers met in Edinburgh at the end of August 1955 and decided that the buying of esparto grass should be concentrated in one firm, or a specially appointed organisation. One hundred thousand tons a year would be needed. Tudor Pole's firm, which had handled 50,000 tons of Libyan grass in 1954, was specially mentioned, and Sir David alerted him to expect an approach. But Tudor Pole pointed out that under such a scheme the Tullis Russell quota would be cut by 30 per cent or more, since his firm had kept the Markinch mills fully supplied, even when other firms were short.

Tudor Pole was asked to go to France for negotiations concerning Anglo–French esparto relations. Sir David told him:

Our fear generally is that, as conditions improve in North Africa, the cost of gathering must inevitably be higher and, even although esparto might be available, the price will probably rise to a figure that we cannot afford to pay as against the cost of wood pulp, and for many years I have made it a point to emphasise to manufacturers of wood pulp the importance of producing a short-fibred wood pulp to take the place of esparto. This would almost necessarily come from a hardwood.

In fact the days of papermaking with esparto were drawing to a close.

Queen Juliana of the Netherlands was interested in the Quest. She offered to use her influence with the authorities in Ankara for another dig. Miss Hofman, a Dutch healer and clairvoyant, whom the Queen regarded as genuine, assured Tudor Pole that the manuscripts were still intact "where you think they are." There seemed to be no end to Tudor Pole's psychic interests. In June he planned to begin "dousing" for oil, using North African maps.

Though he was effectively retired from the mills, Sir David continued to take a deep interest in them. He recalled the railway strike of the 1920s as his son prepared the mills for a rail strike in late May 1955, with 6000 tons of coal in stock, and more being delivered daily. Paradoxically, customers were getting goods in better condition by lorry, because Sir David complained that bales of papers often suffered considerable damage through the rough handling the railway gave them.

Sir David Russell had always encouraged all kinds of activities to develop the talents and interests of the Tullis Russell workers. Here members of the firm's amateur dramatic club play their parts in *Retreat from Moonshine*, 1956.

The Russells went to Iona in August, to spend a week with Sheila and her family. Between Oban and Perth Sir David saw the beautiful colours of the ripe fields, but there was a water shortage, recalling Cadell's remark that "on Iona you either stink or swim." In mid September he read reports of riots in Constantinople, and wondered if the mosaics were safe. In February the Director of Antiquities at Ankara had sent a new expropriation claim of around £3000, but this was still not acceptable. At the end of the month David Talbot Rice wrote, on his return from the Byzantine Congress in Constantinople.

All who saw the mosaic—and I spent a great deal of time showing it to people, and in discussing it with the authorities from Italy, Germany, Russia, and so on—were thrilled, and continued to stress its importance and the value of the work that the Walker Trust had done. Many expressed a hope that it would some day be possible for the work to continue.

But Sir David had turned to Scotland for his archaeological interests. The library of Justinian in Constantinople had not been found, but what about the library of Iona? There is a legend that

Sir David and Lady Russell with some of the family at Christmas 1955, his last one before his death. His son David is on the left.

the books of Iona, including the sacred writings of St Columba, were buried nearly 1000 years ago on Cairn na Burg Mhor, one of the Treshnish Islands off Mull. In the summer of 1953 the Russell Trust supported a dig on the island by 17 students from the four Scottish universities, with St Andrews naturally in the majority. They did not find the library in their six week search of the island, but they found friendships that have lasted for life. Through the Russell Trust Sir David also financed excavations on Iona from 1956 on Torr an Aba, a rock outcrop west of Iona Abbey. The excavators felt that "the details as revealed by digging . . . are consistent with the inscription given by Adamnan of a (if not only) cell, perhaps the living or writing-cell of Columba in the sixth century."

In March 1956 Sir David had bronchial catarrh, and was only allowed out if the weather was sunny, and then for only half an hour. But he was still dealing with correspondence, including a request for a grant for a survey of pre-Classical sites in eastern Turkey.

Pat was never forgotten. He had loved his brief time at the Ygorra Camp of the Grenfell Mission at St Anthony, Newfoundland in 1938–39. He had sailed in a schooner, helped with road-making, fished for food, and taken his turn at the cooking, with stuffed cod a speciality. A new sanatorium had been completed at St Anthony. The occupational therapy room had been furnished by the Russells and their friends in memory of Pat, with a plaque put on the wall. Eskimo and Indian patients attended, with the men carving and the women sewing in the sunny peaceful room.

In April 1956 Sir David's doctor sent him for a change of air to Lochearnhead for ten days. One of his last dictated letters was to Talbot Rice, telling him of Russell Trust grants for archaeology in Transjordan and Harran. He was delighted with the progress on the second report on the Great Palace, which was almost ready for publication.

Sir David Russell had a cerebral haemorrhage in bed. His son David and daughter-in-law Catherine were with him when he died on 12th May 1956, aged 84. He was buried in the little hillside churchyard of Upper below Largo Law. George MacLeod was among the many present. Three days later his long-time friend the Reverend Selby Wright, minister at the Canongate Kirk, Edinburgh, gave an oration at a memorial service in St Andrews University chapel. He recalled:

A fortnight ago, the last night I spent with him, I was allowed to see something of the secret of his life. It was late and I noticed that the light was on outside my door and I went to put it out thinking that by some accident it had been left on and would burn throughout the night. But as I went to turn out the switch, Sir David appeared. He had just come out of a room and he asked if I would like to see it. "Pat's room," he called it. And there I saw his little chapel where in the morning and at night he said his prayers. It was just by chance, and it was all so quiet, so natural, so peaceful.

Part of Sir David's legacy to his family was a paper mill with over 1000 employees. He had succeeded in creating a complete and efficient manufacturing process, consistently producing paper of the finest quality. He could have made the mills even bigger, but early in his business career he had made a decision: he would make enough money, and leave himself enough time for his many other interests.

Not long before he died he told Tudor Pole, with whom he had exchanged almost daily letters for close to 40 years: "What we are here for is the development of what one might call Mind, which includes sympathetic understanding, imaginative purposes and all that these qualities include and mean."

A LIFE CONCLUDED

Though not a church-goer, David Russell was a deeply religious man in the broadest sense. He investigated Indian belief, Theosophy and Steiner's philosophy, and was a New Age thinker long before he met Tudor Pole. He applied his reading and reflections on moral philosophy in his treatment of his workforce. One employee queried why he had not received promotion and was told by David Russell: "because you have not helped your fellow workers." David Russell passed on one of his tenets to his family, advising them always to "expect the best in a person, but to hope for nothing." He himself had so often brought out the best in people.

Miss Bell had worked for David Russell for 37 years as his immensely competent personal secretary and had seen how he had helped so many people privately. She wrote to Tudor Pole: "Sometimes I feel he is near me, but I am not at all a sensitive person in that way. What grieves me is that I shall be getting farther and farther behind him spiritually and that when I get to the Other Side I shall never come near him again."

As a family man David Russell had found fulfilment, though there were the tragedies of Catherine and Pat. In the course of her married life Alison Russell had created a celebration of their marriage. She had sewn printed linen squares, and crocheted them together into a double bed spread. On the back of each square was stitched a piece of tape embroidered with the place and date of its completion. With its different colours, its overall harmony and its extent, the cover was a unique diary of the life she had shared with her husband.

In 1942, in the darkness of war, Myra Hess had written to David Russell: "I think of you always surmounting the sad experiences in this life with your calm inner faith; a light that never seems to fail and which you pass on to us, helping us on our way." One Quest was in abeyance, but he had embarked on the greatest with absolute certitude. For Alexis Aladin's tombstone David Russell had chosen a prayer, his own favourite throughout his long life: "Grant that I may behold Thy Light in the stillness of my heart." But he had once written to Selby Wright: "I should like to associate eternity not only with peace but with useful service. Peace unqualified seems to assume inactivity which I think is very far from what we are justified in anticipating in the glorious hereafter."

Index

Adamnan, *Life of Columba* 106, 115
Aithernie 45, 47
Aladin, Alexis 96–104
Aladin, Alexis junior 103, 104, 208, 211, 216
Algiers 79
alternative medicine: Anderschou 145–6; Artificial Sunlight 139–41; Delawarr Laboratories 243–4; Emion process 220–1; faith healing 246; Kellgren system 10–11, 14, 42; Lakhowsky Oscillator 146–7; radiesthesia 243; Sandor foam baths 141
Amalgamated Society of Paper Makers 41
American Iona Society 193, 194
Anderschou, H. W. 145–6
antiques 53, 55
archaeology: *see* Constantinople excavations; Justinian, House of
Argyll, Duke of 197, 198, 199
Artificial Sunlight clinic 139–41
Associated Paper Mills Limited 54
Auchmuty Mill: acquisition 20–1; developments 22; employment 30; esparto 78; losses 46; post-war 40; production 24, 25, 60, 65, 71; World War I 33; World War II 201, 208–9, 215
Aureliana 133, 135–7, 172, 174

Baha, Abdu'l 37, 51

Baldwin, Stanley 66, 94
Baring, Maurice 96
Barn, David 138
Basiaux Frères, Carl and Ivan 78, 86, 210–11, 216
Baxter, James: Constantinople excavations 126–7, 151–4, 159–71, 182, 184–92; criticised 225; expropriation 182, 184, 189; and Irvine 153, 155; and Leveaux 128; publicity 156, 158, 167; and Russell 123, 124, 184–6, 188, 190; and Tudor Pole 167–8, 188
Beatty, Chester 102, 153
Becker, Sir Frederick 52, 53, 56, 59
Becker & Company Limited 52
Bell, Ilse 70–1, 211, 241–2, 253
Bergengreen, Anatoly: death 222; Paraguay 158, 168, 207; Quest 119, 122–3; and Russell 156
Besant, Annie 31
Bey, Aziz 154, 158
Black, John 61, 69, 79–82, 86
Blyth, Alison (later Alison Russell) 28
Blyth, Ben 28, 222
Blyth, Billy 210
Brampton Park clinic 7–9
British Byzantine Archaeological Committee 190–1, 192
Bruce, Kinleith & Sons Limited 51–2
Buckton, Alice 32, 61–2, 64, 246

·254·

INDEX

Bucolean Palace: *see* Justinian, House of
Budge, Sir Ernest A. Wallace 127, 156
Bullionfield Mill 52, 53, 59–60
Burg Farm 177–8, 196
Bute, Marquess of 197–8

Cadell, F.C.B. 106, 110, 112–13, 114
Cameron, Sir D. Y. 198
Campbell, Iain Gordon 159, 161
Carrongrove Paper Company 52, 53
Chalice Well 31–2, 61–2, 64, 246
Chamberlain, Neville 183
Chill, Mary (née Russell) 39
Chill, Walter 26
Chronander, Gunnar 18, 24, 26, 28
Clayton, Tubby 200, 205
Clifton Bank 1, 2, 3–4
Cnocmor 114–17, 199
Constantinople excavations 118–19; Baxter 126–7, 151–4, 159–71, 182, 184–92; criticism 186; expropriation 182, 184, 189; Golden Gate 152, 156; Great Palace 159–71, 183–4; Leveaux 152, 190–1, 235; mosaic 163–6, 169–71, 175, 185; Quest site 121–2, 151; report 225–6, 229; Walker Trust 127–8, 151, 178–9, 229; *see also* Justinian, House of
Corbett, James 159
Corbett, Spencer 230, 232, 236–7
Craigflower 71, 72
Crimea 99
Cummins, Geraldine 124, 218

de la Warr, George 243–4
Delawarr Laboratories 243–4
Despujols, Jean 67, 76, 131
Doyle, Sir Arthur Conan 123

EANN (Exploitation Alfatieres de L'Afrique Du Nord) 79, 86
Eden, Anthony 182
Edinburgh Castle, Queen Margaret's Chapel 144, 148, 193
Edwards, Harry 246
Emergency Powers Act (1920) 69
Emion process 220–1
Erdal, Alison 220
Erdal, Edward 73–4, 214, 218, 220, 247
esparto grass 21, 77–86, 201, 249
Esparto Paper Mills Limited 50–3

Fairlie, Reginald 110–11, 193, 194, 195, 198
faith healing 246
Federation of Paper Makers 41
First World War: *see* World War I
Fraser, Ian 216–17
Frederick Ernst, Prince of Saxe-Altenburg 185, 188
Fundamental Research Centre 243

Gargano scheme 130–1, 134–5
Gauer, Bernhard 175
General Strike 69–70
Glastonbury 31
Glastonbury bowl 105, 118, 247
Gorton, Neville 206, 210
Great Palace of the Byzantine Emperors 226
Great War, The (Tudor Pole) 123
Grenfell, Wilfred 199

Hatry, Clarence 49–50, 52, 54, 56–7
Henderson, Keith 208
Hess, Myra 242–3, 253
House of Justinian: *see* Justinian, House of 119, 126
Humphris, J. Howard 140–1
Hurd, Robert 197, 207–8

INDEX

Hutchison, Janet (later Janet Russell) 1–2
Hyganic 175, 209

Inveresk Paper Company Limited 51, 65
Iona 105–17, 193–203, 247
Iona Cathedral 110–12
Iona Community 193, 194, 224
Iona Fellowship 109–10
Iona Press 107
Iona Trust 194, 238
Irvine, James Colquhoun 64, 88–95; and Baxter 153, 155; Constantinople excavations 127–8, 228–9; died 242; and Tudor Pole 93; and Walker Trust 166
Irvine, Mabel 89–90, 93, 94–5, 222
Italy: Aureliana 133, 135–7, 172, 174; Gargano scheme 130–1, 134–5; land reclamation 129–30, 134; Romeland 133, 135–6, 137, 172–3

Janson, E. W. 125–6, 191
Justinian, House of: deterioration 157–8, 186, 188; as Quest site 119, 126; Rice 227, 233–40; Russell 170; Tudor Pole 231, 233–40; Walker Trust 192; *see also* Quest

Kellgren, Harry 10–11, 16–17, 34, 42
Kellgren, Jonas 10–11, 14–15, 42
Kellgren, Vera 41–3
Kellgren Institute 10–11, 14, 42
Kennedy-Fraser, Marjory 112, 114

Lakhowsky Oscillator 146–7
Leavey, George 62, 66, 135, 136
Leveaux, Frederick: Aureliana 133, 135; and Baxter 128; Constantinople excavations 152, 190–1, 235; Quest 119, 123
Lewis, Charles 33, 34
Lindsay, Ian 110–11, 198, 202, 247
Lithgow, Sir James 199

Maby, Joseph Cecil 223
Macaulay, William 170, 221
MacLeod, George: factory-community 216–18; Iona Community 193, 194; Iona Fellowship 109; and Russell 216–18, 220, 246; Silent Minute 205; St Mary's College 245; and Vyner 196
MacPhail, Angus 107
Maindy Hill 82–3
Mamboury, Ernest 159, 161, 170–1
Marcault, Emilio 92
Margaret, Queen of Scotland 144, 148, 193
Markinch 139
Martiny, Gunther 184, 185, 186, 188
Men of the Trees 180
Montgomery of Alamein 218
Monymusk Reliquary 145
Muir, Edwin 207
Munro, Hector 141
Mussolini, Benito 129, 130, 136, 172

National Union of Paper Mill Workers 41
Nightingale, E. Constance 98, 102, 104
Nisbet, Nurse 139–41, 179

Oyler, Philip 32

Papermakers Straw Trading Company 215

INDEX

papermaking 1–2; bribery 24; coal shortage 48, 70; combine 51–2; depression 50–1; esparto grass 21, 77–86, 249; industrial relations 40–1; prices maintained 71; raw materials 21; short time 59; wages 40, 43–4; women workers 22–3; World War II 201, 206, 215
Paperworkers' Charter 44
Pecorini, Daniele 129; Aureliana 133, 172, 177; death 177; and Mussolini 136; and Russell 130–3, 134, 136, 137, 172, 174–5, 177; St Margaret antique 144
Perkins, Ward 232, 235, 236
Pilgrim Trust 178, 200, 241
Pio da Pietralcini, Padre 75, 134
Pojidaiev, Michael: death 223; Quest 119, 122–3, 158; and Russells 152–3, 156; and Tudor Pole 154
Pole, Wellesley Tudor: see Tudor Pole
Private Dowding (Tudor Pole) 35–6, 121

Quest 118–28; BB 119, 122, 123; Bergengreen 119, 122–3; Constantinople excavations 121–2, 151; Juliana, Queen of the Netherlands 249; Leveaux 119, 123; Pojidaiev 119, 122–3, 158; *see also* Justinian, House of; Tudor Pole

radiesthesia 243
Rae, James 52
Ramsden cross 202
recession 46
Recording Scotland 241–2
Rice, David Talbot: excavations in Constantinople 119, 120, 226–32; expropriation 250; House of Justinian 227, 233–40; and Russell 183; and Tudor Pole 231
Rice, Tamara Talbot 226, 230, 239–40
Richardson, James 107
Ricketts, Henry 159
Rinman, A. L. 60–1
Ritchie, Alexander and Euphemia 107, 108, 109, 110–11, 180, 206
Robertson, Angus 193, 194
Robinson, Catherine 218
Romeland 133, 135–6, 137, 172–3
Rothes House 29–30, 41
Rothes Mill 21, 25; employment 22–3, 30; losses 46; post-war 40; product range 72; profit 24; rag boilers 65; vulcanising paper 59; World War I 33; World War II 201, 208–9
Rothmill Quarterly Magazine 138, 222
Royal Society of Edinburgh 141, 211
Russell, Agnes 1, 6, 28
Russell, Alison 253; and Aladin 98; and children 67, 115; and Irvine, Mabel 90, 93; Sandor foam baths 141; Dr Swanberg 223; touring 131; World War II 205–6
Russell, Anne (Margaret Anne Oliphant): birth 61; childhood 73, 109, 142; education 173, 201; marriage 221; in Tullis Russell 220
Russell, Catherine Alison 33, 64, 223
Russell, Christian 1; and brothers 6–7, 28; and Chronander, Gunnar 18, 24, 26; death 246; ill-health 4, 39; Kellgren Institute 11; Sanna 15, 16, 18, 24

INDEX

Russell, David xi, 1–4, 5–6, 7–9, 219, 220, 252–3; and Aladin 97–8, 102; alternative medicine 10–11, 14, 42, 139–41, 145–7, 220–1, 243; and Baxter 123, 124, 184–6, 188, 190; botany 5, 7, 143; children's education 64, 65, 68, 71–2, 73–4, 176; and Constantinople 155—6, 163, 175–6, 183–4, 225–6, 229; as employer 65; financing Quest 119, 123; fine arts 67, 144–5, 207–8; ill-health 10–18, 41, 71, 75, 76, 222; Iona 105–17, 193–203, 247; Italy 130–4; and MacLeod 216–18, 220, 246; and Pecorini 130–3, 134, 136, 137, 172, 174–5, 177; and Ramsay MacDonald 168; and science, unorthodox 3, 212, 223, 243, 244; St Andrews University 87–95; Walker Trust 95, 166; World War I 37–8; *see also* Tullis Russell

Russell, David Francis Oliphant: birth 34; childhood 39, 76; in Constantinople 164, 175; marriage 218; as soldier 199, 200, 205, 206, 209–11; at St Andrews University 148, 174; at Tullis Russell 179; wounded 212, 213

Russell, David senior: business ventures 1–2, 6; death 18–19; and papermaking 22–3; stroke 10; Walker Trust 87

Russell, George 1; and Bessie 61; childhood 3; as farmer 7, 24; in Kenya 48; World War I 33

Russell, Janet 1–2, 7, 56, 61, 64–5

Russell, Jenny 1, 7

Russell, John Patrick Oliphant: *see* Russell, Pat

Russell, Margaret Anne Oliphant: *see* Russell, Anne

Russell, Mary 1, 6, 26

Russell, Pat (John Patrick Oliphant): birth 38; in Canada 199–200; clairvoyance 62, 64; died 212, 214–15; education 73–4, 148; ill-health 75, 174; remembered 251–2; as soldier 201, 205, 210, 211; at St Andrews University 176

Russell, Robert 1; and brother 7; died 180–1; ill 10, 27, 32–3, 34, 38–9; as partner 23; and Tullis brothers 58, 66; wax extraction 85

Russell, Sheila Felicity Oliphant: birth 51; childhood 73, 109, 112, 142, 176; education 143, 173; marriage 214, 218; as nurse 208, 209; from Rhodesia 223; World War II 200

Russell Trust 220, 238, 244, 251

Sandor foam baths 141
Sankey Commission 41
Sanna 11–16
Scripts of Cleophas, The (Cummins) 124
Second World War: *see* World War II
Sfax 81
Sieff, Israel 36–7, 156
Silent Minute 204–5, 210, 239, 245, 246
Silverburn 1, 2, 72–3, 142–3
Sissoeff, Dmitry 119, 122–3, 125
Societa Aureliana 133; *see also* Aureliana
soda recovery 23, 60–1
St Andrews University: Russell as benefactor 87–95; Russell's sons as students 148, 174, 176; St Leonard's Chapel 244; *see also* Irvine
St Andrews University Act (1953) 245

INDEX

St James's Literary Agency 55
St Margaret's Chapel 144, 148, 193
strikes 40; dockers 61; general 69–70; miners 47; railway 45
Susa 81–2
Swanberg, Carl 103, 205, 223

Talbot Rice: see Rice, David Talbot
Tebessa 81
Theosophical Society 31
Theosophy 92
trade unions 40, 69
Tudor Pole, Christopher 213
Tudor Pole, Florence 39, 145, 229
Tudor Pole, Wellesley xi, 31; and Aladin 99–102; antiques 53, 55; and Baxter 167–8, 188; BB's writings 234–5; Big Ben Council 247–9; esparto agent 78, 86, 246–7; Glastonbury bowl 31, 32; *The Great War* 123; and Hatry 50, 52; House of Justinian excavations 233–40; Hyganic 175, 209; ill 145–6, 147; intuition 34–6, 37, 64; and Irvine 93; in Italy 74–5, 129, 130, 133, 173; and Leavey 136; mediumship 124–5, 213–14, 218; ozone layer 247; *Private Dowding* 35–6, 121; Quest 118–23, 156–8, 233–40; Silent Minute 204–5, 210; World War II 202, 204–5, 210, 239, 245, 246
Tullis, George 55, 58
Tullis, Robert 20–1, 23
Tullis, Robin 55, 58
Tullis, William 77–8
Tullis Hunter 6

Tullis Russell: in combine 49–50, 54–5; diversifying 46; housing for millworkers 139; as limited company 24; mergers 141; profits 68; relationship with workers 69; Russell buy-out 58–9, 66; Savings Fund 45; supertax 142, 149; women employees 40, 43; World War II 215–16; see also Auchmuty Mill; Rothes Mill

Vyner, Clare 195–6

Wages Temporary Regulation Act 41
Walker Trust: competition 87–8; Constantinople excavations 127–8, 151, 166, 178–9, 229; expropriation 182–3, 184, 189, 238–9, 240, 250; Golden Gate 156; House of Justinian 192; Iona Retreat 106; Irvine 166; and Russell 95, 166; science lectureship 245–6
Warr, Charles 110, 193, 194
Watsons of Bullionfield Limited 52, 53
Watt, James 54, 55, 59, 182, 218
wax extraction 85
Wei-chi 129, 131–2
World War I 32–3, 37–8
World War II: esparto supplies 201; outbreak of 200; paper rationing 201; papermaking 201, 206, 208–9, 215; Silent Minute 204–5, 210, 239, 245, 246; threatening 179–81; Tudor Pole 202, 204–5, 210
Wright, Selby 252

Zytocin 221

N.T.S - 177
178